W9-CNS-774

Immigration Chaos:

Solutions to an American Crisis

by

Neville W. Cramer

ISBN Number 978-0-9762820-1-3

Library of Congress Number: 2007936079

Published by IES Publications, LLC, Scottsdale, Arizona

Portions of this book have been taken from *Fixing the INSanity—America's Immigration Crisis*.

Printed in the United States of America

Dedication

I dedicate this book to my magnificent and loving wife Timea. Her love for America represents the greatest aspect of our heritage of legal immigration.

Immigration Chaos

Introduction

I realize discussing immigration reform is not the hottest topic at most dinner tables, but take a look around your own city or town. If you do not notice a significant change in the demographics, you have probably moved to Iceland. It seems that legal and illegal immigrant populations in the U.S. are larger and more prevalent than ever before. New York, Chicago, Miami, and Los Angeles are not the only places immigrants reside in large numbers. They are also in our small towns, rural areas, and suburbs. We now have large communities of Mexicans, El Salvadorans, Colombians, Cubans, Nigerians, Ethiopians, Lebanese, Israelis, Russians, Bosnians, Indians, Pakistanis, Vietnamese, and Chinese, just to name a few.

U.S. Immigration enforcement activities over the past 30 years have been a disastrous failure. Our government and political leaders have let us down. Whether it was the Cuban Mariel Boatlift or the 12 million plus illegal aliens currently here, politicians have not had the will to deal effectively with our broken borders.

Most Americans have little understanding about our immigration problems. I have written this book to simplify the discussion. It is critical that more Americans understand exactly how our current immigration quagmire evolved, and then realize Congress could authorize innovative programs that will bring sanity back to our immigration system. If we are to maintain ourselves as a world leader, we must curtail illegal immigration to a manageable level, secure our physical borders and allow America to once again become a nation that welcomes immigrants—not a nation flooded with illegal aliens.

Legal immigration has been the lifeblood of the U.S. Any attempt to close our borders is un-American, unrealistic, and virtually impossible. Illegal immigration, however, has cast a bad light on all immigration, forcing many Americans to question whether we should continue our current overly generous legal immigration system. With our current immigration system on the verge of collapse, and illegal aliens pouring into the country unabated,

U.S. citizens are getting extremely frustrated. If anti-immigrant vigilantism breaks out, the results could be catastrophic.

As a nation, we must realize that employment is the magnet that draws most illegal aliens to America. Therefore, Congress must mandate workable compliance programs that allow employers to cooperate with the government. At the same time, we must also understand the needs of certain employers who have become dependent on cheap, physical labor.

I am not a strong proponent of using diplomacy to reduce the worldwide "push factors" associated with illegal immigration. Only a limited amount of success will be gained through these initiatives. In most poor countries, there is massive overpopulation, and the U.S. offers the largest and most lucrative relief valve in the world. It is highly unlikely that Third World leaders will truly implement programs that will reduce emigration to the U.S. For years, I observed our politicians and diplomats meeting with officials from other nations in an effort to stop the flow of illegal immigrants. These meetings seemed to be nothing more than an excuse for our senior government officials, diplomats and politicians to travel around the world and sign useless agreements. Considering the number of illegal aliens in the U.S., the facts seem to favor my conclusions.

The new Department of Homeland Security also needs to take a good hard look at the way the Border Patrol operates on both the Canadian and Mexican borders. Time and time again, we have learned that effective control of our land and sea borders requires increased usage of technology like ground radar systems, night-vision cameras, satellites and sensors. It is far more effective to watch for an incursion and then respond to it, than it is to patrol the border hoping to stumble across a group of illegal aliens or other violators. We also need large scale detention facilities in many areas along our border with Mexico. Common sense tells us it would be much more effective immigration control if we incarcerated illegal aliens instead of immediately sending them back to Mexico to try again and again until they finally get past the Border Patrol.

In 2006, several Democratic and Republican politicians in California, Arizona and New Mexico appeased their constituents by yelling "immigration emergency" and began sending National Guard troops to the assist the Border Patrol. As I will explain, this may have swayed a few impressionable voters, but as a permanent policy it is a mistake. There are many more solutions we should try before we "militarize" our borders.

America's legal immigration system is antiquated, overrun, and unrealistic. Our current policies seem to favor those aliens who will not necessarily benefit the U.S., while it discourages immigrants who will truly make America a better place to live.

The media has also played a significant role in creating a liberalized attitude toward illegal immigration. For decades most reporters viewed immigration enforcement initiatives as racist, inhumane, mean-spirited and un-American. On the other hand, CNN's Lou Dobbs and Fox News' Bill O'Reilly have done just the opposite. Their viewers have been fed a steady diet of programs relating to border control, illegal immigration and its impact on the American middle class. Some competing news outlets like the *New York Times* have even editorialized that Lou Dobbs is doing nothing more than fueling racism and xenophobia. One thing is certain—it is about time America heard the truth about this growing domestic cancer. Whether Lou Dobbs and Bill O'Reilly are truly "fair and balanced" is for the viewers to decide. It is refreshing, however, to finally hear about both sides of the immigration debate.

As we begin the 21st century, there are many significant problems confronting the U.S., and immigration control is near the top of the list. According to a December, 2004, Homeland Security Inspector General report, entitled "Major Management Challenges Facing the Department of Homeland Security," there are an estimated 8–12 million illegal aliens in the U.S. For the sake of argument, I will use this estimate throughout the book.

With a few exceptions, I am going to stay away from statistics, polls and studies about illegal immigration. Despite everything that has been said and done thus far, the immigration problem in America gets worse every day. Studies and polls have done nothing more than muddy the waters.

The tragic events of September 11, 2001, showed that we do not have a clue as to what foreign nationals are in this country. Worse yet, we have no idea what they are planning to do to us. In the wake of the attacks, the Federal government came up with goofball fixes like the establishment of the "Terrorism Threat Level Color Charts." If our government leaders truly believe these initiatives will thwart international terrorism, we are in deep trouble as a nation. Instead of color charts, the U.S. government must fund and implement effective immigration control programs at our borders, throughout the U.S. and even overseas.

I spent more than 26 long years in INS. While I considered it to be one of the most dysfunctional Federal agencies in the history of our nation, I did learn a great deal about legal and illegal immigration. Congress and the President can begin to eliminate the problems if they immediately and responsibly start implementing a series of initiatives similar to those described in Part 2 of this book. Or we can allow the situation to deteriorate even further. Eventually it will reach a point, when we, as a nation, will not be able to control it. If this happens, both our sovereignty and our national security will be gravely at risk.

Whether it is terrorism by foreign nationals, gangs of criminal aliens, or simply millions of illegal aliens living within our borders, we cannot continue to treat these problems as though, one day, they will just disappear. The American immigrant dream is slowly turning into a domestic nightmare. I think it is time we wake up.

Part 1
Chaos in the Making

Chapter 1

Failed Immigration Policies, Ineptitude and the 9/11 Attacks

In individuals insanity is rare; but in groups, parties, nations and epochs it is the rule.

Friedrich Nietzsche, Beyond Good and Evil

Consequences of a broken system

While there is little correlation between terrorism and the millions of hard-working illegal immigrants in the U.S., history has shown us over and over again how dangerous it is for our politicians to take a cavalier attitude toward immigration. Whether it is Mexicans dying of thirst in the Arizona desert or fundamentalist Muslim terrorists crashing airliners into our landmarks, Americans now realize our politicians have failed us.

The photographs on the back cover of this book illustrate a stunning example of how our leaders fail us when serious immigration issues arise. In July, 1980, 194 radical Muslim demonstrators were arrested rioting near the White House. It was suspected most were from Iran and Saudi Arabia and were illegally in the U.S. They refused to give their names or supply passports to U.S. law enforcement. Without question they had come to Washington, D.C., to violently demonstrate support for Iran's Ayatollah Khomeini and test the reaction of the U.S. government. They all vowed to destroy America, no matter how long it would take!

Hours after the riot, the Carter White House dreamed up the idea that detaining these fanatics would somehow lead to the harming of American hostages held in Iran. President Jimmy Carter ordered their immediate release, despite the fact all had violated U.S. immigration laws. Law enforcement officials hastily obtained these "mug shots" before releasing them back onto the streets of Washington, D.C.

To this day, officials cannot identify most of these people. We have no idea where they were living or what they were doing in the U.S. We do not know who organized the riot or how many of them are still here.

Some may believe time has mitigated the danger these fundamentalists pose to America. On the contrary, it may have exacerbated it. Iran's new President Mahmoud Ahmadinejad was one of their cronies, and he is now thumbing his nose at the rest of the world, as Iran moves rapidly toward the production of a deliverable nuclear weapon.

What will happen if the U.S. is forced to take military action against Iran? Could hundreds (maybe thousands) of fundamentalist Iranian Muslim "moles" be living in the U.S.? Could a number of them suddenly become homicidal *jihadists?* Could they be "activated" and strike us from within? Only time will tell.

What we do know is that the 1993 World Trade Center bombing and the attacks on September 11, 2001, were carried out by fundamentalist Muslim extremists residing in the U.S. They all entered and remained here by taking advantage of a completely broken immigration system.

Immigration and the 9/11 attacks

The 9/11 Commission blamed the attacks on intelligence failures of the Federal Bureau of Investigation, Central Intelligence Agency, National Security Agency, and all of the other alphabet-soup agencies in and around Washington, D.C. The fact is no other agency in the Federal government had a better chance of stopping the terrorist attacks than the Immigration and Naturalization Service (INS). In fact, one suspected 9/11 terrorist *was* stopped by INS, and his entry into the U.S. was denied. I believe INS ineptitude was a key factor that allowed the hijackers to enter the U.S., remain here, and carry out their maniacal plan.

Consider two points about INS and the 9/11 attacks.

1. INS Special Agents and immigration intelligence officers working overseas should have compiled and transmitted much more information about *al Qaeda* to the INS Intelligence Division at Headquarters. Had this been done, there was a good chance more of the terrorists would have been denied entry into the U.S.
2. INS Special Agents should have been working more aggressively with other agencies to locate, arrest and deport suspected terrorists residing in the U.S. If INS Agents had skillfully used their unique authority to question, search and detain suspected *al Qaeda* members, the plans for terrorizing us may have been uncovered and the attacks thwarted.

While The 9/11 Commission investigators might not agree, my conclusions are the result of "street" experience. In the early 1980s, I worked closely with counter-terrorism squads of the FBI's Washington, D.C., Field Office. Every time the Bureau developed intelligence that a suspected foreign terrorist was even "breathing the wrong way," we were there to question and, if necessary, arrest the individual for violating his immigration status. We were extremely effective.

After one such arrest in July, 1982, the following wire was sent to then Secretary of State George Shultz.

> *"I would like to draw your attention to the fact that two of your employees Mr. Cramer and Mr. Olech have twice now intimidated and harassed our employees. On Tuesday March 2, they illegally entered our office carrying guns and questioned some of our workers. Today they again arrested and handcuffed one of our part-time, student workers and took him in for questioning. Our office gives information about Palestinian people and has respected all American laws and regulations. We did not know this morning whether our worker was being kidnapped by Israeli agents or other fanatic Jewish groups. We urge you to take*

measures to protect the rights of our office and to stop this campaign of harassment and intimidation of our workers.

Best wishes and regards, Dr. Hatem Hussaini,
Director Palestine Information Office."

Obviously the Palestinian Information Office was not happy that we had arrested one of their "students." (Most of the 9/11 hijackers were also "students" of one kind or another.) The intelligence gathered after this arrest was significant to say the least. Although most of the information obtained is probably still classified, I can freely say the "student" was doing a bit more than studying English 101.

During the years I worked with the FBI counter-terrorism squads, there was not a single foreign terrorist act committed within the U.S. Our success did not go unnoticed at FBI Head-

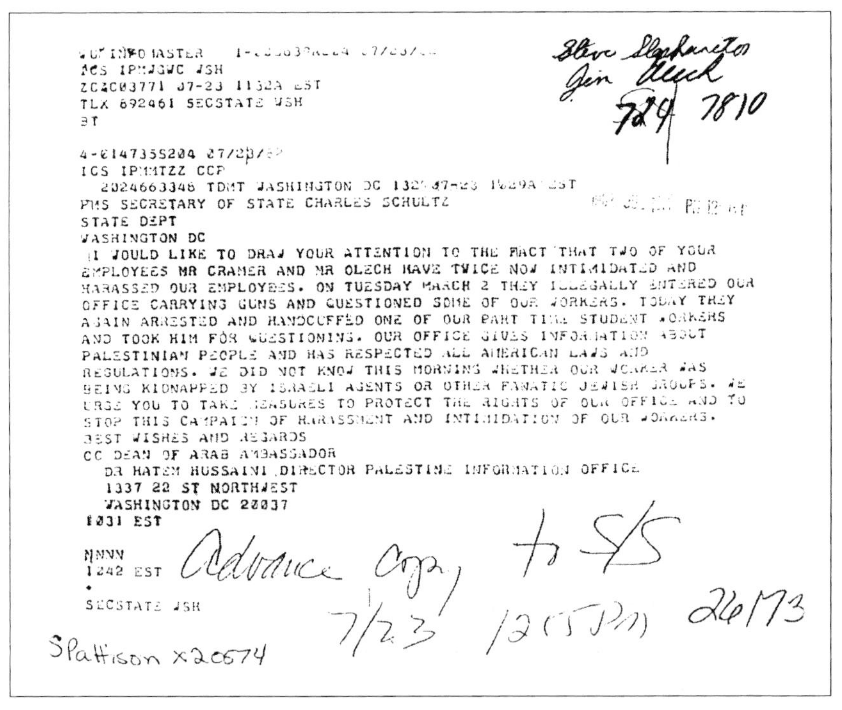
WUI INFO MASTER
ICS IPMJGWC WSH
ZCZC03771 07-23 1132A EST
TLX 692461 SECSTATE WSH
BT

4-014735S204 07/23/
ICS IPMMTZZ CCP
2024663348 TDMT WASHINGTON DC 132 07-23 1029A EST
PMS SECRETARY OF STATE CHARLES SCHULTZ
STATE DEPT
WASHINGTON DC
I WOULD LIKE TO DRAW YOUR ATTENTION TO THE FACT THAT TWO OF YOUR EMPLOYEES MR CRAMER AND MR OLECH HAVE TWICE NOW INTIMIDATED AND HARASSED OUR EMPLOYEES. ON TUESDAY MARCH 2 THEY ILLEGALLY ENTERED OUR OFFICE CARRYING GUNS AND QUESTIONED SOME OF OUR WORKERS. TODAY THEY AGAIN ARRESTED AND HANDCUFFED ONE OF OUR PART TIME STUDENT WORKERS AND TOOK HIM FOR QUESTIONING. OUR OFFICE GIVES INFORMATION ABOUT PALESTINIAN PEOPLE AND HAS RESPECTED ALL AMERICAN LAWS AND REGULATIONS. WE DID NOT KNOW THIS MORNING WHETHER OUR WORKER WAS BEING KIDNAPPED BY ISRAELI AGENTS OR OTHER FANATIC JEWISH GROUPS. WE URGE YOU TO TAKE MEASURES TO PROTECT THE RIGHTS OF OUR OFFICE AND TO STOP THIS CAMPAIGN OF HARASSMENT AND INTIMIDATION OF OUR WORKERS.
BEST WISHES AND REGARDS
CC DEAN OF ARAB AMBASSADOR
DR HATEM HUSSAINI DIRECTOR PALESTINE INFORMATION OFFICE
1337 22 ST NORTHWEST
WASHINGTON DC 20037
1031 EST

NNNN
1242 EST

SECSTATE WSH

Advance Copy to S/S
7/23 1215 PM 26173
Steve Stephanatos
Jim Olech
724 7810
S Pattison x20674

Wire sent by PLO to Secretary of State Schultz complaining about INS intimidation and harassment of one of their "students."

quarters. They realized that INS Agents had far-reaching authority that could be used to aggressively collect intelligence and combat terrorism by foreign nationals living here. Eventually, the FBI requested that INS Agents be assigned to its multi-agency Joint Terrorism Task Force (JTTF).

The Chief of INS Headquarters Investigations saw the JTTF as a waste of manpower. Initially he did everything possible to stonewall the transfer of manpower. It is an understatement to say that the number of INS Special Agents originally assigned to the JTTF was insufficient. And in many cases, the INS Agents came from the "bottom of the barrel." Whether this directly or indirectly led to the 1993 and 2001 World Trade Center terrorist attacks will never be known. However, there is now significant evidence to indicate that ineffective immigration controls can facilitate the ability of terrorists to operate within the U.S. and, on the other hand, aggressive immigration enforcement initiatives can significantly diminish their capabilities.

The 9/11 Commission made several recommendations regarding immigration control. As usual, there was nothing specific about how to implement the suggested changes. As we all know, "the devil is in the details."

For example, the Commission wrote:

> *"Secure identification should begin in the United States. The Federal government should* ***set standards*** *[emphasis added] for the issuance of birth certificates and sources of identification, such as driver's licenses. Fraud in identification is no longer just a problem of theft. At many entry points to vulnerable facilities, including gates for boarding aircraft, sources of identification are the last opportunity to ensure that people are who they say they are and to check whether they are terrorists."*

While I applaud the work of The 9/11 Commission, the lack of specificity in the report indicates the members had little understanding of the complexity of the problems surrounding identification fraud. As I will delineate in Part II, very specific and in some cases, expensive projects must be undertaken if America is going to close this massive security loophole. Curtailing production and use of fraudulent immigration and identification documents will be a large but critically necessary initiative to prevent future terrorism. Simply "setting standards" will accomplish very little, if anything at all.

People were at fault on 9/11—not acronyms!

For those people who have never been part of the Federal bureaucracy, the term Presidential Rank Award has little meaning. The best way to describe one is a multi-thousand dollar "pat-on-the-back" that is passed out annually to "deserving" U.S. Government Senior Executives—many of whom are political appointees or are politically connected in one form or another. Presidential Rank Awards are just one example of the many ways that senior level Federal employees add significant cash to their bank accounts.

For the most part, these nifty cash bonuses are given to individual employees, and the award ceremonies are nothing short of a West Point graduation. If it is not the President himself handing out the checks, it is a Cabinet Secretary, the Secretary of State or the Attorney General. The accolades usually flow for an hour or two, while lower-graded employees in attendance shake their heads in disbelief of what is being proclaimed. Then most attendees clap gratuitously—probably to take their minds off the fact they want to throw up.

What do Presidential Rank Awards have to do with the 9/11 attacks? Americans were duped into believing that systematic failures at different government agencies (FBI, CIA, NSA, etc.) allowed the 19 hijackers to enter the U.S. and carry out the attacks. Nothing is further from the truth. Not a single three-letter agency was responsible. The *people* in those agencies were responsible, and the *people* should have been held accountable. After all, when the awards are given out, Senior Executives take the credit . . . and the cash. Maybe it is time we started to hold our government Senior Executives accountable for their ineptitude as well.

While I am pleased The 9/11 Commission did not carry out a "witch hunt," in some cases they should have named individuals responsible for critical failures. By not doing so, the Commission inadvertently implied no one was at fault. Many INS employees should have been mentioned in the Commission's report, and the list would have been quite revealing. It would have named District Directors who were not qualified for their jobs, Immigration officers in very sensitive positions who had no formal training, and other INS officials who completely misunderstood their function in the Immigration and Naturalization Service. By not naming specific individuals, the Commission virtually approved their ineptitude, and allowed them to continue to operate unnoticed in the new Department of Homeland Security. In fact, it would not surprise me if some of those responsible have since received Presidential Rank Awards or other similar accolades.

Chapter 2
The U.S. Border Patrol

Insanity is doing the same thing over and over again and expecting different results.

Albert Einstein

On the front page of *USA Today,* Monday, February 2, 2004, one headline read:

"Border Patrol catches, then releases, illegals; System creates gap in national security."

In Kevin Johnson's article, it states:

"Thousands of illegal immigrants, mostly from Central and South America, are being released into the USA almost immediately after they are picked up by the Border Patrol as part of a policy that U.S. officials acknowledge represents a significant gap in homeland security.

"D'Wayne Jernigan, the sheriff in Val Verde County, Texas seemed to sum up the whole issue when he stated, 'During these times when everybody's concerned about who's coming into this country, I think you have to question the wisdom of this policy.'

"Remember, these are the same policy makers who created the terrorist threat level color chart and who require each and every seventy-five year old woman passenger to remove her shoes at the airport!

"I don't mean to be sarcastic, but this is ludicrous!"

In a September 20, 2004, issue of *Time* magazine, reporters Barlett and Steele began their article "Who Left the Door Open?" with the following paragraph:

"The next time you pass through an airport and have to produce a photo I.D. to establish who you are and then must remove

your shoes, take off your belt, empty your pockets, prove your laptop is not an explosive device and send your briefcase or purse through a machine to determine whether it holds weapons, think about this: 4,000 illegal aliens will walk across the busiest unlawful gateway into the U.S., the 375-mile border between Arizona and Mexico. No searches for weapons. No shoe removal. No photo-ID checks. Before long, many will obtain phony identification papers, including bogus Social Security numbers, to conceal their true identities and mask their unlawful presence."

The Border Patrol smokescreen

Washington politicians always equate immigration control with the U.S. Border Patrol. It is simply political rhetoric. Whenever and wherever the illegal immigration issue is raised, representatives always seem to answer the tough questions by advocating more Border Patrol Agents. I found it fascinating that during the 2004 U.S. Presidential debates, President Bush proudly stated that, since the 9/11 attacks, he has added a thousand Border Patrol Agents to the Mexican and Canadian borders. There was an implication that this increase would make America safer and would curtail illegal immigration.

In 2005, Congress passed sweeping intelligence reform legislation based on the recommendations of The 9/11 Commission. President George W. Bush signed the bill into law. Immigration reform was supposed to be part of the final bill, but it was removed during the last days before passage. The only immigration-related part of the legislation that did survive authorized (you guessed it) more Border Patrol Agents.

Hiring more Border Patrol Agents is little more than a smokescreen for real immigration control. While it may give politicians and their constituents a warm and fuzzy feeling, it does little to truly secure our borders, and virtually nothing to solve our growing problem of illegal immigration.

Some politicians are actually swayed by Hollywood. They truly believe the way to eliminate illegal immigration and protect the country from George W. Bush's "evildoers" is to mass thousands of Charles Bronsons along the Mexican and Canadian borders. The truth is, Americans are fed up with these failed policies and are demanding much more security than increased manpower can provide.

I certainly do not advocate downsizing the Border Patrol. However, history has shown that as the U.S. increased the number of its Border Patrol Agents, the number of illegal aliens increased as well. Facts are facts, so let's take a look at them.

- The Canadian and Mexican land borders have not changed in decades.
- In 1976 (when I joined the Border Patrol), there were approximately 2,000 Border Patrol Agents and an estimated 2 million illegal aliens in the U.S.
- In 2007, the Border Patrol had approximately 14,000 agents stationed mostly on the Mexican border, and there were an estimated 12 million-plus illegal aliens in the U.S. (This does not include the 2.8 million illegal aliens granted legal status under the 1986 amnesty.)
- If we keep going at this rate (and there is no reason to believe we will not), by the year 2030, we will have close to 50,000 Border Patrol Agents and at least 50 million illegal aliens.

We are well on our way. In almost every version of "comprehensive immigration reform" legislation considered by Congress in 2007, there was a call to add 18,000 new Border Patrol Agents by 2012. The legislation may have failed, but solving our immigration problems by simply deploying more Border Patrol Agents is a concept that has a life of its own.

It does not take a degree in statistics to see that the Border Patrol represents one of the biggest failures in U.S. law-enforcement history. For various reasons, the Patrol has done a miserable job in fulfilling its primary mission—stopping illegal immigration.

This chapter is dedicated to revealing why the Border Patrol has failed. I hope the anecdotes will give Americans some insight into why the U.S. Border Patrol became so large, so powerful, and so inept, all at the same time.

I also have no intention of demeaning the dedicated men and women of the U.S. Border Patrol. In fact, agents themselves are not happy about the situation. In a 2004 survey conducted by the American Federation of Government Employees, 64% of the Border Patrol Agents surveyed said they had not been given the tools, training and support that they need to do their job. Another 62% said that Homeland Security could be doing much more to stop potential terrorists from entering the country.

The new Customs and Border Protection of the Department of Homeland Security

The United States Border Patrol is now under Homeland Security. Their new parent division is called Customs and Border Protection (CBP). But fear not, no matter what name they give it, the U.S. Border Patrol is still the "same old Patrol." (Many of us who served in the Patrol referred to it as the "mean green," despite the fact that the epithet became "politically incorrect" during the Clinton presidency.)

The more the Border Patrol changes, the more it stays the same

Several months before I retired, I received a call from a young friend in Florida. He called to say that he had decided on a career in law enforcement and was going for his oral interview with the U.S. Border Patrol. He asked me if I had any advice.

Jokingly I told him about a trick question that was presented to me during my oral interview in 1975. As the hypothetical question goes, there was an alien drowning in the Rio Grande River and the agent's supervisor had given the agent a prior order to remain at his lookout post. I warned my young friend (if they presented him with the same scenario) to disregard the supervisor's order and save the alien drowning in the river.

Within hours after he finished his exam he phoned to thank me for warning him about the question. I could not believe my ears. Almost 30 years had passed and the Border Patrol was still using the same stupid hypothetical situations. While this might not seem like a big deal, it indicates how little the Border Patrol has changed over the years.

The U.S. Border Patrol Academy

As a graduate of the 110th Session of the U.S. Border Patrol Academy, I believe I have a right to give my opinion about this revered institution. I am proud that I successfully passed, but some of the Border Patrol's training is misguided at best.

The Patrol likes to think it is a paramilitary organization. It is not. It is a law enforcement agency. Yet, the Patrol is the only agency at the Federal Law Enforcement Training Center that requires its agents to march in formation around the campus screaming unintelligible rhymes. As much as this seems like a good thing for *esprit de corps*, it sends the wrong signal to many recruits. The Border Patrol promotes a military mentality, and many graduates head for the U.S. borders thinking they are heading to war.

When most agents arrive at their first duty station, it does not take long before the mystique wears off. While most are proud to be walking around their communities as Border Patrol Agents, they usually dread going to work. For every hour spent on patrol, they spend six hours doing tedious paperwork. And talk about culture shock. After being trained for a war, they find themselves interrogating Mexican dishwashers for the first three years on the job.

Some Border Patrol Agents are brutal to the illegal aliens they apprehend. When I served at INS Headquarters, complaints of beatings by Border Patrol Agents used to keep the Justice Department's Office of Professional Responsibility a busy place. Admittedly the U.S.-Mexican border is a very dangerous place, and there are drug smugglers and other serious criminals operating along the river and other border areas. I believe, however, that some agents have difficulty understanding that the vast majority of the people they encounter are not "the enemy." They are simply poor, illegal immigrants looking for a better way of life. They are to be processed administratively, detained and eventually sent back home.

The Border Patrol Academy would do a much better job at preparing trainee agents for their job if they would tell the recruits the truth about life in the Patrol, and train them as law enforcement officers, not soldiers.

Some parts of Border Patrol Academy were wonderful. I learned a lot about immigration law, and I had an opportunity to expand my Spanish language skills. I also met my training instructor Gene Corder. To this day, I consider him to be one of the finest men I have ever met in my life. Gene and two of his brothers were career Border Patrol Agents and he was a great mentor at the Academy. (He subsequently became a Chief Patrol Agent in Yuma, Arizona, before his retirement.) I am especially grateful to him for giving several of us his best advice, hours before we graduated. He told us privately to get out of the U.S. Border Patrol as fast as we could. He obviously knew something.

The numbers game

In July, 1976, I arrived in Eagle Pass, Texas, after graduating from the Border Patrol Academy, located then in Los Fresnos, Texas. I learned Rule #1 about the Border Patrol. We were in a numbers game, and nothing else mattered. If Border Patrol Agents arrested and processed enough illegal aliens and caught an alien smuggler along the way, no one questioned where they went or what they did.

Border Patrol management in the Del Rio Sector Headquarters, in the Dallas, Texas, Regional Office and in Headquarters in Washington, D.C., were all playing the same game. The more illegal aliens arrested, the more manpower would be forthcoming from Congress. Astronomical numbers of arrests would start the bureaucratic domino effect. More Border Patrol Agents meant

"Border Patrol Headquarters," Quemado, Texas, 1976.

more supervisors; more supervisors meant more chance for advancement; more advancement meant higher pay; higher pay meant bigger budgets; bigger budgets bought faster cars and bigger guns; and so on and so on. Border Patrol management could have cared less that they were doing little to control illegal immigration. They had found a way into the U.S. Treasury, and no one was going to stop them.

Most Patrol Agents I worked with were extremely hard-working men and women. They would go out on the border each night looking for loads of aliens being smuggled into the U.S. Considering the fact that there were 50 or 60 loads being smuggled each night, finding one was not the most difficult work in the world. In fact, catching illegal aliens and their smugglers on the Mexican border was similar to catching bartenders and drunks in New Orleans during Mardi Gras. There were plenty to go around.

However, there were agents who worked the day shift, and they also needed numbers to keep Border Patrol management happy. I had not been in Eagle Pass a week before I was introduced to the "day game."

My first day-shift training officer was Agent Bill. He was a seasoned Patrol agent and had spent most of his career in Eagle Pass. He had been around a long time and was disheartened that the Border Patrol was not more progressive in its attempts to stop the flow of illegal aliens. He had also become a master at producing "numbers" for management.

Bill showed me two quick ways to arrest all of the illegal aliens I needed to eventually get promoted: (1) "dump rats" and (2) the photocopy machine.

"Dump rats" were illegal aliens who crossed the Rio Grande almost daily. They loved to rummage through a small dump on the U.S side of the Rio Grande near Eagle Pass. Many locals on the U.S. side used the dump to discard everything from old tires to coffee makers. The Mexicans would swim across the river at all hours of the day and night, grab what they could, and head back home. They also knew the Border Patrol "game" and were happy to play.

If Patrol Agents were a little short on apprehensions they would head down to the dump, arrest nine or ten "dump rats" (who would never run), and head back to the office with their load of illegal aliens. The Mexicans knew the Border Patrol Agents were not going to hurt them, and they all looked forward to the meal they received while in INS custody.

At the office, the agents completed their I-213s (Record of Deportable Alien), submitted them to their supervisors, and received credit for stopping the entry of another group of illegal aliens. The Mexicans were driven back to the U.S. side of the international bridge and were told to walk back to Mexico. The whole process was nothing but a complete fraud.

For those agents who didn't like the "dump rat" scheme, there was the photocopy machine. Agents would erase the names and supervisor signatures from previously submitted forms. They would then add different Mexican names, and submit them to a "cooperating" supervisor. Once again, numbers of arrests were all that mattered.

The arrest records were proudly forwarded to Sector Headquarters in Del Rio, Texas, then on to the Dallas Regional Office, and eventually to Washington, D.C. The agents in Eagle Pass looked great, the Sector looked great, the Region looked great and INS Border Patrol in Headquarters had plenty of impressive statistics to use to obtain more resources from Congress.

Public relations and the U.S. Border Patrol

The Border Patrol likes to portray itself as a paramilitary organization. As such, it attracts many young veterans into its ranks. The Border Patrol has not only hired a few thousand soldiers after their military service, the Patrol's Senior Executives apparently went straight to the Pentagon for lessons in public relations. The brass at the Pentagon taught the brass at the Border Patrol a very important lesson about politicians. If a Congressman or Senator is taken on a flight in an F-16 fighter, or given a ride in a nuclear submarine, there is a very good possibility he or she will vote favorably on the agency's next appropriation requests on Capitol Hill.

The Border Patrol doesn't have fighter jets or submarines, but they have something just as good. Every night near San Diego, California, thousands of aliens line up on the Mexican side of the border and wait for darkness. Shortly after the sun goes down, the mass of humanity starts across the desert and attempts to get by the Border Patrol.

Years ago, Border Patrol brass realized this race to America had tremendous entertainment value for politicians—especially new Attorney Generals and political appointees at Homeland Security.

South of San Diego, in a small California city named Chula Vista, the U.S. Border Patrol can put on a show that makes Disney's fireworks at Epcot Center look meager. Before heading down to the desert, dignitaries are first awarded everything from a green baseball hat to a $300 Border Patrol leather bomber jacket. (Janet Reno looked stunning in her outfit.) Soon comes the night-vision goggles, the four-wheel drive all-terrain vehicles, and a high-speed romp across the dunes to rendezvous with Patrol Agents on horseback—just to give the flavor of the "Old Patrol."

Suddenly one agent receives a call on his radio that a "load" of illegal aliens has been spotted. With wide-eyed civilians safely strapped in the back seat, the Border Patrol driver rips the vehicle's gear box to shreds as he hastily places it into gear, and speeds through the desert, allowing all the passengers to experience horrific air turbulence without ever leaving the ground. After several minutes, all arrive at the final part of the show.

There on the desert floor sit 25 illegal aliens with their hands cuffed behind their backs. While the aliens sit waiting to be taken to the Border Patrol station for processing, the "show-and-tell" agents relate stories about drug smugglers and gun fights. Within an hour, the Border Patrol has everyone convinced that they are the finest law enforcement agency this side of the NYPD. It is impressive—especially when they tell their guests to keep the $300 bomber jackets.

Every Attorney General, politician and media pundit who ever went through this tour came out vowing to get more resources for the Border Patrol. It was, and still is, one of the finest public relations gimmicks I have ever seen.

Unfortunately, this Border Patrol game is doing little to truly curtail illegal immigration.

Guarding our borders

Once again I refer back to my days in Eagle Pass, Texas. I have vivid memories of one landmark known as the Black Bridge or *El Puente Negro*. It was a black railroad bridge that spanned the Rio Grande River.

The Border Patrol had planted several radio transmitting sensors at strategic places on the bridge. When illegal aliens tried to cross, they inevitably stepped on the sensors, sending a signal of "M-24" to the receiver we carried in the patrol car. As soon as the sun went down, the sensors went off, and the nonsense began.

First, it was a high-speed run down the highway and through the city streets of Eagle Pass. Then we would shut off the headlights, roll down the dirt road to a parking lot at river level. Finally, we would quietly walk down and hide in the bushes at the bottom of the bridge's staircase.

Before too long the aliens who had set off the sensor would come down the stairs and walk right past us. As soon as the entire group had passed, we would sneak up behind them with guns drawn and yell, *"Parate, parate! Patrulleros de la Frontera!"* ("Stop, stop, Border Patrol!")

I was never sure at this point who was more afraid, me or the aliens. Despite the fact I was 6'3" tall, had a fully loaded .38 Colt in my hand, and carried all the authority of a U.S. Federal officer, my finger was cautiously on the trigger. Staring me in the face were 10 or 15 frightened illegal immigrants and usually one very cunning smuggler. (No matter how many times I went through this routine, I never got used to it. I always thought there had to be a better way.)

There was also a very high hill in Eagle Pass that looked down on the Black Bridge. Frequently, Border Patrol Agents would park on the hill to look out across the Rio Grande into Mexico for groups gathering on the other side. I noticed after weeks of working near the bridge that while the Border Patrol vehicles were visibly parked on the hill, no aliens ever attempted to cross *El Puente Negro*.

One evening when I was sitting with a journeyman Border Patrol training officer named Roy, I asked a stupid question. "Why don't we just sit here all night? Then the aliens will never come across the bridge."

I may as well have shot someone. Roy became enraged and advised me that if we guarded the border we would not get paid as much. Furthermore, we would not apprehend any aliens or not get "our numbers."

Roy's ideas and attitude about patrolling the Mexican border are as pervasive today as they were in 1976. While I am not about to blame the illegal immigration problem on the Border Patrol, their inability to change old habits is partially to blame for their inability to curtail the flow of illegal aliens. For the sake of maintaining their federal pay grade, they refuse to grasp the concept that, in some areas, it would be better to guard the border than to patrol it. Most of the senior management are so wrapped up with their Border Patrol traditions they cannot admit they are failing in their primary mission.

The tragedy of Border Patrol Agents Ignacio Ramos and Jose Compean

The date of February 17, 2005, will go down in history as one of the darkest and most destructive days in the history of the U.S. Border Patrol. According to several different sources, Patrol Agents Ignacio Ramos and Jose Compean attempted to stop a vehicle that was being driven in Fabens, Texas, near the U.S.-Mexico border. After failing in an attempt to flee in his vehicle, the driver subsequently jumped out and started to run back to Mexico with the agents in hot pursuit. At some point in the foot race, the suspect apparently turned toward one of the pursuing agents, and waved what was perceived as a firearm. Shots were fired at the suspect, but he continued back to Mexico, supposedly unharmed. Shortly after the shooting incident, agents searched the abandoned vehicle and found almost 750 pounds of marijuana.

Patrol Agents Compean and Ramos then made the biggest mistake of their lives. They failed to complete the necessary paperwork regarding the shooting.

Had it not been for some coincidental relationships, the incident would not have been heard about again. As court documents show, however, the suspect Osbaldo Aldrete-Davila was actually shot as he was fleeing and was apparently wounded by the Border Patrol Agents. His mother, Marcadia Aldrete-Davila, contacted the mother-in-law of another Border Patrol Agent who then notified Homeland Security officials. The wounded suspect was contacted by investigators, brought back to the U.S. for medical treatment, and offered immunity to testify against the Border Patrol Agents—despite the fact the suspect was a known drug dealer.

After an extremely questionable investigation and trial, Compean and Ramos were indicted, convicted and sent to Federal prison. Both were sentenced to more than a decade in jail because the law requires a minimum sentence of ten years when a gun is involved in a crime. Despite enormous media coverage and a plea to President George W. Bush for a presidential pardon, the two agents went to prison.

It is not for me to agree or disagree with the jury in this case. I was not there and I can only hope that justice will prevail in the end. This case does give a clear indication that Border Patrol Agents are working in a very dangerous and unpredictable job. Our government has created extreme confusion on our border with Mexico, where Border Patrol Agents are forced to make life-and-death decisions on a regular basis.

As a final note regarding this case, I believe U.S. Attorney Sutton and his fellow prosecutors intended to make an example of the agents for political purposes. Illegal immigration is one of the most sensitive issues facing the U.S. and Mexico, and our government chose to appease Mexican politicians by destroying the lives of agents Compean and Ramos. A review of the court records indicates clearly that the agents were convicted with evidence that did not even come close to "proof beyond reasonable doubt." On the other hand, I believe that Compean and Ramos should have been punished for their failure to follow the procedures of the U.S. Border Patrol. But, to send these two dedicated officers to prison, based on the testimony of an illegal-alien drug dealer, is one of the greatest miscarriages of justice in U.S. history.

"Hold the Line"—1993: El Paso, Texas

One of the most progressive men in the history of U.S. immigration law enforcement was El Paso Chief Patrol Agent Sylvester

"Silver" Reyes. In December, 1995, Silver retired from the ranks of the U.S. Border Patrol to become a U.S. Congressman. His popularity in the El Paso area was partially due to his bold initiatives when he was Border Patrol Chief in El Paso.

In September, 1993, Chief Reyes implemented a commonsense program called "Hold the Line." He simply moved most of his Border Patrol resources to the most active crossing areas around El Paso and told the agents to guard the border, not patrol it. As the Mexicans lined up on the other side waiting for the agents to begin their patrols, they soon realized the agents and their cars were not moving. In fact, they did not move for days.

Suddenly, the usual "cat and mouse" game had changed, and the Border Patrol virtually shut down illegal crossings between El Paso, Texas, and Juarez, Mexico. The complaints could be heard loud and clear. The wealthy homeowners in El Paso had no maids and their babysitters could not get across the river. The landscaping crews never showed up and most of the construction stopped. It did not take long before the "crap hit the fan" in Washington, D.C.

Operation "Hold the Line" was working so well that the Mexican government vigorously protested to the U.S. State Department, and every immigrant-rights group within a thousand miles of El Paso yelled Border Patrol racism. One problem—Silver Reyes is an American of Mexican descent, so the racist name-calling immediately went out the window. Reyes was simply a professional Border Patrol Agent who was fed up with illegal immigration and was willing to take a huge risk to bring the situation in El Paso under control.

I was in Glynco, Georgia, at the time. I remember hearing that Commissioner Meissner was livid about Reyes implementing a program that she never approved. Friends of mine stationed in Headquarters at the time said she was walking around threatening to remove Reyes from his position. However, a few days after "Hold the Line" began, many residents in El Paso realized that the program was creating unexpected and favorable results. Shoplifting arrests went down, and car thefts took a plunge. El Paso police reported a significant drop in violent crimes. “Hold the Line” had worked. Meissner not only withdrew her criticism of Reyes, but was forced to thank him publicly for his law enforcement professionalism.

Sylvester Reyes not only risked the wrath of the politicians in Washington, but more importantly, he did something the Border Patrol had feared for decades. Reyes showed that the best way to control certain areas of the border is to “guard” it, not “patrol” it.

Chapter 3
What Happened to Employer Sanctions?

Our porous borders are only part of the reason we have 12 million-plus illegal aliens in the country. It is the opportunity for employment in America that has brought us to our current crisis. After listening to debate after debate about "comprehensive immigration reform," Americans should realize that most illegal aliens have jobs here. In a nutshell, the economics are simple. Many employers want hard-working people to do menial or back-breaking labor for moderate wages. Most Americans are just not willing to do the work, and illegal aliens show up to fill the void.

This is not the first time the U.S. has had to deal with this problem. More than 20 years ago, Americans were listening to the same arguments and contemplating the same solutions. History has shown that our politicians and government leaders failed us—and failed us miserably. If I do not accomplish anything else by writing this book, I hope Americans will finally understand what happened, who was responsible, and what we need to do to prevent it from happening again.

Congress passed the Simpson-Mazzoli Immigration Reform and Control Act in 1986. Wyoming Republican Senator Alan Simpson (I think he was one of the smartest and most thoughtful politicians to ever grace the halls of Capitol Hill), and Kentucky Democrat Congressman Romano Mazzoli, took the lead in crafting one of the most controversial revisions of U.S. immigration law in almost 30 years.

In the months before the Act was passed, I was serving at INS Headquarters developing the Systematic Alien Verification

Illegal aliens arrested paving Pennsylvania Avenue—it is not just a border issue.

for Entitlements program, in hopes of making it part of the new legislation. I had the opportunity to meet and discuss America's immigration problems with Senator Simpson, Congressman Mazzoli and many others on Capitol Hill.

As I listen to the current debates about "comprehensive immigration reform," it seems like a flashback to1986. Some of the characters have changed but the rhetoric is still the same. Senator Edward Kennedy from Massachusetts was promoting amnesty and Senator Simpson was promoting security of our borders and employer sanctions to prevent more illegal aliens from entering the country. Immigrant advocacy groups like *La Raza* were accusing everyone who opposed amnesty of being a racist, and Dan Stein's Federation of Americans for Immigration Reform (FAIR) was trying their best to convince Americans that the amnesty was nothing more than a huge reward for big business and a free pass to the U.S. for millions of law breakers. Sound familiar?

The 1986 Immigration Reform and Control Act had two major components:

1. amnesty for illegal aliens, and
2. employer sanctions.

The theory behind the legislation was to have a complete overhaul of our immigration system by approving an amnesty to wipe the slate clean for millions of illegal aliens who were working here, and to implement employer sanctions to punish employers who knowingly hired illegal aliens.

The employer sanctions program was supposed to create a system where employers would be required to check the documents of all their workers to make certain they had the legal right to work here. Those who did not comply would be subjected to fines and possible criminal prosecution. The Employment Eligibility Verification Form (I-9) was born from this legislation.

In the years that followed the passage of the Immigration Reform and Control Act, the amnesty was successfully implemented. Approximately 2.8 million illegal aliens were granted permanent residence in the U.S.

The employer sanctions program was another story. It was purposefully sabotaged at the Immigration and Naturalization Service. Ineptitude may have played a small part in its demise, but stupidity can only do so much to dismantle meaningful legislation.

The failure to properly implement the employer sanctions portion of the Immigration Reform and Control Act of 1986 is a historical lesson that must be carefully studied, as we move America toward implementation of yet another employer-sanctions program and more "comprehensive immigration reform." As a nation, will be making a huge mistake if we simultaneously legalize millions of people who thumbed their noses at our immigration laws, and again allow the powerful lobbies in Washington to reduce the immigration enforcement mechanisms to another

U.S. Department of Justice
Immigration and Naturalization Service

OMB No. 1115-0136

Employment Eligibility Verification

Please read instructions carefully before completing this form. The instructions must be available during completion of this form. ANTI-DISCRIMINATION NOTICE: It is illegal to discriminate against work eligible individuals. Employers CANNOT specify which document(s) they will accept from an employee. The refusal to hire an individual because of a future expiration date may also constitute illegal discrimination.

Section 1. Employee Information and Verification. To be completed and signed by employee at the time employment begins.

Print Name: Last | First | Middle Initial | Maiden Name

Address *(Street Name and Number)* | Apt. # | Date of Birth *(month/day/year)*

City | State | Zip Code | Social Security #

I am aware that federal law provides for imprisonment and/or fines for false statements or use of false documents in connection with the completion of this form.

I attest, under penalty of perjury, that I am (check one of the following):
- ☐ A citizen or national of the United States
- ☐ A Lawful Permanent Resident (Alien # A______
- ☐ An alien authorized to work until ___/___/___
(Alien # or Admission #) ______

Employee's Signature | Date *(month/day/year)*

Preparer and/or Translator Certification. *(To be completed and signed if Section 1 is prepared by a person other than the employee.) I attest, under penalty of perjury, that I have assisted in the completion of this form and that to the best of my knowledge the information is true and correct.*

Preparer's/Translator's Signature | Print Name

Address *(Street Name and Number, City, State, Zip Code)* | Date *(month/day/year)*

Section 2. Employer Review and Verification. To be completed and signed by employer. Examine one document from List A OR examine one document from List B and one from List C, as listed on the reverse of this form, and record the title, number and expiration date, if any, of the document(s)

	List A	OR	List B	AND	List C
Document title:	______		______		______
Issuing authority:	______		______		______
Document #:	______		______		______
Expiration Date *(if any)*:	___/___/___		___/___/___		___/___/___
Document #:	______				
Expiration Date *(if any)*:	___/___/___				

CERTIFICATION - I attest, under penalty of perjury, that I have examined the document(s) presented by the above-named employee, that the above-listed document(s) appear to be genuine and to relate to the employee named, that the employee began employment on *(month/day/year)* ___/___/___ **and that to the best of my knowledge the employee is eligible to work in the United States. (State employment agencies may omit the date the employee began employment.)**

Signature of Employer or Authorized Representative | Print Name | Title

Business or Organization Name | Address *(Street Name and Number, City, State, Zip Code)* | Date *(month/day/year)*

Section 3. Updating and Reverification. To be completed and signed by employer.

A. New Name *(if applicable)* | B. Date of rehire *(month/day/year) (if applicable)*

C. If employee's previous grant of work authorization has expired, provide the information below for the document that establishes current employment eligibility.

Document Title:______ Document #:______ Expiration Date (if any): ___/___/___

I attest, under penalty of perjury, that to the best of my knowledge, this employee is eligible to work in the United States, and if the employee presented document(s), the document(s) I have examined appear to be genuine and to relate to the individual.

Signature of Employer or Authorized Representative | Date *(month/day/year)*

Form I-9 (Rev. 04/06/00)Y Page 2

The I-9. Virtually useless without automated verification of documents.

LISTS OF ACCEPTABLE DOCUMENTS

LIST A

Documents that Establish Both Identity and Employment Eligibility

1. U.S. Passport (unexpired or expired)
2. Certificate of U.S. Citizenship *(INS Form N-560 or N-561)*
3. Certificate of Naturalization *(INS Form N-550 or N-570)*
4. Unexpired foreign passport, with *I-551 stamp or* attached *INS Form I-94* indicating unexpired employment authorization
5. Alien Registration Receipt Card with photograph *(INS Form I-151 or I-551)*
6. Unexpired Temporary Card *(INS Form I-688)*
7. Unexpired Employment Authorization Card *(INS Form I-688A)*
8. Unexpired Reentry Permit *(INS Form I-327)*
9. Unexpired Refugee Travel Document *(INS Form I-571)*
10. Unexpired Employment Authorization Document issued by the INS which contains a photograph *(INS Form I-688B)*

OR

LIST B

Documents that Establish Identity

1. Driver's license or ID card issued by a state or outlying possession of the United States provided it contains a photograph or information such as name, date of birth, sex, height, eye color and address
2. ID card issued by federal, state or local government agencies or entities, provided it contains a photograph or information such as name, date of birth, sex, height, eye color and address
3. School ID card with a photograph
4. Voter's registration card
5. U.S. Military card or draft record
6. Military dependent's ID card
7. U.S. Coast Guard Merchant Mariner Card
8. Native American tribal document
9. Driver's license issued by a Canadian government authority

For persons under age 18 who are unable to present a document listed above:

10. School record or report card
11. Clinic, doctor or hospital record
12. Day-care or nursery school record

AND

LIST C

Documents that Establish Employment Eligibility

1. U.S. social security card issued by the Social Security Administration *(other than a card stating it is not valid for employment)*
2. Certification of Birth Abroad issued by the Department of State *(Form FS-545 or Form DS-1350)*
3. Original or certified copy of a birth certificate issued by a state, county, municipal authority or outlying possession of the United States bearing an official seal
4. Native American tribal document
5. U.S. Citizen ID Card *(INS Form I-197)*
6. ID Card for use of Resident Citizen in the United States *(INS Form I-179)*
7. Unexpired employment authorization document issued by the INS *(other then those listed under List A)*

Illustrations of many of these documents appear in Part 8 of the Handbook for Employers (M-274)

Form I-9 (Rev. 04/06/00)Y Page 3

The I-9 list of acceptable documents. A counterfeiter's dream come true!

"paper tiger." It happened in 1986, and it will happen again if certain business interests have their way.

Jack, "Bud Light" and Marianne

The current chaos with legal and illegal immigration cannot be blamed on some non-entity acronym like "INS." Government employees, not acronyms, must be held accountable. To simply say that a government agency is responsible may be "politically correct", but it does nothing to prevent mistakes from occurring again and again.

It has been decades since I worked at the Immigration and Naturalization Service Headquarters, implementing the provisions of the 1986 Immigration Reform and Control Act. However, I have vivid memories (and copious notes) regarding the development and implementation of the employer sanctions program.

Considering the current debate about re-implementing "employer sanctions", it would be a serious mistake not to discuss those responsible for past failures of the program. After all, it is one of the most useless initiatives ever created by the Federal government. Hopefully, we will never allow a similar situation to evolve again. (It is not my intention to be retributive. I decided to use only aliases and nicknames, as the specific identity of the employees is far less important than where they came from and how destructive they were to the implementation of the program.)

Overseeing the implementation of the employer sanctions program mandated by the 1986 Immigration Reform and Control Act was "Jack." Like so many others in INS Headquarters, he never graduated from the U.S. Border Patrol Academy or the Immigration Officer Basic Training Course. Even worse, he never served a day in the field as an Immigration officer.

Before Jack arrived at INS he served a short time as a Special Agent in the Federal Bureau of Investigation. He had difficulty at the FBI for allegedly writing a paper about the Bureau without first getting permission from Director J. Edgar Hoover. (Jack eventually won a lawsuit against the government, but his hatred of the FBI was evident to me during his entire tenure at the INS.) He also seemed uninterested in immigration law enforcement, and told me in private he could have cared less about illegal immigration, alien smuggling, document counterfeiting or employer sanctions.

How did Jack end up overseeing the sanctions program? After spending some "purgatory time" at the Department of Justice he was transferred to the Immigration and Naturalization Service and simply appointed Assistant Commissioner for Investigations. (Not bad for a guy who never conducted a single immigration-related investigation in his life.) With the passage of the 1986 Reform Act, Jack suddenly became the point man for employer sanctions implementation—despite the fact he knew virtually nothing about immigration law enforcement.

INS Agents knew there were three closely connected elements to a successful employer sanctions program: (1) employers must be required to review and verify work documents of all employees;(2) employers must complete and sign Form I-9: and (3) employers must be fined for failing to comply with the verification requirements and/or knowingly employing illegal aliens.

Whether it was done to be purposely destructive or out of shear stupidity, Jack stopped any attempt to develop a verification system for employers. Individuals who had experience with such systems were intentionally kept as far away from the employer sanctions program as possible, and the program was sabotaged from day one.

The result was inevitable. Immigration and identity document counterfeiters began coming out of the woodwork. Illegal aliens knew they could still get a job anywhere in the U.S. using nothing more than a fraudulent Social Security card and a fake "green card." Employers simply recorded what was shown to them on the Form I-9, and both the employer and the illegal alien were home free. The entire employer sanctions program was rendered virtually useless.

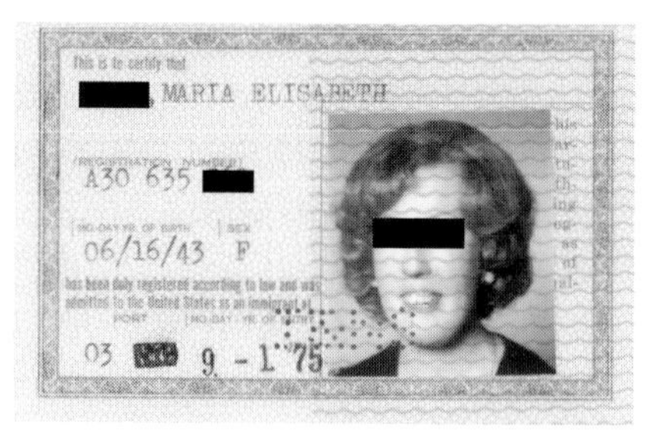

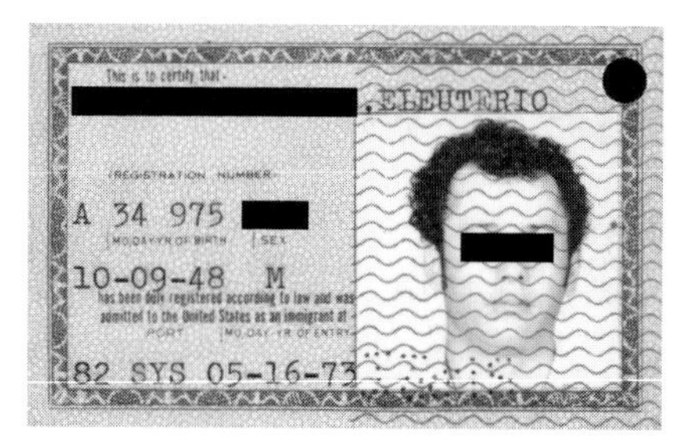

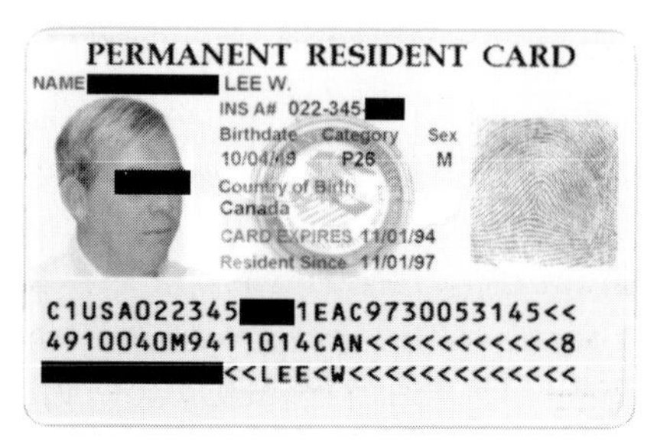

Various immigration and Social Security cards—some real, some fake!

I could ramble on for pages about the issue of fraudulent documents, but David Simcox summed it up completely in his Center for Immigration Studies report entitled "Secure Identification; A National Need—A Must for Immigration Control."

> *"Pervasive document fraud seriously impairs effective sanctions against employers of illegal aliens. Well-intentioned employers are hard-pressed to judge the validity of a multiplicity of I.D. documents submitted by applicants, while others knowingly accept false documents with little fear of successful prosecution."*

Since 1987, Immigration and Naturalization Service Special Agents (now Immigration and Customs Enforcement Special Agents) simply became disenchanted and chose to investigate everything but employer sanctions violations. The I-9 process has become a complete waste of time, and illegal immigration has continued to grow to unprecedented levels.

It seems that Jack had an agenda. Whether it was his desire to see the Department of Justice fail because of his previous problems with J. Edgar Hoover, or some other hidden reason, he quietly and effectively emasculated the employer sanctions program.

Could Jack have done this on his own? Where were his supervisors when all of this was happening?

Jack's supervisor was a man nicknamed "Bud Light." His nickname had more to do with his perceived intelligence level than the fact he weighed about 90 pounds. He also had an uncanny resemblance to Barney Fife on the Andy Griffith Show.

Bud had reportedly been a police chief in the Midwest before coming to Washington, and had moved around within the Federal law enforcement system before coming to INS.

According to Commissioner Nelson, Bud cornered him in an elevator at another law enforcement agency and asked the Commissioner for a job. Being "Mr. Nice Guy", Nelson inquired about him and Bud's employer gave him a fantastic recommendation. (Later they admitted they were just trying to get rid of him.)

Commissioner Nelson not only hired Bud, he subsequently appointed him as Associate Commissioner for INS Enforcement—overseeing Jack and the implementation of the employer sanctions program. (Once again, we had a Senior Executive in charge of all INS enforcement who had no basic knowledge of his job.)

One of my first direct encounters with Bud took place when I was working with several other officers to stop illegal aliens from obtaining valid Social Security cards. In August, 1989, we presented Bud with a memorandum for the Commissioner. The memo focused on two issues.

1. Illegal aliens were obtaining Social Security cards with counterfeit immigration documents and using them to get jobs. (The memo advocated that the Social Security

Administration use the Systematic Alien Verification for Entitlement database to verify immigration documents before issuing the Social Security number to alien applicants.)

2. Immigration and Naturalization Service Records Division was making slow progress updating the main INS Central Index database, and it was causing problems to the users of the Systematic Alien Verification for Entitlements program.

We wrote the following:

> *"The legislative history of IRCA [the Immigration Reform and Control Act] indicates that border control and employer sanctions could control illegal immigration into the United States. Considering the present IRCA mandated employer responsibilities (completing the I-9), the availability of counterfeit documents, the importance of the Social Security card, and the lack of alien status verification by the Social Security Administration, IRCA's enforcement provisions are fast becoming a paper tiger.*
>
> *"Corrective action in this area is critical to present immigration enforcement. Without a database that is accurate, up-to-date and readily accessible, the Service will ultimately fail in one of its most important areas of operation."*

On November 7, 1989, the memo finally made it to Bud's desk. At 10:00 A.M., I was summoned to his office. As I walked towards his desk, he threw the memorandum at me, and said "If you ever write another piece of shit about verification again, I'll have you working *under* this building. Now get out of my office and take this verification crap with you. Your ideas are politically unacceptable." From that day forward I stayed as far away from Bud as possible—and continued to watch the employer sanctions program decline.

As a last straw, Jack and Bud hired a Special Assistant. "MaryAnn" came from some unrelated division in the Department of Justice, and her job was to review all proposed federal regulations regarding employer sanctions implementation. For those of us who worked with her there was no doubt about her intentions. She was there to "roadblock" everything that made effective employer sanctions even remotely possible. No one seems to know whether she acted on her own or under orders from Jack and Bud.

The SAVE program—Testing automated status verification

During my first few years at INS Headquarters, I developed, tested and implemented a verification system using alien registration numbers. The Systematic Alien Verification for Entitlements (SAVE) program still exists and represents one of the most successful verification systems ever created at the former INS. (Obviously one of my predecessors at Headquarters had way too much time on his hands and came up with the acronym.) Here is a brief account and history of the SAVE program.

Early in my INS career, I realized that the U.S. could not control illegal immigration without some sort of "work authorization" verification system for employers. It was evident to me in the late 1970s and early 1980s that chasing illegal aliens through the streets of Washington, D.C., was not doing anyone any good. Unfortunately, the people who ran INS at that time were mostly former Border Patrol Agents. The majority had what I refer to as the "Border Patrol mentality." They believed that the more illegal aliens INS agents arrested, the more resources they could obtain from the Justice Department and Congress. Whether the INS was really doing anything to stop illegal immigration did not matter. Resources meant more people, more people meant more chances for advancement, and more advancement meant more money. Stopping illegal aliens from obtaining entitlement benefits was not on their agenda.

In 1981, I was promoted to Supervisory Special Agent. My Assistant District Director for Investigations was a Greek American named Stephen D. Stephanadis. He was not a former Border Patrol agent, and saw the entire internal immigration enforcement program in a very questionable light. Stephanadis also realized that some of us had new ideas about immigration enforcement, and he was usually supportive of our experiments. He always told us to be creative and to make certain what we did was legal and in the best interest of the U.S. government.

Following Steve's sage advice, I developed a unique little system to prevent illegal aliens from collecting unemployment compensation in the District of Columbia. One of the intake workers at the Labor Department suspected many El Salvadoran aliens were using fraudulent documents to collect unemployment benefits. Whenever an alien presented "green cards" or other INS paperwork to prove they had the right to work, this intake worker would photocopy them and mail them to me at the INS District Office. In turn, I would verify the documents using INS databases, actual alien files, and security features visible on the photocopy. I would then mail them back to her within a few days with a notation as to whether the documents were valid or not. The applicants never knew their immigration documents had been sent for verification, and the benefits were never delayed while the document was being verified.

Even back then, privacy was a huge concern, so the legality of the program had to be cleared with the legal beagles. I checked with some INS attorneys, and they advised me that as long as the immigration documents were the only items being verified, and I was not divulging that the applicant was applying for unemployment benefits, I was on safe ground.

This cooperative effort with the D.C. Labor Department also provided proof of another problem—that fraudulent immigration documents were being used to obtain government social service benefits. While all INS Special Agents knew that counterfeit "green cards" were used to obtain Social Security numbers and employment, we were never able to obtain sufficient evidence that illegal aliens were also using them to get different types of public assistance.

Within weeks of starting the verification program, our efforts resulted in the removal of more than 100 recipients from the unemployment compensation rolls. In addition, the "green cards" being utilized were not even good quality counterfeits. (We used to call the cards "50 footers" because Immigration inspectors on the Mexican border used to claim they could tell they were counterfeit from 50 feet away.) Unfortunately, since no one at the unemployment office knew anything about "green cards," they never had any reason to question their validity.

It was not long before the D.C. Labor Department workers began to spread the word about counterfeit immigration documents. The success they had with our verification program soon spread to several other agencies. In 1981, it was going so well, I had to enlist the help of a GS-4 Record Searcher named Phyllis Lancaster. Many nights Phyllis would stay with me until 9:00 P.M., checking documents and reviewing alien files. I mention Phyllis' dedication in those early days because she too believed in the value of the program. (Note: In August, 2004, after more than 23 years of working with the SAVE verification system, Phyllis Lancaster became Director of the program. She retired from that position in January, 2007.)

In those early days, I realized we had created something valuable. Not only did the verification system work, but the photocopies gave us great intelligence concerning fraudulent immigration documents. We were also able to determine the types of counterfeits being produced and the different nationalities using them. Unfortunately, it was very difficult to demonstrate the usefulness of the verification system to INS management. As I mentioned earlier, they were mostly former Border Patrol Agents who believed that the only real immigration law enforcement was to apprehend illegal aliens and put them back across the Mexican border. It was an uphill battle to say the least.

The Nelson mandate

Around 1983, Alan C. Nelson became Commissioner of INS under the Reagan Administration. Nelson had worked with Attorney General Ed Meese in Alameda County, California, and was quite glib when it came to discussing illegal aliens and how they impacted California's social services. When he arrived in Washington, he indicated he wanted to establish a program to prevent illegal aliens from obtaining welfare benefits.

Nelson's staff was befuddled. They did not know anything about welfare programs, and even less about immigration status verification. Despite their continuous attempts to sidetrack Nelson with other issues, the Commissioner pressed on. He enlisted two people at Headquarters to set up a verification system. He tagged Walt Wondolowski, an analyst working in the Office of Plans and Analysis, and Jim Olech, a Senior Special Agent in the Office of Investigations. They both hated the verification program and were under constant pressure to produce a viable system for Commissioner Nelson.

Eventually someone came up with the catchy abbreviation of SAVE (Systematic Alien Verification for Entitlements) and a slide presentation showing how much money the government would save by removing illegal aliens from Federally funded welfare programs. The slide presentation made some very questionable conclusions and estimated that implementation of the system would create $2.5 billion in savings the first year. The data used to make this assertion was straight from Disneyland, but it didn't matter. Nelson loved it.

During the time the slide show was being created, Wondolowski and Olech were praying that someone would come in, take over Nelson's folly, and get them the hell away from what appeared to be a career-ending program. At the same time, I was at the local D.C. immigration office looking for the right opportunity to demonstrate my pilot verification system to the powers-that-be at INS Headquarters.

I remember getting the phone call at the District Office from Rick Norton, Deputy Assistant Commissioner for Investigations. We were friends, as both of us had worked in the Investigations Section in Chicago in 1977. Rick asked me if I was interested in coming to Headquarters temporarily to work on a new system. As soon as I realized it was the SAVE system, I agreed.

When I arrived the following Monday, I was called into a meeting with Rick Norton, Jack Shaw, Assistant Commissioner for Investigations, and Ray Kisor, Associate Commissioner for Enforcement.

Ray Kisor simply told me, *"Commissioner Nelson is on my ass about this crazy SAVE program. I don't care what you have to do, where you have to go, or how many people you need, just get him off my ass."*

I was in heaven. I knew how successful my little project had been in D.C., and I couldn't wait to try it on a much larger scale. For the next several months, I worked day and night with a secretary named Marianne Martz, an INS contract specialist named Bertha Reed (now deceased), and Ray Gross, a representative from Martin-Marietta Data Systems.

Within months, the automated SAVE verification program became a reality.

"Why the strange look, Mr. Cramer?"

There are moments in everyone's life that they never forget. I had several thrilling ones as a Special Agent. However, as innocuous as it was, the SAVE program provided me one of the most amazing moments in my government career.

Commissioner Nelson had convinced Missouri Governor John Ashcroft (subsequently the U.S. Attorney General) to implement the SAVE program throughout his state welfare system. Kansas City INS District Director Ron Sanders had arranged for a meeting with Ashcroft in his office at the State Capitol. Ron was a great guy and a good friend and had done much of the leg work to get the Governor to promote the system. At the time, Ron never knew it, but all of us at Headquarters were promoting a SAVE computer system that had never actually worked.

For weeks prior to the Ashcroft meeting, and despite all of the efforts of Martin-Marietta Data Systems, every time the toll-free telephone number was dialed to access the SAVE system, it simply gave a busy signal. No matter how many times we tried and no matter how many promises Martin-Marietta made, the phone line always gave a busy signal.

Then I received the call from Ashcroft's office. Before I knew it, I was on a flight to the Missouri State Capitol to meet with Director Sanders and Governor Ashcroft to sign a Systematic Alien Verification Program proclamation. (Nelson had apparently used his Republican influence and convinced Ashcroft to support the system.)

Before I departed Washington, D.C. (the day before the meeting), I checked the system for the one hundredth time—busy signal. When I landed in Missouri, I checked it again—busy signal. I checked it five more times before I finally went to bed—busy signal every time. (As I remember I did not sleep very well!)

The next morning it was busy signal after busy signal. I called Martin-Marietta's help desk and nervously explained that the Governor of Missouri was going to use the system in a few hours and it had to work. They told me not to worry . . . everything would be fine.

Immediately after we arrived at the Capitol, I found a pay phone on the way to the Governor's office. I called the access number one last time. My heart sank as the damned busy signal came on once again. That was it . . . I began internally conjuring up excuses. Ashcroft would understand. Right? Wrong!

In conjunction with the Governor's Proclamation, Ashcroft wanted to test the system himself. And instead of having a nifty little private meeting, he had invited several members of the T.V. media into his outer office, including cameras, lights and the all impressive silver umbrellas. When I saw the set-up, I almost got sick.

Within minutes, Ashcroft signed the paperwork and went to the demonstration table to test the system. I stood over his shoulder and watched him dial the SAVE automated access phone number, knowing that a career-ending disaster was only seconds away.

As I nervously anticipated the annoying busy signal, I almost lost my lunch on the Governor's shoulder. Suddenly, I could not believe my ears. The phone actually rang. Then it rang again. Just before the third ring, the phone answered and a female recorded voice pleasantly stated, *"Welcome to the INS Alien Status Verification Index. Please enter your Access Code . . ."* Despite the fact I

Director Ron Sanders and Governor John Ashcroft signed SAVE Agreement while I closed my eyes and thanked God the system worked!

was in total disbelief that the system actually worked, I assisted Governor Ashcroft in performing two live verifications—one of a valid "green card" and another of a counterfeit. The system worked beautifully, as it verified the valid document and detected the counterfeit immediately.

Shortly afterwards, Ashcroft answered a few questions from the media, and then called an end to the session. Governor Ashcroft said he was impressed and expressed his appreciation that the entire demonstration went flawlessly. I was the only one who knew it was the very first time the SAVE system had actually operated.

As we were departing the office, a young female reporter came up to me and asked, "Mr. Cramer, that's a pretty impressive system. Why did you have such a troubled look on your face when the Governor was dialing the phone?" I simply smiled at her and left the building—as fast as my lucky ass would go.

Lobbying Congress—The next big step

During the time I was developing the Systematic Alien Verification for Entitlements (SAVE) program, momentum was growing in Congress to pass an overhaul of U.S. immigration laws. Commissioner Nelson told me he wanted the SAVE program to be included in the new immigration legislation. I did not have the slightest idea how to proceed, so I asked for guidance from Tom Perrelli, Nelson's lead INS liaison person on Capitol Hill.

Perrelli told me, "It is illegal as hell for you to lobby Congress. But, the only way the SAVE program will be included in the new legislation is if *you* lobby Congress." Perelli then gave me a few hints as to how to proceed, and sent me on my way to Capitol Hill. Despite the fact I was supposed to be an INS Senior Special Agent, I took on the challenge and soon began one of the most fascinating periods in my INS career. I virtually lobbied Congress to include the verification system in the Immigration Reform and Control Act of 1986.

Overcoming "garbage in-garbage out"

The biggest hurdle I had to overcome was the knowledge on Capitol Hill that INS databases were horribly inaccurate. (See Chapter 10.) If aliens were to be checked against databases filled with errors, thousands, if not millions, of legal immigrants could be erroneously denied welfare assistance. Democrats and Republicans both expressed concern about the reliability of INS databases.

I reverted back to my original days in the Washington District Office. I remembered that I had never made a mistake when I had a photocopy of the immigration document sent in to me for verification. I saw no reason this mail-in program could not be used as a back-up to alleviate the problems associated with INS records.

I convinced a few members on Simpson and Mazzoli's staff to make the mail-in "secondary verification" process part of the program. They agreed that this process would be an excellent way to prevent erroneous denials. Subsequently, under the proposed legislation, any INS document that could not be validated by the INS computer system, would be photocopied and mailed to INS for further examination. Entitlement agencies would be required to pay the benefits to an alien applicant until positive or negative written authorization was returned from the INS.

There was also a great deal of skepticism that any real conclusions could be drawn from a photocopy of an immigration document. I knew differently, and I knew I could prove it.

The undotted "i"

"Green cards" are actually INS forms. The old ones were Form I-151 and new fancy ones are Form I-551. Every version of the "green card" ever made had at least a few sneaky security features built in, to thwart counterfeiters. One of my favorites was the "undotted i" on the Form I-151.

On the reverse side of a genuine Form I-151, the word "immigration" in the fourth line was *not* dotted on the valid card. Due to the fact this was a security feature, only INS officers were supposed to have this information. Counterfeiters did not know about this "mistake" for years, and produced tens of thousands of counterfeit cards with the "i" dotted. A trained Immigration officer used to take less then a second to spot a counterfeit. To everyone else the cards looked valid—and "everyone else" included young impressionable Congressional staffers who couldn't wait to get some "top secret" information from a government agent.

During my lobbying efforts, I would make appointments to meet with Congressional staffers who were responsible for working on the new IRCA legislation. As soon as I arrived at their office, I would ask them to take me to a private room that was "secure" because I had classified information to discuss with them. Their eyes almost popped out of their heads.

In the "secure" room, I would speak very quietly and show the young workers two "green cards"—one genuine, one counterfeit. Most staffers, like most people, admitted they had never seen a "green card"—genuine or not. I would then tell them about the "i" without the dot and explain that INS had purposely left it off to thwart counterfeiters. You would have thought I had

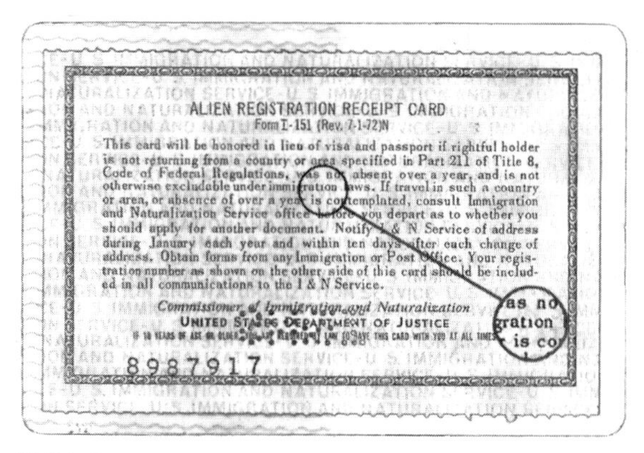

ALIEN REGISTRATION RECEIPT CARD
Form I-151 (Rev. 7-1-72)N

This card will be honored in lieu of visa and passport if rightful holder is not returning from a country or area specified in Part 211 of Title 8, Code of Federal Regulations, was not absent over a year, and is not otherwise excludable under immigration laws. If travel in such a country or area, or absence of over a year is contemplated, consult Immigration and Naturalization Service office before you depart as to whether you should apply for another document. Notify I & N Service of address during January each year and within ten days after each change of address. Obtain forms from any Immigration or Post Office. Your registration number as shown on the other side of this card should be included in all communications to the I & N Service.

Commissioner of Immigration and Naturalization
UNITED STATES DEPARTMENT OF JUSTICE

8987917

Valid document with undotted "i."

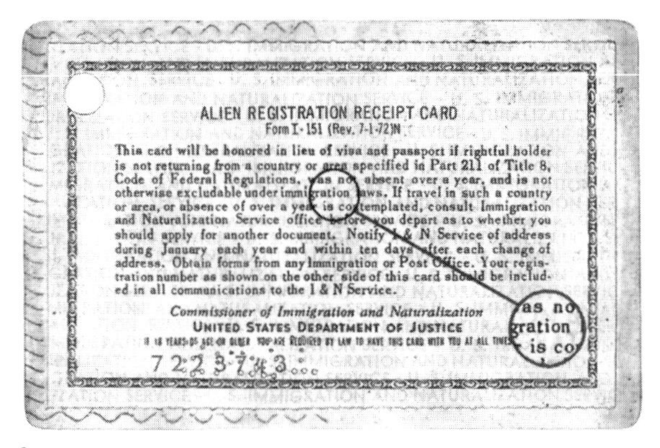

ALIEN REGISTRATION RECEIPT CARD
Form I-151 (Rev. 7-1-72)N

This card will be honored in lieu of visa and passport if rightful holder is not returning from a country or area specified in Part 211 of Title 8, Code of Federal Regulations, was not absent over a year, and is not otherwise excludable under immigration laws. If travel in such a country or area, or absence of over a year is contemplated, consult Immigration and Naturalization Service office before you depart as to whether you should apply for another document. Notify I & N Service of address during January each year and within ten days after each change of address. Obtain forms from any Immigration or Post Office. Your registration number as shown on the other side of this card should be included in all communications to the I & N Service.

Commissioner of Immigration and Naturalization
UNITED STATES DEPARTMENT OF JUSTICE

Counterfeit with dotted "i."

given them plans to a nuclear bomb. They started whispering and telling me they thought it was so cool. They all promised not to tell anyone. (As my fisherman brother describes it, "The bait was taken, the hook was in their gills, and all I had to do was gently reel them in.")

After giving them this secret information (it wasn't secret at all), I then explained that the SAVE program would make it almost impossible for illegal aliens and criminals to use fraudulent "green cards" to get entitlement benefits. I demonstrated that the automated system would prevent them from using a fraudulent Alien Registration number, and when a photocopy of their document was mailed in for secondary verification, all the dotted "i"s would be caught immediately.

The vast majority of staffers went back to their respective Congressmen and Senators and told them to vote for the SAVE program.

Did it work? SAVE was included in the 1986 Immigration Reform and Control Act. Commissioner Nelson took all of the credit and I was given the program to implement nationwide.

I subsequently served for four years as the Director of the SAVE program. I was supported by a dedicated staff, including Senior Special Agents Lena Berkholtz, Keith Roberts and Jim McClain. My Records Specialist was Phyllis Lancaster and our only secretary was Rene Scheming. This small staff was responsible for implementing the verification system throughout the U.S. and in five major cabinet level entitlement agencies. We succeeded and the program is still in operation today. Since its inception, it has saved American taxpayers billions of dollars.

The SAVE program demonstrated that "status verification" works and it can be a significant tool to curb illegal immigration. In the 1990s, the SAVE program was used as the foundation for the congressionally mandated Basic Pilot Program used by employers who desired immigration status verification of their employees. (See Chapter 4.) The Basic Pilot Program has lasted for more than a decade and has also successfully proven that employment status verification using Social Security numbers and other data is the next logical step.

The day that changed me forever

If you don't think a Social Security Number Verification System creates horror in the eyes of liberals and conservatives alike, consider what happened to me. In the summer of 1990, I wrote a proposal suggesting that we set up a Social Security Number Verification pilot program and attempt to verify the Social Security numbers of every employee working for Shirley Construction on government contracts in and around the Washington,

D.C. area. Every time I passed one of their sites I would wonder how many illegal aliens were being paid with our highway funds.

I knew Shirley Construction was responsible for building many of the major roadways in the area, and their projects were at least partially funded by Federal highway dollars. I did not think anyone would deny me the right to check the records of a Federally funded construction project. After all, who would care if I wanted to make certain taxpayer funds were being used to create jobs for people legally in the U.S.? Who would care? Read on.

My proposal described in detail how a review of a Shirley Construction road project could be conducted using an automated Social Security Number Verification System. I even researched the use of a toll-free phone number, right down to the cost per call.

The concept paper was submitted "through official channels" to Commissioner McNary's staff. I found out later that Tom Perrelli, INS point man for the IRCA legislation, had also forwarded it to some Congressional staffers who had expressed an interest in the concept.

Late the following Thursday afternoon, I was summoned to the office of Joe Sylvester, the Associate Commissioner for INS Management. Since I had done nothing wrong, I thought maybe I had hit the jackpot with my suggestion.

When I entered Joe's office I observed him sitting pleasantly behind his desk. He was flanked by his confidant and "get-it-done" guy, Jim Caffrey. Both were smiling at me, and Caffrey was twirling his long handlebar moustache—something he was apt to do before the "crap hit the fan."

Joe asked me how I was doing with my golf game. He was familiar with my exploits on the course and was a fair golfer himself. I knew immediately, however, I was not there to get an invitation to his next Member-Guest tournament.

Joe Sylvester then got serious. He congratulated me and my staff on the superb job we had done over the past five years developing and implementing the SAVE program. Then he let the other shoe fall and advised me that the job we had done may have been "too good."

He asked me about the plan to verify Social Security numbers at Shirley Construction and then questioned me, "Do you realize how many people in the U.S. government are upset with your proposal?"

I did not realize it, but several powerful liberal members of Congress were well aware that I was the brains behind the Systematic Alien Verification for Entitlements program, and they were still upset that the "welfare-busting" program had made it successfully into the 1986 Immigration Reform and Control Act legislation. Just the thought that I wanted to expand the idea and create a pilot program to verify Social Security numbers was enough to send them into orbit. Implementation of such a system might actually curtail illegal immigration. They were not about to give it a chance.

Sylvester told me that the phones in Commissioner McNary's Office "rang off the hook" with demands from people on Capitol Hill, the Justice Department and the White House to kill the Shirley Construction proposal.

McNary's staff wasted no time in appeasing the callers. Joe got the word to move me out of Headquarters, move the SAVE program out of the Enforcement Division and disregard any proposal even remotely associated with an enforcement action against Shirley Construction.

Sylvester advised me in a fatherly way, "Pick any vacant position in the United States that is not associated with verification systems, and I'll make sure you get it. You've pissed off the White House, Justice Department, members of Congress, and even the ACLU."

Jim Caffrey kindly added, *"We'll take care of you. Just get out of here."*

After five years of dedicated service to the program, I was removed as Director of SAVE. My reassignment and transfer was based solely on my desire to expand the verification system and create an automated process that would be used by employers to verify the Social Security numbers of their employees. In so doing, I knew it would eventually curtail illegal immigration.

A Social Security Number Verification System makes sense to most people in the U.S. Unfortunately, most people are not in Congress or the White House.

I will never forget what happened in Joe Sylvester's office that day. It changed my view of our government forever.

Sea Island golf, here I come

Faced with Sylvester's haunting words, I began to look at other jobs within INS. I was informed that Jim Murphy, Chief of the Immigration Officer Academy, had suddenly retired. He had been Chief of the Immigration Academy since its inception in the late 1970s, and his job was coveted by many.

The thought of living on St. Simon's Island and playing golf at Sea Island Golf Club seemed to be a lot more appealing than running some beleaguered INS office on the Mexican border.

The Friday following my "massacre," I returned to Sylvester's office and advised him that I would take Murphy's job at the Federal Law Enforcement Training Center. I entered on duty as Chief of the Immigration Officer Academy three weeks later.

The next logical step

I am still proud I was responsible for the development and implementation of the Systematic Alien Verification program. It was built on very sound principles. Despite what happened to me, the program continued to operate and remains today a valuable part of the Department of Homeland Security. More importantly, the Systematic Alien Verification system proved that employer sanctions together with an automated employment verification system could be the most effective enforcement mechanism available for preventing the employment of illegal aliens in the interior of the U.S.

Chapter 4

Understanding More about Illegal Immigration

"Undocumented" workers are not undocumented

It is also about time the "open border" crowd and the media got over their politically correct "undocumented worker" nonsense. Under immigration law, there is no such thing as an "undocumented worker."

During the reign of Commissioner Leonel Castillo (President Carter's Commissioner of INS), Castillo decided that the term "illegal alien" was demeaning to his fellow Mexicans who had crossed the Rio Grande illegally. In its place, Mr. Castillo and his friends came up with "undocumented worker" and decided to use it when referring to illegal aliens.

The term "illegal alien" seems quite appropriate to me. Consider for a moment that everyone in America is either a citizen or an alien. If you are an alien, you are either here legally or illegally. If you are here illegally, you are an illegal alien. It's not rocket science. And besides, I arrested hundreds of illegal aliens, and they all had some kind of documents—they just weren't the right ones.

This little debate has recently resulted in one of the most interesting "Catch-22s" I have seen in my life. In the interest of political correctness, advocacy groups (and many in the media) still call illegal aliens "undocumented workers." Recently, however, illegal aliens have become so emboldened that many are now applying for home mortgages. Can someone please explain to me how an illegal alien can be "undocumented" and still come up with the wheelbarrow full of paperwork needed to qualify for a home loan?

Once and for all . . . they are not undocumented. They are illegal aliens.

Immigration 101: legal aliens versus illegal aliens

Before we continue any further, I believe my readers need a little lesson in immigration law.

Lesson #1: Legal Aliens. Legal aliens fall into two very broad categories.

- *Non-immigrants* are citizens of other countries who come to the U.S. legally and temporarily (to visit, to study, to compete in athletics, etc.).
- *Immigrants* are citizens of other countries who come to settle permanently in the U.S. They must get a "permanent residence visa" commonly known as a "green card."

Lesson #2: Illegal Aliens. There are three types of illegal aliens.

- Aliens who sneak into the country without being inspected.
- Aliens who come to the U.S. as non-immigrants, and then violate the conditions of entry or overstay their allotted time.
- Aliens who enter using counterfeit documents, a fake identity, or some other fraudulent method.

Illegal aliens—Who needs them?

America needs thousands if not millions of workers who are willing to do tough physical labor at moderate wages. Illegal immigrants seem to be the ones most willing to provide these services. To deny this is simply ridiculous.

When it comes to proving illegal immigrants help or hurt our economy, no one knows the truth. Immigrant advocacy groups claim that the cheap hard labor provided by illegal immigrants keeps our economy growing. On the other hand, anti-immigration advocates show evidence that hidden costs associated with these illegal immigrants are shifted to other places in our economy. One fact is clear—there are millions of illegal aliens here, and their numbers are getting bigger and bigger by the day.

One misconception is that illegal immigrants are slaves. They are far from it. In fact, the vast majority of illegal aliens I arrested during my career were earning a lot more than minimum wage. The bigger issue is what are the illegal aliens doing with their money?

Illegal immigrants usually have no roots in the U.S. If the data was available, I believe it would indicate that illegal aliens (compared to U.S. citizens and legal aliens) send a disproportionate part of their wages home to foreign countries.

On Tuesday, June 8, 2004, Cox News Service reported that Mexican President Vicente Fox said, "*. . . poverty has been eased by a doubling in the money that Mexican immigrants in the United States send their families in Mexico. Remittances from migrants rose from $7 billion in 2000 to an estimated $14 billion in 2004.*" At last report (2006) the number had swelled to an incredible $24 billion.

I am not an economist, but I do understand one or two things about the American economy. Every dollar that a person spends is spent again several times over. In other words, when I pay for groceries, the grocer uses my dollars to pay his employee. That employee in turn pays her car loan at the bank, and the bank in turn pays the teller. In very simple terms, this is how economists determine our gross domestic product or GDP.

Dollars sent directly out of the U.S. are simply taken out of the system and never have the chance to be spent again and again in our economy. So, while Mexican President Vicente Fox was proud that his emigrants were sending $14 billion home, our politicians sat by and gleefully watched about $80 billion getting siphoned straight out of our economy. Admittedly, not all of the money is being sent south by illegal immigrants, but I am certain they account for a large part of the export.

Mexico is also a huge trading partner with the U.S. Once again, it is difficult to determine what effect it would have on our economy if Mexicans did not have the dollars to purchase U.S. goods and services. Reliable economic data in this area is scarce because it is impossible to know how much money is sent to Mexico by illegal aliens. However, in this cross-border economic duel, I believe the U.S. is getting the short end of the stick.

One Arizona Republican politician recently warned me not to advocate an end to illegal immigration. He stated that the cost of a car wash could go from $10 to $25. He admitted to me that his comments were not based on reliable research. However, his sentiments are typical of what many employers and politicians say when discussing the economic impact of curtailing illegal immigration to the U.S. There are so many unknown factors when it comes to illegal immigrants, no one really knows what will happen to our economy if we bring illegal immigration under control.

One thing is certain. The Labor Department and our labor unions must be more realistic and truthful about America's labor needs and our insatiable appetite for tough physical labor at moderate wages. And speaking of labor unions, illegal aliens are now pouring into the rank and file, and union leaders love it. Illegal aliens are usually docile, don't ask questions and faithfully pay their dues. With no immigration enforcement to worry about, many unions and their illegal immigrant members have recently become close allies.

At the current time, several major industries in the U.S. would struggle to exist without illegal aliens. Aside from the work they do in agriculture, illegal aliens are commonly found working in construction, landscaping, restaurants, hospitals, domestic service, gas stations, hotels, road work, cable wiring, car washes, and taxi cabs, just to name a few.

Illegal aliens and crime

In Chapter 17 I will explain in greater detail why there is very little historical data linking illegal immigration to crime. Immigrant advocates have known for years that without statistics no one could positively make the connection between the two entities. In other words, if you cannot quantify it, it does not exist. However, ask any police officer who works in a large immigrant community and the anecdotes will flow about alien gangs, international drug smuggling, human trafficking and other crimes associated with illegal immigration.

Have America's 12 million illegal immigrants created an inordinate amount of serious crime? If the answer is "yes", it is one more reason we should all be concerned about curtailing this human invasion.

The connection between crime and immigration has always been a topic for debate. At the turn of the century, New York City gangs of Irish and Italian immigrants controlled the streets of The Big Apple. In later years, Hollywood glamorized such characters as Al Capone, and turned mobsters from the Italian Mafia into American folk heroes. No one should forget, however, that they were murderous gangsters who displayed little respect for American laws.

Over the past three decades, immigration-related gangs have been growing in size and popularity and, as of 2007, they became one of the most significant law enforcement problems in America. Law enforcement sources are well aware that vast numbers of gang members are illegal aliens with serious criminal backgrounds. Immigration and Customs Enforcement Agents have been working closely with state and local authorities to try and combat this crime wave, but their efforts do not seem to be having a significant impact on the illegal alien gang population in the U.S.

The magnitude of this problem was exemplified during some California raids conducted by Homeland Security Immigration and Customs Enforcement Agents during June, 2007. The story in the Napa Valley Register stated that 124 illegal alien gang members were arrested in the Los Angeles area. The aliens were mostly from Mexico and Central American countries and many of them had been previously deported from the U.S. The article states:

> *"Acting U.S. Attorney George Cardona gave the example of a gang member who had been deported nine times to Mexico between sentences for drug possession and unlawfully driving a vehicle."*

Obviously the failure by Homeland Security to keep these individuals from re-entering the country makes their deportations nothing more than an inconvenient joke for the gang members and a huge frustration for law enforcement.

Who are the supporters of open borders and/or illegal immigration?

Whenever I discuss the topic of illegal immigration, I often make the mistake of saying "they" do not want effective immigration controls, and I fail to delineate some specific organizations. I will not make the same mistake here. During my work in Washington, D.C., and on Capitol Hill, I found lobbyists who not only supported illegal immigration, but in some instances threatened anyone who suggested otherwise. The following is a list of organizations that wield incredible influence in Congress and have lobbied for years to keep immigration controls to a minimum. While the list is far from complete, it is virtually a "Who's Who" of power on Capitol Hill.

- American Association of Retired Persons
- U.S. Chamber of Commerce
- National Council of Agricultural Employers
- National Association of Home Builders
- National Restaurant Association
- American Hotel and Lodging Association
- U.S. Council of Catholic Bishops

Changing our immigration laws has always created strange bedfellows. Consider the fact that in 2007, Senators Edward Kennedy (D-Massachusetts) and John McCain (R-Arizona) worked together on "comprehensive immigration reform." This is nothing short of miraculous, as Kennedy and McCain are usually diametrically opposed to each others views.

Illegal aliens and income taxes

This is another crazy argument that raises its ugly head every so often. I do not think anyone really knows if illegal aliens pay their fair share of taxes. Immigration advocates love to point out illegal immigrants "pay taxes" because of Social Security tax withholding requirements. This is partially true, but the whole story is seldom told. Millions of illegal aliens pay Social Security and income taxes by way of payroll deductions. The problem is illegal aliens usually pay their fair share of Social Security taxes, but not their proper share of state and Federal income taxes. (This is the main reason why the American Association of Retired Persons lobbies so hard against initiatives that will curtail illegal immigration.) What is usually never discussed is the amount of taxes withheld from the paychecks of illegal aliens. They learn very quickly to claim as many exemptions as allowed on Federal and state tax withholding forms. As a result, very few withholding taxes are withdrawn from their paychecks.

When audits are conducted of large companies that utilize illegal immigrant labor, the trend becomes quite apparent. Illegal aliens claim far more exemptions than their legal counterparts, resulting in a small amount of withholding tax being taken from their paychecks. Come April 15, the number of tax returns filed by the illegal aliens is miniscule as well. (Almost all owe more taxes.)

In other words, illegal aliens may pay some taxes (if the laborers are not illegally paid "under the table"). They simply do not pay enough.

Nannies and maids

During the last 20 years, we have seen more and more American women enter the U.S. workforce. At the same time we have done little to promote programs that support day care and working parents. (And surprisingly Bill Gates and friends have not come up with a robot or a computer that tends to young children or cleans houses.) "Domestic help" is at a premium, and the shortage has created a huge opportunity for illegal immigrant women to find work in the U.S.

Most families will deny that their nannies and housekeepers are illegal aliens. Some of the most law-abiding and respected members of our communities employ illegal immigrants. They know they are breaking the law, and seem ambivalent to the fact they are creating a huge employment magnet for female illegal immigrants. Several Presidential appointees in recent years (Zoe Baird, Clinton nominee for Attorney General, and Bernard Kerik, Bush appointee for Homeland Security Secretary) were forced to withdraw their names from consideration because investigators discovered evidence that both of them had employed illegal aliens as domestic help prior to their nominations.

For those who don't know it, there is a U.S. immigration program that allows families to bring *au pairs* into the country *legally*. I have discussed this initiative with several people who attempted to use the system, and they advised me that it was so cost prohibitive, they simply gave up. First, there was the $6,000 fee for the agency that did the interviewing, recruiting and hiring. Then, there were the travel expenses, health insurance, and school tuition. When all the initial expenses were tallied, $10,000 was spent, and the babysitter had not even arrived yet. This program is a perfect example of how our government turns great ideas into expensive bureaucracies that do nothing more than pad the pockets of middle-men and immigration lawyers.

Some activities related to illegal immigration will probably never stop, and I have no intention of advocating that we start arresting and deporting maids who do the chores for working parents. It is important, however, that Americans realize that we have created yet another labor crisis, and we need to do something about it. The *au pair* program as it is currently operated is not a solution. It is an expensive joke.

"Anchor babies"—Children born in the U.S. to illegal alien parents

If there has ever been an immigration issue that strikes at the heart of America, this is it. "Anchor babies" are children born in America to illegal alien parents. For decades, pregnant women from Mexico and Central America have been coming across the U.S.-Mexican border for the purpose of delivering their babies here. At birth, the baby is automatically a U.S. citizen. This entitlement has a Constitutional foundation, as the Fourteenth Amendment clearly states, *"All persons born or naturalized in the United States and subject to the jurisdiction thereof, are citizens of the United States and of the State wherein they reside."*

The term "anchor baby" came about because after the birth of the child, the parents *seem* to be "anchored" in the U.S. By law, however, the newborn does not give the parents any legal right to remain. The parents have to wait until the child is at least 21 years of age before they become eligible for any immigration benefits.

Deportations of parents of U.S. citizens are very difficult, but they must be carried out. Inevitably the deportation brings the media and immigration advocates out of the woodwork, and the officers are immediately portrayed as jackbooted Nazi thugs, dragging the parents off to some concentration camp. In reality, the parents are simply being sent back to their country of citizenship and they have every right to take their U.S. citizen child with them.

Immigration advocates love to appeal to our emotional senses by advocating that the parents should be allowed to stay here to promote "family reunification." This is total nonsense. There is no difference if a family stays together here or in another country. Parents who return to their native country with their U.S. citizen children are still a united family.

The answer to problems related to "anchor babies" does not lie with the U.S. Border Patrol. Anti-immigration advocates suggest that the Patrol should somehow locate these women and immediately deport them back to Mexico. This is easier said than done. To most law enforcement officers, pregnant women violators of any kind are problematic and must be handled with the utmost care. Any attempt to arrest a pregnant woman could lead to trauma for both the mother and/or the unborn child. (In the past, civil litigation lawyers have had a field day collecting millions of dollars from law enforcement agencies after a pregnant woman was arrested and the child was subsequently born with a malady.)

"Anchor babies" are also adding to our health-care crisis. Medical costs associated with delivering and caring for "anchor babies" are crippling the health care systems in cities and towns located near the Mexican border, and in other jurisdictions with large concentrations of illegal immigrants. Emergency rooms and hospitals are being forced to close because they can no longer absorb the financial losses associated with this growing problem. The losses are now in the hundreds of millions of dollars.

Are there solutions? Can we somehow reduce the number of "anchor babies?"

The answer is "yes." Congress needs remove the benefit that creates the "anchor." The simplest way to achieve this is to entirely eliminate the visa category that allows a U.S. citizen to bring his or her parents to the U.S. In 2007, during the debates over "comprehensive immigration reform", the proposal to eliminate this benefit created some of the strongest reaction from those in favor of more open immigration policies. If the U.S. ever wants to curtail this growing problem, elimination of the visa category is the easiest and most effective way to do it.

Some members of Congress have also considered legislation that would create a far more restrictive definition of "*under the jurisdiction thereof,*" thereby preventing "anchor babies" from gaining U.S. citizenship at birth. I think this initiative is questionable at best. Should Congress successfully proceed and limit the definition, I am certain there will be an immediate challenge to the constitutionality of the new law. Furthermore, issues about the practicality of the new law will also come into question. Are we really going to implement a program where hospital officials are required to determine the immigration status of every pregnant woman who delivers a baby? I don't think so.

In the event that politics wins out over reason, and the visa category for U.S. citizen parents is not eliminated, "anchor babies" are here to stay.

Overstays—The other illegal aliens

Some immigration experts believe that 40% of all the illegal aliens in the U.S. came as non-immigrants and just decided to stay. It is not hard to understand why some young guy from halfway around the world loves America and wants to take root here. After a hundred trips to Wendy's, multiple six-packs of cold beer, and six months of sex with Jennifer (because she thinks his accent is cool), it is no wonder he wants to stay. After all, getting a visa, coming to the U.S., working here illegally and eventually beating our immigration system is "as American as apple pie."

Most Americans do not seem to equate overstaying a visa and getting a job here with their view of aliens who crossed the border illegally. This may have to do with our European immigrant heritage. Whatever the reasons, aliens who overstay their visas find it much easier to get jobs in the U.S. than illegal immigrants, and those who overstay their visas are seldom arrested by immigration authorities. As far as immigration law is concerned, the alien overstay is no less deportable than the poor migrant who is smuggled across the Rio Grande.

Immigration experts—The far right, the far left, and the far out

Another major political problem is that moderate immigration experts are almost extinct. The only people who seem to speak out about the issue are right-wing "close the border" fanatics who play to near-totalitarian themes, or immigration "open-border" advocates, who want virtually no controls.

Black leaders in America are not helping the situation, either. Many civic leaders continuously complain about the numbers of unemployed minority youth. At the same time, millions of illegal immigrants are pouring into the U.S. and locating jobs almost immediately. Despite the claims from black community leaders that illegal aliens work for substandard wages, most illegal aliens seem to make enough money to live here and also send money back home.

The idea that illegal aliens all have "dead-end" work is also absolute nonsense. The longer an illegal alien remains in the U.S., the more likely he or she will eventually move out of their so-called "dead-end" jobs, and move into more lucrative positions. Why can't unemployed American black youth do the same thing?

Black politicians promote the idea that blacks and illegal immigrants should all be on the same team. If the Congressional black caucus and black community leaders like Rev. Jesse Jackson and Rev. Al Sharpton are sincerely interested in reducing black youth unemployment, they will push for legislation to create many of the programs advocated in Part II of this book. Political correctness aside, if black leaders in America want to help their unemployed youth, they will demand that Congress significantly curtail illegal immigration.

In the U.S. House of Representatives, very few of our elected officials have any experience with the realities of immigration enforcement, with the exception of Congressman Sylvester Reyes (D-El Paso, Texas). "Silver," as he was affectionately called, is a retired Border Patrol Chief who made a name for himself in the Border Patrol in El Paso, Texas, with a project called "Hold the Line." I have discussed "Hold the Line" in Chapter 2 of this book and will say more about it later.

Congressman and 2008 presidential candidate Tom Tancredo from Colorado has recently emerged as a spokesman for the immigration control advocates on Capitol Hill. He has expressed his adamant opposition to President George W. Bush's "guest worker" program and has advocated putting the military and National Guard on our borders. Surprisingly, at one time Representative Tancredo did not support a mandatory electronic employment verification system to strengthen the employer sanctions program. This is quite unusual, as most experts agree that, with a more effective employer sanctions program, we could significantly curtail illegal immigration. It is quite possible that Tom Tancredo has since changed his views, but when I met with his staff on Capitol Hill several years ago, he had advised them he was opposed to any such verification system for employers. I give Congressman Tancredo credit for his willingness to deal with such a difficult issue. However, with regard to some matters (i.e., "guest workers"), his unyielding attitude is not winning any concessions from his fellow representatives on the other side of the aisle.

Aside from Congressmen like Reyes and Tancredo, most politicians know very little about immigration enforcement, and even less about solving immigration-related problems. Most of them consider it a "no-win" issue and would prefer to stay as far away from it as possible.

Then there are T.V.'s talking heads who love to theorize about immigration policies and procedures. How many times have we heard CBS's Katie Couric tell us that "America is a nation of immigrants." (I think we already know that, Katie.) On the other hand, Fox's Bill O'Reilly frequently complains that we have millions of illegal aliens pouring into the U.S., and has called on Congress and the President to militarize the U.S.-Mexico border.

The latest high-profile journalist to tackle the immigration issue is none other than Lou Dobbs of CNN. During 2006 and 2007, he has been airing several pieces about "Broken Borders." Through his hard-hitting journalism, Dobbs and his associates have opened viewers' eyes to our growing immigration nightmare. (One thing, however, both Dobbs and O'Reilly seem to overlook. There are those of us who served long careers in the INS, and spent nearly three decades complaining about the same issues.)

Proponents of increased immigration are a much smarter crew. While they love to debate right-wing inflammatory rhetoric, they know that recent polls have shown Americans are strongly in favor of reducing illegal immigration. In response, immigration advocates quietly and efficiently lobby Congress for laws and amendments that seem like immigration enforcement, but actually open the "Golden Door" even wider.

One example of skillful political maneuvering by the "open border" crowd is to always support hiring, training and deploying more Border Patrol Agents. This appears enforcement-minded, and by agreeing to this manpower increase, legislators receive concessions for their liberal agenda. The fact is, these advocates know only too well that no matter how many Border Patrol Agents line the U.S.-Mexico border, the illegal aliens will continue to get in.

Whether an organization is for or against more immigrants, there is usually no question where they stand on the issues. Immigration-control proponents will not listen to any argument about increased immigration, and increased-immigration advocates want virtually open borders. Unfortunately, not one organization represents a moderate and reasonable view of how to better control U.S. immigration.

My alien is better than your alien

U.S. immigration law is very complex. With the exception of the government employees who work with it every day and the cadre of private immigration lawyers, it is a puzzle to the rest of America. Despite this, many Americans seem to know exactly which aliens should be allowed to remain and which ones should immediately be forced to leave. To this day, I am amazed at how many Americans truly believe that their "alien" is above the law.

A close relative recently asked me to assist a foreign student from Turkey. The alien was being asked to leave the country because he had completed his studies in the U.S. His allotted time was about to expire. From the description of the young man, one would have thought he was Einstein's reincarnation. Apparently he spoke three languages and knew more about computers than Bill Gates. Despite all this brainpower, and in accordance with Federal regulations, the student had received a letter from Homeland Security advising him to leave the country.

Immediately after his friend received the letter, I received a call from my relative. He started the same speech I have heard a thousand times in my career. He said, *"This guy is one of the nicest guys I have ever met in my life. He helped me with my exams, he loaned me 50 bucks, and he is truly someone who will improve America. Why is the U.S. government asking my friend to leave, and allowing 12 million unskilled illegal aliens to remain here?"* I knew better than to attempt an answer.

The fact is, the Turkish friend came to America legally as a foreign student. When he initially completed his application for his student visa he promised our government he would come to the U.S., get an education, *and then leave*. Despite this explanation, my relative was in total disbelief that his friend actually had to fulfill his promise to our government and return to his country.

Congress decides which aliens stay and which ones must leave and the Federal government will always require many aliens to depart the country—as they promised they would when they received their visas. It should not matter how many languages an alien speaks or how many toilets they have cleaned, when it comes time to leave they should leave.

I know we are a nation of immigrants. However, we are also a nation of laws, and it baffles me that there are so many Americans who cannot grasp the fact that *all* aliens in the U.S. should obey our immigration laws. People might not like to read the cold hard facts, but your friend from another country is no better than some other American's friend. If they cannot find a legal means to remain here, they should return home. It's as simple as that.

Political backlash and illegal immigration

When I first went to work at INS in the 1970s, complaints about illegal immigration were mostly confined to our southwestern states and Florida. Illegal immigration was not a topic of discussion in the other states, and anyone who even suggested passing a law that would restrict benefits to immigrants was considered un-American, racist and mean-spirited. How times have changed.

One of the first significant indications of political backlash from illegal immigration appeared in California in 1994. Proposition 187 was a grassroots initiative that required the State of California to deny certain social welfare benefits to illegal aliens residing in the state. Despite a massive attempt to discredit the initiative as xenophobic, voters overwhelmingly passed Proposition 187. In March, 1998, the proposition was declared unconstitutional, but the political "shot across the bow" had been fired, and the notice was loud and clear—Americans citizens were beginning to realize the negative aspects of illegal immigration.

The popular political backlash has now grown nationwide, and anti-illegal immigrant legislation by local and state governments has reached an unprecedented level. Places like Hazleton, Pennsylvania, Riverside, New Jersey, and Valley Park, Missouri, are experimenting with laws intended to drive illegal immigrants from their communities.

Gettysburg, Pennsylvania, may be the site of the most famous battle in the American Civil War, but 120 miles away miles in Hazleton, Pennsylvania, another civil war is brewing. Mayor Louis J. Barletta and his City Council became so fed up with the problems associated with the influx of illegal immigrants into their former mining town, they passed city ordinances imposing fines on landlords who rented to illegal aliens and denied business permits to businesses who hired them. As expected, the battle began.

The American Civil Liberties Union and several other pro-immigrant advocacy groups filed suit in federal court to block the implementation of the laws. In July 2007, Federal Judge James Manley issued a 200-page ruling. Not only did he strike down the law (citing the Federal government's Constitutionally mandated responsibility for regulating immigration), but he allowed the plaintiff's to remain anonymous—as they were probably illegal aliens. (The judge's decision was hailed by pro-immigrant rights groups as a defeat against all local ordinances dealing with illegal immigration. However, legal experts have expressed doubt that Manley's opinion will set precedent for the rest of the country.)

No sooner had the decision been announced than the second part of the battle began. The Mayor and his legal team expressed their dismay with Judge Manley and advised they would be appealing the decision to the Third Circuit Court of Appeals in Philadelphia. It should not surprise anyone if this case ends up in the U.S. Supreme Court.

On July 6, 2006, *USA Today* published an article entitled "States Take Action on Immigration Issue." The article listed 35 states that now have at least one type of state law aimed at curtailing the influx of illegal immigrants.

Arizona serves as a great example of this growing trend. State representative Russell Pearce (R-Mesa, Arizona) stands as one of the fervent opponents to illegal immigration in both Arizona and the U.S. Despite being labeled as everything from racist to bigot by many immigration advocates, he continues to forge ahead with his anti-illegal immigrant legislative initiatives, and his successes are notable.

On November 2, 2004, voters in Arizona overwhelmingly passed an anti-illegal immigration initiative titled Proposition 200. One purpose of the proposition was to stop illegal immigrants from obtaining valid driver's licenses and other forms of legal identification. Once again, the measure was publicly debated for months before the election, and despite well-coordinated attempts by the local media, Mexican-American organizations, and a host of other pro-immigration advocacy groups, the measure passed by an alarming majority.

In addition to Proposition 200, Arizona voters in November, 2006, again passed anti-illegal immigrant legislation in the form of Proposition 300—an initiative to cut off higher education subsidies for illegal alien students attending state-sponsored schools.

Representative Pearce's biggest prize came in June, 2007. The Arizona legislature passed House Bill 2779, "Fair and Legal Employment Act," and Democratic Governor Janet Napolitano signed it into law on July 2. After January 1, 2008, all Arizona employers will be required to verify the immigration status and validity of Social Security numbers of all of their employees. The employers will be required to use the Department of Homeland Security's *voluntary* E-Verification System (previously called the Basic Pilot Program.) The punishment for failing to use the system will be an initial fine. Subsequent violations can result in the revocation of an employer's business license.

The nation's business and political leaders will be carefully watching what transpires in Arizona. In the absence of a Federal mandate, Arizona's successful implementation of this law will likely lead to other states doing the same.

I have my worries about the successful implementation of these initiatives. The biggest obstacles will be uncooperativeness and ineptitude on the part of the Federal government. Citizenship and Immigration Services (CIS) of the Department of Homeland Security controls most immigration records including the E-Verification System. Sources advise me that these systems are now being overseen by senior managers who have little if any understanding of simple verification processes. (States and localities need to access these records to successfully implement their new laws.) It will be interesting to see if state officials can convince Homeland Security to put qualified people in charge and to support their verification requirements.

Despite the clear Constitutional authority that immigration control is the responsibility of the Federal government, state and local jurisdictions are pushing ahead with their own immigration-related legislative initiatives. According to CNN and the National Council of State Legislatures, *"In 2007, state legislators in all of the 50 states had introduced at least 1169 bills and resolutions related to immigration or immigrants and refugees. This is more than twice the total number of introduced bills (570) in 2006."*

One thing seems perfectly clear. There is an anti-illegal immigrant sentiment spreading across America.

The Minutemen Civil Defense Corps

Whenever I am asked about controlling "illegal immigration," the next question is usually about the "Minutemen." Their website is http://www.minutemenhq.com, and their mission is *"To secure the United States borders and coastal boundaries against unlawful and unauthorized entry of all individuals, contraband, and foreign military."*

NOTICE TO EMPLOYERS

Laws 2007 Chapter 279
Fair and Legal Employment Act (HB 2779)

On January 1, 2008, a new state law prohibits employers from intentionally or knowingly employing an unauthorized alien. An "unauthorized alien" is an alien who does not have the legal right or authorization under federal law to work in the United States.

If a complaint is filed with the County Attorneys or Attorney General an investigation will be conducted. Upon determining that a complaint is not frivolous, a civil action may be instituted. Any judicial proceedings will be governed by the Rules of Civil Procedure.

A judicial determination of a violation of this new state law will subject the employer to probation, and may subject the employer to a suspension or revocation of all licenses as defined in section 23-211, Arizona Revised Statutes depending on the following conditions:

1. For a first violation of an employer **knowingly** hiring an unauthorized alien, the court shall order mandatory three years probation and may suspend all licenses held by the employer for a maximum of ten days. The employer must file a signed sworn affidavit with the county attorney within three business days, stating that the employer has fired all unauthorized aliens and that the employer will not intentionally or knowingly employ any unauthorized alien.
2. For a first violation of an employer **intentionally** hiring an unauthorized alien, the court shall order a mandatory five years probation and order the appropriate licensing agencies to suspend all licenses held by the employer for a minimum of ten days. The employer must file a signed sworn affidavit, stating that the employer has fired all unauthorized aliens and that the employer will not intentionally or knowingly employ any unauthorized alien with the county attorney. A license that is suspended will remain suspended until the employer files a signed sworn affidavit.
3. For a second violation of this new state law committed during a period of probation, the court will order the appropriate licensing agencies to permanently revoke all licenses that are held by the employer.

All court orders will be available on the Attorney Generals website at www.azag.gov.

Employment Eligibility Verification (E-Verify)

E-Verify is the new name for the employment eligibility verification formerly known as the Basic Pilot Program. After December 31, 2007, every employer, after hiring an employee, is required to verify the employment eligibility of the new employee through the E-Verify program, as defined in section 23-211, Arizona Revised Statutes, as added by this act. Proof of verifying the employment authorization of an employee through the E-Verify program will create a rebuttable presumption that an employer did not violate the new state law.

How to Enroll

E-Verify is available on the Internet for all U.S. employers seeking to verify the employment eligibility of new hires. Employers using E-Verify must first register online and sign a Memorandum of Understanding (MOU) with the United States Citizenship and Immigration Service (USCIS) and the Social Security Administration (SSA). There is no cost to use E-Verify. To register and complete a MOU for participation in the Employment Eligibility Verification (EEV) go to https://www.vis-dhs.com/EmployerRegistration, and follow the instructions as outlined.

Upon completion and online submittal of the MOU, the employer will receive email confirmation of his or her company's participation in the E-Verify including a new User ID and temporary password.

You can obtain a copy of the fair and legal employment act (HB 2779; Laws 2007, Chapter 279) at www.azleg.gov.

09/07

Arizona's Notice to Employers about their new Employer Sanctions law.

I have met many members of their organization and I respect them for what they have achieved. In less than a few year's time, their leaders Mr. Simcox and Mr. Gilchrist have created tremendous media attention about America's porous southern border. By setting up a virtual "border neighborhood watch" program, the Minutemen created a media frenzy in the southern Arizona desert, and their story spread across America like wildfire.

Aside from their "Border Watch Operations," the Minutemen have become politically active in many other parts of the country. When the U.S. Senate was about to vote on the "comprehensive immigration reform" legislation in the summer of 2007, the Minutemen were partially responsible for creating the barrage of negative emails and faxes that almost shut down Capitol Hill's electronic communication capabilities. The bill failed and the Minutemen succeeded.

The Minutemen have been accused of being "vigilantes," but so far this has not been the case. As long as the organization maintains itself as a law-abiding group of citizens who wish to *legally* protest America's current immigration policies, their Constitutional rights must be respected.

Violent backlash and illegal immigration

The President, the Secretary of Homeland Security, and the Director of the FBI can proclaim all kinds of successes in their efforts to combat terrorism. I personally believe it is only a matter of time before foreign terrorists hit us again . . . and again, and again. If this should happen, it could create massive anti-immigrant violence that will make the political initiatives seem like child's play.

Considering the number of guns in circulation and the readily available ammunition, no one doubts that Americans are the best-armed people in the world. We are also a nation that allows our authorities to enforce our laws . . . so far.

As a retired law enforcement officer, I am adamantly opposed to any reactionary activity by the general public. However, if foreign terrorists strike us again, and tens of thousands of Americans die as a result, U.S. law enforcement could face a new nightmare. Certain elements in America could randomly unleash their firepower, targeting innocent civilians living in areas populated mostly by immigrants. A few attacks occurred immediately following 9/11, and our law enforcement agencies were able to locate, apprehend and prosecute the perpetrators. In the event of more foreign terrorism within our borders, I doubt that law enforcement will have the same success.

As an example of immigration-related reactionary violence, look no further than Holland. When it comes to immigration, the Dutch had one of the most progressive and liberal nations in the world. That was until early November, 2004. Dutch filmmaker Theo Van Gogh was shot and stabbed to death by a Muslim fanatic. Apparently, the killer was upset that Van Gogh had produced a movie critical of Islam's treatment of women. The usually tolerant and peaceful Dutch population reacted quickly and unexpectedly. Within days after Van Gogh's death, Fox News reported that there were more than 20 attacks on mosques throughout Holland. (It was also reported that the Dutch Secret Service had been infiltrated by a fundamentalist Muslim extremist who was closely related to the killer.) The Dutch are now being forced to review and revise their long-standing tolerance for open immigration.

The rioting in Holland is but a small example of how quickly foreign-based terrorism can turn peace-loving, tolerant people into intolerant revenge-seeking mobs.

Fundamental changes in the heartland

In order to control legal and illegal immigration, the U.S. government must change not only the way we enforce our immigration laws, but more importantly *where* we enforce them. Immigration is no longer a border issue. Every single state is being impacted by both legal and illegal immigration, and effective immigration enforcement throughout the entire country is critical to the overall security of the U.S.

Chapter 5

Professionalism Abandoned—from the INS to Homeland Security

Mission impossible, ineptitude and politics

Is it any wonder that the first three letters of insanity are INS? We have an estimated 12 million illegal aliens in the U.S., and the Federal government does not know who they are, where they are, or what they are doing.

In the early part of the 20th century, the idea of having an agency to control immigration appealed to most Americans, especially since waves of immigrants were hitting our shores. Congress created what subsequently became our Immigration and Naturalization Service under the Department of Justice. The INS was tasked with enforcing America's immigration laws.*

While the INS mission *seemed* simple, it was impossible. One lowly government agency had responsibility for patrolling our borders, inspecting millions of aliens legally entering the country, giving out a multitude of immigration benefits authorized by Congress, and locating and deporting aliens who failed to comply with our laws. All of this was to be done with limited funding, disgruntled employees, and an American business community that prayed every day for the agency's demise.

Over a period of years, INS became the most inept bureaucracy in the Federal government. Those of us who worked there

---

*Most of the agency's basic authority was created in the Immigration and Nationality Act (INA) of 1952. Several other pieces of immigration legislation have been enacted in the last 15 years, such as the Immigration Reform and Control Act of 1986 (IRCA).

joked that INS stood for "I'm Not Sure," because the agency could never get anything straight.

> *Dear Abigail,*
>
> *I recently got engaged and I have to tell my fiancé about my family.*
>
> *My father is in prison for murder and my mother is a convicted drug dealer. I also have a brother who works for the Immigration and Naturalization Service.*
>
> *My fiancé is quite status conscious, and while I have no problem telling him about my mother and father, how can I admit I have a brother who works for the INS?*
>
> *Yours truly,*
> *Concerned*

It is very difficult to truly convey what it was like working at the former INS. Every year the career employees would wonder if INS could get any worse, and every year the agency went further downhill. During even the best of times, we wondered if people would believe us if we ever tried to explain how bad it was.

Even Hollywood put us down. While all of my friends in the FBI and Secret Service were beating their chests about heroes like Clint Eastwood and Robert Stack, I was enduring such classics as *The Green Card* and *Men in Black.*

Many in the government called INS the "stepchild" of the Justice Department. Let's face it, if you were the Attorney General, which agency would you support—the FBI as they tracked down the likes of John Dillinger, or the INS as they chased your waiter across Pennsylvania Avenue?

When I first entered the Service, the agency had insurmountable problems and a meager budget. Twenty-five years later, INS had a multi-billion dollar budget and the same insurmountable problems. For those who believed that every problem in the Federal government could be solved with money, INS was the exception to the rule.

One amazing INS phenomenon was the propensity of the INS Budget Office to get money from Congress and the Justice Department for completely useless projects, while, at the same time, the backlog of immigration applications was growing by the millions and illegal immigration was getting worse by the day. As an example, INS had enough money to hire Ph.D. psychologists to study the effectiveness of the Border Patrol's "artificial language test." At the same time, our deportation officers were forced to release convicted and dangerous criminal aliens because the agency did not have sufficient funds to pay for their detention.

Another problem was one of identity. Half of America, including most of the U.S. government, thought we were part of the Customs Service. As a Senior Special Agent in Headquarters, I went to numerous meetings with high level Justice Department and White House officials. Without fail some political appointee would question me about why INS dogs were sniffing luggage at the airport. When I tried to explain that Customs used dogs at the airport, my comments were dismissed as bureaucratic finger-pointing.

The Customs thing was small potatoes. Every day, INS employees had to deal with the fallout from at least one of these truisms.

- The *INS Personnel Manual* was nothing more than a copy of *The Peter Principle.*
- INS was a dumping ground for inept employees from other agencies. (These "transferees" unfortunately were usually placed in important managerial positions.)
- Congress and the White House hated us—no matter who was in power.
- The Office of Management and Budget and the Justice Department never authorized sufficient positions to handle the number of applications for legal immigration benefits (green cards, naturalization, etc.) There was always a huge backlog of paperwork.
- Our central database was accurate 75% of the time or less, and at least 20% of all alien files were at some stage of being "lost."

- Members of the American Immigration Lawyers' Association (AILA) constantly defeated our *best* lawyers in court and basically emasculated INS enforcement initiatives.
- The media had difficulty supporting any deportations—unless, of course, a T.V. personality had been scammed by an alien.

To say the least, working at INS was a struggle.

INS Commissioners

The job of INS Commissioner was a Presidential appointment and it was well known among the Washington elite that the person who took the job was looking for something other than a future. Bearing this reality in mind, consider the quality of executives selected to head the INS in recent years. Here is a list of those "special" people.

- Leonard F. Chapman was a retired Marine General (Nixon/Ford).
  November 29, 1973–May 12, 1977
- Leonel J. Castillo was a Houston politician (Carter).
  May 13, 1977–October 1, 1979
- Alan C. Nelson (deceased) was a government lawyer from Alameda County, California, and a friend of Attorney General Ed Meese (Reagan).
  February 22, 1982–June 16, 1989
- Gene McNary was a Missouri politician (Bush).
  October 26, 1989–January 20, 1993
- Doris Meissner was working in a liberal Washington think-tank when she was selected (Clinton).
  October 18, 1993–November 18, 2000
- James W. Ziglar was Sergeant at Arms for the U.S. Senate (G.W. Bush).
  August 6, 2001–November 30, 2002

Without question, one of the most significant reasons for America's failed immigration policies during the last three decades lies in the fact that our Commissioners knew virtually zero about enforcing our immigration laws. If anyone thinks this was not a problem, think again. Gene McNary, who became our Commissioner during the first Bush Administration, stated that one of his first priorities was to fix the Puerto Rican immigration problem. (Hey, Commissioner, Puerto Ricans are U.S. citizens, but what difference should that make?)

Even the Commissioners' pictures were scary. At INS Headquarters, located at 425 "I" Street, N.W., Washington, D.C., all of the former Commissioners had their portraits or photographs on the wall in one of the meeting rooms. I was embarrassed to bring guests there—the photos closely resembled Post Office "Wanted" posters rather than pictures of distinguished government leaders.

Riddled with politicals

The Commissioner nonsense I understood. After all, the President has the right to choose his own ideologues to fill "Schedule C" political appointments in the Federal service. These jobs are at a very senior level and the appointees deal mostly with administration policy.

The politics went a lot deeper at INS. We not only had "Schedule C" political appointees, we had their children, their friends, their cousins, their neighbors, and anyone else who wanted a job in Washington, D.C.

There is no better example of this problem than one Commissioner's selection for the INS Associate Commissioner of Enforcement. Many highly qualified Immigration officers applied for this coveted and powerful Senior Executive position.

Twenty-four hours after the job announcement closed, all applicants were notified "Gil" had been selected (or I should say "pre-selected"). Who was "Gil?" Was he a Supervisory Special Agent? A Deportation Officer? Or maybe even a Senior Inspector?

It was not long before we learned that our new leader was none other than a police official from St. Louis, Missouri. His most significant immigration-related qualification was his friendship with the Commissioner.

Gil was not alone. Many high-level INS law enforcement officials were "competitively selected" despite the fact they knew absolutely nothing about immigration enforcement. In fact, for a period of twenty-years (1983–2003) not a single Immigration officer ever served (permanently) as the Associate Commissioner for Enforcement.

Since I am a great fan of examples and comparisons, I want to make one here. One of the finest and most respected law enforcement agencies in the world is the Secret Service. Their Special Agents are very well trained and highly motivated men and women.

To move through the ranks of the Secret Service, one must have started as a probationary Special Agent and completed both basic training at the Federal Law Enforcement Training Center in Georgia and "special" training near Beltsville, Maryland.

The Secret Service has several missions, and the one most of us are familiar with is the protection of the President, Vice President, and their families. These divisions within the Secret Service are known as the Presidential and Vice Presidential Protection Details.

Secret Service protection responsibilities are supervised and managed by higher-level supervisory Special Agents, and it will be a cold day in hell when anyone but a career Secret Service Agent heads those details. Secret Service Agents understand that outside intervention by unskilled and untrained personnel is the fastest way to get one of their protectees injured or killed.

Whether it was by design or by accident, our Commissioners (under the watchful eye of the Justice Department) continuously selected untrained and unqualified people to lead INS enforcement. Doing so eventually crippled almost every aspect of America's immigration law enforcement capabilities.

"Hot dog" Hal and "Machine gun" Marty

This "political appointee" nonsense was not just confined to Headquarters. INS had many other colorful leaders in the field who were dropped into the agency after a national election. Two of the most famous worked during the Reagan Administration as Regional Commissioners in Texas and California.

For people in law enforcement the term "hot dog" has a distinct meaning, and it has nothing to do with "tube steak." It describes individuals who love to show off their authority and frequently their stupidity.

"Hal" was a "hot dog" in every sense of the word. Before coming to INS he had worked for Der Weinerschnitzel fast-food hot dog chain in California. It was rumored that he was given the job at INS because he had made significant contributions to the Reagan presidential campaign. (What a revelation!) Hal was also a guy who thought he knew it all.

It was not long after Hal accepted the position at INS that he realized he was in charge of thousands of Border Patrol agents and other immigration law enforcement officers. He certainly took his responsibility to heart. Within weeks after his swearing in ceremony he ordered a fully-equipped, unmarked police car, complete with hidden emergency lights, siren and two-way radio. He designated himself on the Border Patrol frequency as RC-1 (Regional Commissioner), and began showing up at numerous Border Patrol traffic stops and surveillance operations.

Hal also loved the spotlight. He told *Time* Magazine that the Border Patrol should treat illegal aliens like fish. He said something similar to "The Patrol should catch 'em, fry 'em and throw 'em back." Needless to say he got into the spotlight with that one.

"RC-1" had one other trait that had nothing to do with hot dogs or immigration. He was hatefully vindictive. In one episode he attempted to fire one of the most respected Special Agents in the INS, simply because the agent followed orders from the White House and not from him.

In the 1980's, Supervisory Special Agent David Dec happened to be serving as the Assistant District Director for Investigations in Honolulu, Hawaii, when Ferdinand and Imelda Marcos fled there from the Philippines. The White House and the FBI became fearful that Marcos would eventually violate the Anti-Neutrality Act and attempt a return to power in Manila. A law enforcement task force was formed to keep an eye on the former dictator, and Dec was selected as the INS representative.

Due to political sensitivities involving Marcos, his wife and the Reagan Administration, clear instructions were given that all communication about Marcos was to go *first* to the White House Press Office. Dec was advised NOT to communicate any task force information to anyone—especially to Hal.

On the other hand, Hal was a close friend and fervent supporter of President Marcos. He told the INS District Director he wanted Dec to disregard the White House mandate and report everything to him first.

It was not long before Hal realized Dec was not going to compromise the task force's mission. Hal went ballistic and immediately flew to Hawaii from Southern California. After checking into his hotel suite at the Hilton Hawaiian Village, he went directly into the INS District Director's office on Ala Moana Boulevard and announced, "Fire Dec."

The Director knew enough about the situation and told Hal he couldn't fire Dec. Hal became frustrated, returned to California and immediately transferred Dec to the El Paso Intelligence Center in Texas. (As expected, the White House refused to come to Dec's defense.)

Shortly after Dec's removal, Hal displayed his respect and friendship for the former dictator. While Marcos' house was still under surveillance by the task force, Hal convened a meeting there of all Western Regional Border Patrol Chiefs and INS District Directors. (Quite a place to hold a meeting of U.S. government law enforcement officials!)

Then there was "Marty." He was another politically appointed Regional Commissioner, and he too had a penchant for punitive transfers. However, the story that best symbolizes his professionalism took place in the Big Bend National Park near El Paso, Texas. While floating down the Rio Grande River in a Border Patrol boat, Marty decided to impress another high-level INS official with his shooting skills. He proceeded to blast the river bank on the U.S. side with several bursts of machine-gun fire. The incident would never have been reported had it not been for the terrified campers sitting nearby. (Imagine being on the receiving end of the automatic weapon fire, as you pointed out to your wife and kids the benefits of camping in a National Park.)

The rest is history. Marty resigned shortly thereafter—alleviating the fears of INS employees and campers alike!

No basic training—No basic understanding

Cronyism and ineptitude was not just reserved for INS political appointees and their friends. One of the most destructive and widespread practices at INS was promoting employees into operational law enforcement positions without ever requiring them to graduate from an accredited basic training course. In Federal law enforcement agencies (FBI, Secret Service, Drug Enforcement Administration, etc.), Special Agents and other officers are required to graduate from basic training and then work a probationary period of time in the field to gain practical experience. (Basic training is a critical element in the life of every law enforcement officer. People who do not or cannot successfully complete an accredited basic training course should not serve as sworn operational law enforcement personnel.)

So what happened at INS? Using a whole host of personnel anomalies, INS employees wangled their way into jobs they did not deserve or understand. Whether it was Equal Employment Opportunity complaints, political pressure, "parachuting in" from another agency, "burrowing in" as a political appointee or just plain ineptitude on the part of INS management, Immigration officers seemed to be created out of thin air.

In simple terms the people at the Immigration and Naturalization Service developed several ways to become law enforcement officers and knowledge, skills and abilities usually never entered into the process. INS had Special Agents, District Directors, Officers-in-Charge and a whole host of other "officer corps" employees who were nothing more than untrained "wannabes." (As in "Daddy, I wanna be a policeman!") Let's just say INS operated with a different set of rules than everyone else in Federal law enforcement.

Some of the most prestigious and important officer corps positions were in the Office of International Affairs. INS employees, serving in our embassies abroad, were frequently called upon to make life-and-death decisions. In some cases they were also responsible for our overseas intelligence gathering efforts—like obtaining and reporting information about terrorists.

Before Homeland Security swallowed INS whole in 2003, the following overseas positions were occupied by individuals who had never graduated the U.S. Border Patrol Academy or the Immigration Officer Basic Training Academy. (Domestically it was even more scandalous.)

1. District Director, Bangkok, Thailand
2. District Director, Rome, Italy
3. Deputy District Director, Rome, Italy
4. Officer-in-Charge, Moscow, Russia
5. Officer-in-Charge, Athens, Greece
6. Officer-in-Charge, Accra, Ghana
7. Officer-in-Charge, Copenhagen, Denmark
8. Officer-in-Charge, Guangjou, China
9. Officer-in-Charge, Johannesburg, South Africa

As in most organizations, success or failure rests with the people who work there and INS was no exception. I have a great deal of contempt for many of my former INS co-workers because they accepted jobs for which they knew they were not qualified, and simply took advantage of a personnel system that was horribly mismanaged.

If INS had been responsible for managing a deserted island, it would not have made much of a difference. Unfortunately, our mission involved controlling U.S. immigration and therefore directly impacted our national security.

The new Homeland Security—more political than ever!

The anecdotes I have related in this chapter are but a few of the thousands of stories about the crazy employment practices at the former INS. Soon after the Department of Homeland Security swallowed INS whole, personnel specialists began to hear these horror stories. According to some, they began to sift through INS employee records and shortly thereafter many District Directors, Special Agents, officers in charge, and a host of other unqualified employees, were quietly offered the door out of law enforcement.

The jury is still out on the benefits of establishing Homeland Security, and according to some accounts, Homeland Security is even more "political" than the former INS.

In a June, 2007, edition of the *Government Executive*, Shane Harris' article, "Homeland Security could face transition problem," explains the level to which the agency has been politicized. *"From its inception, Homeland Security was run by political appointees . . . Former officials and experts recognize that haste dictated those early (personnel) decisions. The problem, they say, is that the trend toward political appointees never ended."* In September, 2004, Homeland Security had 180,000 employees of which 360 were political appointees. This might not seem like much, but when compared to the Veteran's Administration (64 appointees for 235,000 employees), Homeland Security is scary.

Political appointees or not, I certainly hope somewhere along the way Homeland Security completes a purge of the old INS wannabe's, and continues to professionalize the highly-skilled, trained and dedicated Immigration officers who were forced to serve for so many years under such miserable leadership. Never again should the Federal government allow so many untrained men and women to serve in positions so critical to our national security.

Homeland Security and illegal immigration

If Americans are getting all warm and fuzzy about how the new Homeland Security will handle the problems associated with illegal immigration, my sources tell me it will be five years before all the employees know where to sit, let alone do anything about the 12 million illegal aliens.

Within Homeland Security, there are now three separate dysfunctional immigration-related entities: (1) Citizenship and Immigration Services (CIS); (2) Customs and Border Protection (CBP); and (3) Immigration and Customs Enforcement (ICE). (I apologize for all of the acronyms.) My many friends who still work in these divisions all relate the same sentiment. However bad INS used to be, Homeland Security is five times worse.

Customs and Border Protection and Immigration and Customs Enforcement have been quietly "Customized." By this I mean the vast majority of high-level law enforcement positions were given to former Customs officers. (The former U.S. Customs Service was also taken in its entirety from the Treasury Department and loaded into Homeland Security.) For example, of the original 27 Immigration and Customs Enforcement Special-Agent-in-Charge positions, 23 were given to former Customs Agents. This lopsided "takeover" was not just coincidental. It signaled a very ominous future for immigration law enforcement. For the most part, U.S. Customs Special Agents could care less about human smuggling or illegal immigration. If the truth be known, they would stay as far away from immigration investigations as they possibly could—no matter how important they are to our national security. There is no doubt that this conquest by former Customs Special Agents will further weaken America's immigration enforcement capabilities.

INS "legacy" Special Agents were also hoping that Homeland Security would end political cronyism that infested their ranks for 30 years. Keep dreaming! As if the Michael Brown and the Hurricane Katrina fiasco never happened, on January 4, 2006, President George W. Bush made a "recess appointment" of 36-year-old Julie Myers to head the Immigration and Customs Enforcement Division. (The "recess appointment" sidestepped the necessity for the U.S. Senate to hold confirmation hearings.)

I am certain Ms. Myers has many qualifications that make her well-suited for the position, and I am more than willing to give her the benefit of the doubt. However, Myers' most outstanding qualifications were listed in a September 20, 2005, *Washington Post* article entitled, "Immigration Nominee's Credentials Questioned." Staff writers Dan Eggen and Spencer S. Hsu noted the following qualifications.

1. Her uncle is retired Joint Chief of Staff Air Force General Richard B. Myers;
2. She worked in several unspecified political jobs at the White House; and,
3. She is married to John F. Wood, former Chief of Staff to Secretary Chertoff of Homeland Security.

Obviously, cronyism is still alive and well in Washington, D.C. However, I am very surprised that General Myers would have had anything to do with the shenanigans surrounding the appointment of his niece to head Immigration and Customs Enforcement. After all, would General Myers have allowed his niece to be "appointed" as wing commander of a fighter squadron without her ever having flown an airplane?

For the sake of Immigration and Customs Enforcement and our national security, I pray Ms. Myers does not "crash and burn."

Different faces—Same old game

Assistant Secretary Julie Myers is just one small example of a trend that professional Immigration officers hoped would end with the establishment of the Department of Homeland Security.

Earlier I noted that in thirty years INS did not have a single Commissioner who served as a career Immigration officer. Political appointees and their friends multiplied at INS like cockroaches in a pantry. They created a "glass ceiling" that blocked career officers from specific Senior Executive positions and did little more than spread ineptitude throughout the agency.

A review of two immigration-related Homeland Security websites reveals that the White House still desires to run our immigration agencies with appointees who are untrained, unskilled and have no experience as Immigration officers.

Under the term "Leadership" at Immigration and Customs Enforcement, Assistant Secretary Myers is pictured with eighteen other cohorts who virtually run the agency. I recognize *one* of them as a trained Immigration officer.

Dr. Emilio T. Gonzales is listed as Director of Citizenship and Immigration Services. His biography is five paragraphs long, praises his "distinguished career in the U.S. Army that spanned twenty-six years" and notes he is a "Knight of Malta." The word "immigration" does not appear in his biography.

Citizenship and Immigration Services also has a "Leadership" page on their website. Under Dr. Gonzales' picture are eleven other officials. Again, only *one* of them is a career Immigration officer.

Earlier in this chapter I made reference to the U.S. Secret Service, as I consider it to be one of the finest government agencies anywhere in the world—law enforcement or otherwise. During my research in Homeland Security's cyberspace, I happened to look at their website. Since they are responsible for protecting the President and his family, I was curious how many of their "Leadership" positions were filled with "Knights of Malta." The Secret Service lists only two leaders—Director Mark Sullivan and Deputy Director Brian Nagel. Both of them are career Special Agents with 25 and 23 years of Secret Service experience respectively. Need I say more?

Chapter 6

Immigration, Religion and Political Power

One citizen, one vote

The first part of this chapter is about our electoral process, and it might seem a bit trivial. In fact, had it not been for the 2001 Presidential election between George W. Bush and Al Gore, I would not even be mentioning it. If Americans learned anything that year from the "hanging chads" in Florida, they learned that every vote counts.

A U.S. citizen's right to vote is one of the most sacred privileges in our democracy. Or is it?

Creating a new identity in the U.S. is a very easy thing to do. Birth certificates can easily be obtained through the mail, and anyone can buy or create a fraudulent (and unverifiable) Social Security card. With these two documents, an imposter can obtain a driver's license, credit cards, and, yes, even a voter registration card. During my career, I arrested hundreds of illegal aliens in Texas, Illinois, Maryland and Virginia, and many had registered to vote in the U.S.

I am not a historian, but I do understand for decades blacks in America have been subjected to threats of violence to prevent them from voting. In order to stop this type of harassment, Congress passed voting rights legislation and made it a Federal crime to deny a citizen the right to vote. Unfortunately, the law made it easy for anyone to vote—including aliens (who don't have the *right* to vote.) Currently, all anyone has to do is raise their right hand, swear they are a U.S. citizen, display a valid driver's license and vote. The system is wide open to abuse by aliens, and they know it.

How many legal and illegal aliens actually do go to the polls is unknown. Just as statistics are unavailable regarding illegal aliens and crime, the same vacuum of data exists when it comes to aliens illegally casting ballots in the U.S. Whether the voting fraud actually occurs is not the issue. The fact that aliens could be used to rig an election should be a matter of grave concern to every American citizen.

Under our current system, aliens have a very real capacity to illegally influence our election process. Through the use of voter fraud, an official could easily be elected who does not represent the majority of U.S. citizen voters in a particular jurisdiction.

Since voter registration is not an issue with which I am familiar, I am not going to propose any method to stop voter fraud by aliens. I simply think the American public should be aware that we have tens of millions of legal aliens in the U.S. and approximately 12 million illegal aliens. As dramatic as it sounds, if a large percentage of our alien population decided to illegally vote in a national election, it could have serious consequences for our democracy.

Immigration and votes

Immigration affects American politics more than most people realize. Allow me to point out why certain organizations consider immigration critical to their political survival in the U.S.

- The vast majority of U.S. permanent resident aliens eventually become U.S. citizens.
- One U.S. citizen equals one voter.
- Citizens vote for candidates who have a similar ideology to their own.
- With the exception of the Presidential election (where the electoral college decides), the candidate with the

most votes wins the election and becomes the elected representative.

- The more elected representatives with a particular ideology, the more chance future legislation will reflect that ideology.
- If enough immigrants of a particular race or persuasion eventually become U.S. citizens, they can change America's political and legal landscape.

Influencing immigration policies by religious organizations for political gain

It has always amazed me that groups who advocate a separation of church and state have not objected more vigorously to the way religious organizations impact the administration of America's immigration laws. For decades, Catholic, Jewish and other religious affiliations have quietly and efficiently supported both legal and illegal immigration to the U.S. Whether it is Senator Edward Kennedy of Massachusetts pushing the Catholic immigration agenda or Senator (formerly Congressman) Charles Schumer of New York vociferously supporting the immigration agenda for the American Jewish lobby, these politicians and others have used their political positions to enact religiously supported immigration legislation.

In the name of the Statue of Liberty and humanitarianism, religious entities (along with others) have been able to liberalize our immigration policies to such an extent that our legal immigration process is overwhelmed and illegal immigration has reached unprecedented levels.

Our Constitution requires a separation of church and state. Therefore, the government grants religious organizations tax-exempt status. The same government, however, allows religious organizations to turn right around and use their tax-free income to directly influence America's immigration laws. Needless to say, this is not a separation of church and state.

If Americans can get past the usual "humanitarianism" smokescreen, it is obvious that some religious organizations are involved in developing immigration policy simply to enhance their own political power. Liberty, justice, freedom and huddled masses have nothing to do with their lobbying efforts.

The Catholic Church

I have tremendous respect for people of the Catholic faith. However, when it comes to U.S. immigration policy, the leaders of the Catholic Church seem far more interested in getting the faithful into America than into Heaven.

Let's take a quick look at the countries that have the most illegal immigrants living in the U.S.—Mexico, El Salvador, Guatemala, Honduras, Bolivia, Colombia and the Philippines. Notice anything strange? They are countries that have three things in common.

- They are all poor.
- They are all overpopulated.
- They are all predominantly Catholic.

During my travels, I also noticed that the largest and most opulent structures in the cities, towns and villages in most of these countries were Catholic churches. I was frequently told that the money to build and support the local churches came directly from legal and illegal immigrants living and working in the U.S.

In the September 20, 2004, *Arizona Republic,* journalist Daniel Gonzalez wrote a front page article entitled "Giving back: Immigrants in U.S. revitalize hometowns with billions they send back to Mexico." The picture under the article showed a beautiful church in the background, and the statement under the picture read, "Alfredo Chalico stands in front of the San Jose de Mendoza Catholic Church. The church is being reconstructed with money raised from former residents like Chalico who have immigrated to the United States."

While it does not specifically say it, the picture and the statement underneath it indicate that the Catholic Church is a strong supporter of mass legal and illegal immigration to the U.S. Allow me to use a hypothetical example to demonstrate the point.

Let's suppose you are a priest in the town of Intipuca, La Union, El Salvador. Hundreds of your parishioners live (legally and illegally) in the Washington, D.C., area. Every week, your church receives tens of thousands of dollars in donations from residents who receive their money from illegal immigrants working in America. Why would you or any other clergyman in your position support initiatives that would curtail illegal immigration to the U.S.? On the contrary, you would be foolish if you did anything other than support the migration, whether it was legal or not.

Is the Catholic Church openly interjecting itself into our government's immigration policies in clear violation of our Constitutional requirement of separation of church and state? The answer is "yes." Look no further than http://justiceforimmigrants.org website. Within seconds of a mouse click, readers can see for themselves that the Catholic Church has every intention of using every available methodology to influence U.S. immigration policy. On July 1, 2007, the website stated, *"This website is designed to help achieve the goals of the Justice for Immigrants Campaign. It provides tools and information for diocesan and community-based organizing, education, and advocacy efforts. You will find information about Catholic teachings that underpin this Campaign, as well as proposals from the Catholic Bishops to achieve reforms in our nation's immigration laws and policies that better reflect our values as a nation of immigrants. We encourage you to visit this site often, as we will be updating it frequently, with resource materials, action alerts, and other information we hope you find useful."* This is blatant interference in our government policymaking. I could not have described it better myself.

This website is just the beginning. The Catholic Legal Immigration Network spends big dollars every year on "immigrant services." While the title sounds innocuous and humanitarian, a good portion of their tax-free dollars is spent to oppose the enforcement efforts of U.S. immigration authorities and to keep as many illegal aliens as possible in the U.S.

Washington Post reporter Karin Brulliard, incidentally, wrote about this quiet intervention in her January 8, 2007, article entitled, "Battling deportation often a solitary journey." In her story about legal representation for aliens fighting deportation, one of the people she interviewed was Donald Kerwin, Executive Director for the Catholic Legal Immigration Network, Inc. His organization is one of the many charities that offer free or low-cost legal services to aliens fighting to remain here. Why does such an organization even exist? Is there a Catholic Legal *Customs* Network to help people through their import/export woes? Or how about a Catholic Legal *Environmental* Network, to help businesses figure out if they are in compliance with Federal clean air laws?

While no one should object to lawyers offering free legal services to illegal aliens, there must be strong opposition to the use of tax-exempt dollars from religious organizations being used to meddle in U.S. government affairs.

The Catholic Church is also in the business of assisting political candidates who support legalizing as many illegal aliens as possible. It is no secret that when it comes to immigration reform, Senator Kennedy is the Church's main man on Capitol Hill. At the end of the 109th Congress in 2006, the U.S. Senate passed a "comprehensive immigration reform bill" called the Kennedy-McCain Act. (The bill did not become law.) At the beginning of the 110th Congress, Senator Kennedy posted the following on his Senate website:

> *"From our country's very beginning to the present day, immigrants have helped build our nation, and made us strong. Their labor is vital to the economy, and it will continue to be needed to sustain our economic growth. The American people demanded action on this critical issue, and the Senate answered with a bipartisan solution to the problem. Business and labor, Republicans and Democrats, and religious leaders strongly supported our bipartisan plan to strengthen our borders, provide a path to earned citizen-*

ship for workers who are here illegally, and put in place a realistic guest worker program for the future."

Why are "religious leaders" getting involved, and who are they? According to CNN's Lou Dobbs' March 7, 2007 commentary, Senator Kennedy was consulting none other than the Archbishop of Los Angeles, Cardinal Roger Mahoney. This is the same Cardinal Mahoney who openly advocates that U.S. towns and cities declare themselves as "sanctuary" localities and openly refuse to assist in the enforcement of U.S. immigration laws.

Intervention in U.S. immigration policy is no small issue. There are hidden but far-reaching domestic and international implications related to these political activities. Consider the huge benefits to the Catholic Church in both the "sending countries" and in the U.S.

In sending countries:

- Legal and illegal aliens in the U.S. send tens of billions of dollars home (2007 estimate for Mexico alone was $24 billion).
- Money is donated by the faithful to the local Catholic Church, making it one of the wealthiest and most powerful institutions in each country.
- Local overpopulation is relieved when large groups of poor illiterates leave and settle in the U.S.

In the U.S.:

- The Church acts as sanctuary for illegal aliens, and many immigrants feel forever indebted to the Church.
- The Church continuously fights for programs, such as amnesty and temporary protected status to legalize as many illegal aliens as possible.
- Through the efforts of the Church, many illegal aliens eventually become legal aliens and U.S. citizens.
- Catholic U.S. citizens subsequently bring large families to the U.S. by applying for immediate relative family reunification visas.

- The Church gains political power because the number of U.S. citizen Catholics increases faster than the rest of the U.S. population.
- Catholic U.S. citizens use their voting power to elect candidates who support the teachings of the Church.

Considering these factors, the Pope to the parish priest (including Cardinal Mahoney) all know they have everything to gain and nothing to lose by openly supporting illegal immigration to the U.S.

With regard to the Catholic Church's claims about humanitarianism and family reunification, Americans must ask a serious question. Why doesn't the Church begin using their tax-free dollars to repatriate illegal aliens to their home countries, so their families can again be reunited? Good question.

It seems that the Catholic Church is adamant about continuing to take part in civil disobedience in support of illegal immigration. The U.S. government's response should be an immediate suspension of their tax-exempt status until the civil disobedience and government meddling ceases. Then and only then will Americans find out whether the Catholic Church is sincere about its humanitarian initiatives or whether the almighty dollar takes precedence.

The Elvira Arellano story

If anyone doubts my assertion that illegal immigration has seriously eroded our Contitutionally mandated separation of church and state, look no further than the case of Elvira Arellano. In 2002, she was convicted of using a fake Social Security card to obtain employment at O'Hare International Airport, and was sentenced to three years probation. In August, 2006, she was also ordered to appear before an immigration judge and instead moved into the Adelberto United Methodist Church of Chicago. Despite the fact she was a federal fugitive, the church decided to give her "sanctuary" from the authorities.

On August 19, 2007, Arellano decided to leave the church "to attend several speaking engagements" in Los Angeles, California. Sometime during her travels she was reportedly apprehended by immigration authorities and immediately deported to Mexico.

Elvira Arellano was not just another illegal alien from Mexico. According to Wikipedia, the online encyclopedia, she was deported back to Mexico in 1997. More importantly, her resume lists her as president of *La Familia Latina Unida* (United Latino Family), "a group that lobbies for families that could be split by deportation." She is the mother of a young U.S. citizen child, and before her deportation was fast becoming the poster lady for every illegal alien woman who was smart enough to give birth to a child in the U.S. (According to one Mexican representative by the name of Jose Jacques, there are 4.9 million U.S. citizen children whose parents are subject to deportation from the U.S. This statistic has not been verified by reliable data.)

During her year long stay in the church, Arellano was able to access many of our media outlets and played to the hearts and minds of every benevolent American citizen who ever dropped a coin in a Salvation Army bucket. It seemed to work. In lieu of being tagged as jack-booted thugs, Immigration and Customs Enforcement agents decided to allow the woman to remain in the church.

Was this truly a case about "family reunification?" No! There was nothing stopping Arellano from taking her son and returning to Mexico. She also knew at the time her son was born that he could not convey any immigration benefits to her until he reached adulthood. Was this about some mean-spirited and overzealous government agents? Absolutely not! Immigration and Customs Enforcement was lenient with her, to say the least. Or maybe it was about racism? Apparently it was not. Ms. Arellano never claimed her race was an issue. So what was her case all about?

Elvira Arellano was about U.S. politics, plain and simple. Her supporters wanted her to stay in America and they want Congress to allow millions like her to remain as well.

Shortly after Arellano's deportation, *Newsweek's* Jennifer Ordonez wrote an August 23, 2007, article about the growing "sanctuary movement" in the U.S. The article entitled, "A Movement Takes a Hit", explains that this case was a lot more than a simple deportation back to Mexico. Ordonez describes that Arellano was "*. . . one of 22 carefully chosen illegal immigrants living on the grounds of various churches as part of what's being called the New Sanctuary Movement. It's a group vetted by a team of lawyers working with the religious congregations involved in the movement, which range from Roman Catholic to Jewish to Mennonite. To be the face of the estimated 12 million illegal aliens now living in the United States, as organizers call them, the small crew now in sanctuary have either overstayed their visas or never had one in the first place. They are the men and women with steady work histories, who pay taxes and are parents to children born in the United States—a profile designed to help mitigate the fact that each had broken the law in various ways to establish their lives in the United States, including using fake Social Security numbers.*"

I hope Americans can see through these "sanctuary" cases. Some religious leaders are testing the government's resolve to see just how far they can go in the name of God. While it may appear as though Immigration and Customs Enforcement did the right thing by waiting until Arellano left the church, they actually set a very dangerous precedent. What's next—"sanctuary" for drug dealers because they have a perfect attendance record at church or synagogue? Or, how about giving "sanctuary" to pedophile clergymen simply because they pay their taxes?

Church or no church, illegal aliens like Elvira Arellano should be arrested, given due process, and if so ordered, deported to their homeland. As far as their minor U.S. citizen children are concerned, the parents have a choice—take the child back with them for the sake of "family reunification" or leave the child with relatives in the U.S.

With regard to politically motivated issues like Arellano's, if religious organizations feel so compelled to violate our immigration laws, they should be stripped of their tax-exempt status. Furthermore, the clergymen responsible should be arrested for harboring Federal fugitives. Once and for all, separation of church and state has its foundation in the U.S. Constitution and we should keep that separation sacred and well-defined.

The Jewish lobby

During the 1970s and 1980s, the Jewish political lobby in America had two major initiatives when it came to the U.S. Congress. The first involved support for the State of Israel, and the second involved the more relevant issue of Russian Jewish emigration.

Maybe it is just coincidental, but Jewish Congressional leaders have consistently been members of the House Judiciary Committee and the Immigration Subcommittee. History will show that during the House of Representative debates about the Immigration Reform and Control Act of 1986, and subsequent pieces of immigration reform legislation, Charles Schumer of New York, Howard Berman of California, and Barney Frank of Massachusetts were ever present and participating. And, until 9/11, they were seldom, if ever, proponents of increased immigration enforcement activities.

In the name of preventing another Holocaust, the U.S. took in thousands of Jews from the former Soviet Union during the 1980s. While I am certain that many of the Jewish Soviet refugees had been subjected to some form of persecution, I am also certain that many others who came to the U.S. were not Jews at all.

Unfortunately, just as Fidel Castro emptied his jails into America during the Mariel Boatlift, the Russian government used our benevolent immigration system to quietly send hundreds of KGB agents and Russian mobsters to North Miami Beach, Florida, Los Angeles, California, and Brighton Beach, New York. And it was all done under the Soviet Jewish émigré refugee program.

I want to relate just one personal anecdote about a family of "Jewish refugees" who were allowed to come to the U.S. after fleeing Russia.

My mother had a friend who arranged for several such families to immigrate to Connecticut. With the help of the rabbis and several other politicians, these "Russian Jews" were granted refugee status, processed in Vienna, Austria, and sent to central Connecticut to start their new life.

Just before the families arrived, I had an opportunity to discuss the situation with my mother's close friend. She told me that she was so pleased that U.S. Immigration had allowed so many people to escape from Russia. She felt as though she was preventing another Holocaust, and could not wait to begin teaching the families about Judaism.

One week later she received a little dose of reality when the "Russian Jews" finally arrived. Judaism was the last thing they wanted. As soon as they got their feet on the ground, they collected every conceivable gift and government benefit they could get their hands on, and left for sunny Los Angeles, California. It turned out they were all members of an Armenian crime syndicate and did not know a thing about synagogue, sabbath, and the *Torah*.

My mother's friend was livid. She called me and wanted them all deported. Apparently the "Jewish refugees" had bribed Russian government officials, who then created documents indicating they were persecuted Russian Jews. I do not know what eventually happened to them, but there is little likelihood they were deported.

By now, most of the refugees who wanted to leave Russia and the former Soviet Union have left and settled in the U.S. and Israel. While the Jewish lobby succeeded in liberalizing U.S. immigration policies, they may have made the mistake of the century. These liberalized policies that were meant to prevent another Holocaust are now being applied to tens of thousands of refugees from the West Bank, Lebanon, Sudan, Afghanistan, Iraq, and Iran. These refugees are mostly devout Muslims, who openly call for the demise of the Jews and the destruction of the State of Israel. As the human tide from these Muslim countries increases, it will be interesting to see if the Jewish lobby on Capitol Hill rethinks their initiative to open America to all who claim political persecution.

When it comes to religious organizations influencing U.S. immigration policy, Catholics and Jews are not alone. Many other religious organizations have powerful lobbyists working these issues on Capitol Hill. Our founding fathers warned us to maintain clear lines of separation between church and state, as they evidently understood the problems that can occur when the line is crossed. Unfortunately when it comes to U.S. immigration policy, the line has recently emerged as a dangerous blur.

The Hispanic vote

Two days after the 2004 Presidential election, Lou Dobbs announced on CNN that the vast majority of the 7 million Latino voters voted for George W. Bush. Amazingly, immigration was not the core issue. Exit polls indicated that "family values," "integrity" and other issues were important to Hispanics, much as they are to mainstream America. This is a change from years past.

In the months preceding the 2004 elections, Americans were bombarded with nationally syndicated articles about how the Hispanic vote might impact the election. And, of course, one of the major issues discussed in each article was illegal immigration.

In the November 9, 2004, *New York Times* staff writer Kirk Johnson proclaimed, "Hispanic Voters Declare Their Independence." In the article, he wrote about everything from Mexican-American and Cuban-American Catholics to Latinos in the Marine Corps. By the end of the article, he had covered so many issues and made so many conclusions about Hispanics, I could not discern what specific ethnic group he was discussing.

Admittedly, I am not a politician or a journalist, but discussing the Hispanic vote is absolute nonsense. When it comes to the issue of illegal immigration and a host of other similar issues, there is no such thing as "Hispanic."

U.S. citizens of Mexican and Latin American descent are usually in favor of liberalized immigration policies. However, there are a great many Spanish-speaking U.S. citizens in the Western states who vote against increased immigration. They realize better than anyone that they are the ones who are most affected by the artificially low wages created by illegal immigration.

Next are the U.S. citizens of Cuban descent. They are concentrated mostly in the Miami metropolitan area and northern New Jersey. Cuban-Americans are usually one-issue, conservative voters. Their big concern is not education, it is not jobs, and it is not illegal immigration. It is Fidel Castro, plain and simple. For journalists to include U.S. citizens of Cuban descent in a discussion about Hispanics and illegal immigration shows how little they understand the Cuban-American community. Besides, when Cuban nationals flee Castro and subsequently set foot on American soil, they are automatically granted legal status. With few exceptions, there is no such thing as an illegal alien from Cuba.

The last large group of Hispanic voters could also care less about illegal immigration. They are Puerto Ricans, and they are U.S. citizens at birth. Illegal immigration is not even in their vocabulary.

The vast majority of Latin and Hispanic voters I have interviewed are interested in immigration policies that will make *legal* immigration easier and are not in favor of rewarding illegal immigrants. If our politicians believe that the majority of Hispanic voters support illegal immigration, come election time, they may be in for a rude awakening.

So the next time you hear television pundits discussing illegal immigration and the "Hispanic" vote, you might want to ask, "What 'Hispanics' are they talking about?"

Immigration and U.S. politics—look closely

Immigration is a powerful tool that can significantly influence our political system. For the most part, America's legal immigrants eventually become U.S. citizens and that equates to votes. Groups seeking more political power in the U.S. fully understand these facts and will do everything they can to legalize as many illegal aliens as possible. After all, a new U.S. citizen will be easy to influence politically, especially if the citizen feels indebted to an organization for helping him or her obtain their legal status.

In the future, when any group claims they want to help illegal immigrants, Americans should always look beyond the rhetoric and the claims of humanitarianism. More than likely they will find an organization seeking more political power.

Chapter 7

Legal Immigration—A System in Crisis

America's legal immigration process is completely broken. Whether it is the long lines at immigration offices or notices telling applicants that it will be years before they will get an answer, the system is in a state of collapse.

The vast majority of immigration professionals I have interviewed advocate a complete overhaul of our immigration laws. In other words, throw out the Immigration and Nationality Act and all the other subsequent "band-aid" legislation. Congress should get to work and pass a new comprehensive law for the 21st century. It will never happen, so I will simply advocate it here, and then get back to reality.

I admit that during my years at INS I had little to do with the actual adjudication of applications for immigration benefits. However, I did work closely with examiners during my tenure as Chief of the Immigration Officer Academy. I was responsible for the training of these officers and became quite familiar with their issues and their problems.

Since my retirement, I have kept in touch with many of those who are still responsible for adjudicating applications in the new Citizenship and Immigration Services (CIS) division of Homeland Security. Several have told me that despite the glowing reports to Congress and the claims of backlog reduction, Citizenship and Immigration Services is just another Titanic waiting to sink.

Even the Homeland Security Inspector General paints a somewhat bleak picture of Citizenship and Immigration Services.

I know I promised to stay away from statistics, but the following data is mind-boggling. In his December, 2004, report, "Major Management Challenges Facing the Department of Homeland Security," the Inspector General states:

> *"USCIS is challenged with processing immigration benefit applications and petitions in a timely manner. As of May 2004, USCIS had pending 5,696,066 applications and petitions. Of these, 233,696 were for asylum; 671,107 for naturalization; and 4,790,663 for immigration benefits. The Administration announced the aim of meeting a six month standard from start to finish for processing applications for immigration. The President pledged $500 million over five years, beginning with $100 million requested for fiscal year 2002, to support USCIS in eliminating the backlog by the end of 2006.*
>
> *"USCIS issued a 'Backlog Elimination Plan' in June 2004, that reframed how USCIS counts the backlog and proposed the following backlog elimination strategies: (1) new management tools;(2) improved processes and procedures; and (3) better use of technology. USCIS' backlog reduction plan is ambitious and is based on numerous assumptions about application receipts, increased productivity and the success of some pilot programs currently being conducted. Many of these assumptions would be severely disrupted if global immigration patterns or U.S. immigration law encountered significant changes. For example, a proposed new guest worker program would permit many currently illegal aliens to apply for some form of immigration status. If USCIS were suddenly inundated with potentially millions of unexpected immigration benefit applications, its efforts to eliminate current backlogs would be severely hindered."*

Despite what the Inspector General says, here is what USCIS says about the problem. A November 9, 2004, letter posted on the U.S. Citizenship and Immigration Services website states:

> *"By completing more than 600,000 more cases than we received in the first three quarters of Fiscal Year 2004, U.S. Citizenship and Immigration Services (USCIS) announced today that the backlog has declined for the processing of immigration benefits*

such as work authorization, permanent residency, and naturalization. In the update issued to Congress, USCIS reported the backlog, which had reached a high of 3.8 million cases in January 2004, had been reduced to 3.2 million cases as of June 30, 2004." Director Aguirre added, "I'm confident that the momentum we're building now will carry us to our goal of completely eliminating the backlog and maintaining a six-month or less cycle time by the end of 2006."

The Director of Citizenship and Immigration Services and the Inspector General should get their facts straight or maybe purchase some new calculators. Is the backlog 6 million or 3 million? Using *their* calculations, the backlog will be reduced in 2009, not 2006. (Imagine being told by a motor vehicle department that your driver's license will be ready in 2009.)

This massive backlog has created not only frustration and distrust of our government, but also increased illegal immigration. Many citizens and aliens alike feel it is better to violate U.S. immigration laws than to have family members wait in a foreign country for years for an immigration benefit that should take only a few weeks to process.

The immigration multiplication factor

For those Americans who are not involved in our legal immigration process (first thank God you are not involved), it is difficult to imagine how any Federal agency could get so far behind in its work. One examiner told me there are close to 6 million applications sitting in boxes waiting to be adjudicated. The disorder is bigger than we all realize.

There is one major cause for this crisis and I call it the "immigration multiplication factor." In simple terms, it means that immigration leads to more immigration. If a U.S. citizen marries a citizen of another country, the alien spouse can come to the U.S., get permanent resident status (a "green card") and almost immediately start petitioning for other immediate relatives. The process continues until the entire family immigrates to the U.S. This is what policy makers call "family reunification."

This family reunification concept seems very humanitarian, and has been one of the foundations of our immigration policy for decades. Unfortunately, it is being abused, and it is one of the reasons we have a huge backlog of immigration applications waiting to be processed. There is no better way to demonstrate this problem than to describe a real case.

In 1978, I was assisting with a marriage-fraud investigation of a 25-year-old Iranian student named Reza. Shortly after finishing his degree at a northern Virginia college, and knowing his time in the U.S. was short, Reza went out in search of the love of his life.

This thin, dark, handsome Iranian had no trouble finding "Barbara," who was wearing her heart on her sleeve and checking out every gin mill in Old Town Alexandria, Virginia. She was an unattractive and grossly overweight 40-year-old, but she had the one trait that Reza loved. She was an American citizen.

Three months after their "love affair" began, they were married. Within three more months Reza had his "green card." (Back in those days, aliens received their "green cards" shortly after the relative petition was approved.) Within days after receiving his "green card," he was out the door and heading for a divorce lawyer. INS was never able to prove his marriage was fraudulent. However, less than a year after they tied the knot, Reza and Barbara ended their marriage.

Reza decided to make good use of his new U.S. resident alien status. He headed for Tehran, Iran, and once again Reza fell in love. This time it was with an Iranian woman with seven children. Reza petitioned for his new love and her entire crew. (Years ago, it took only months before Reza's new nine-member family were all legally settled in the U.S. With the huge backlog of immigrant visas, it might now be years before his family could immigrate.)

This is an example of the "multiplication factor." Within two years, one fraudulent marriage resulted in the immigration of eight people, all in the name of "family reunification." (Eventually, Reza became a U.S. citizen, and his mother, father and several brothers and sisters immigrated as well.

By approving Reza's one "green card" application, the U.S. Immigration Service gave rise to many more applications. And, without a doubt, several of the new immigrants Reza brought in eventually filed new petitions of their own. Considering the number of similar situations throughout the U.S., it is easy to see how this immigration "multiplication factor" has created a huge workload for the agencies responsible for legal U.S. immigration.

Despite the massive increase in immigration benefit applications, Congress and the White House refused to exponentially increase the size of the INS. The agency did grow, but never fast enough to keep up with the rapidly growing number of applications. Now the backlog is incomprehensible.

Adjudication fee account

During the 1980s, and especially after the amnesty in 1986, Congress and the U.S. government decided to impose application fees to offset the rising administrative costs associated with increased immigration. They implemented a "user fee" that required applicants to pay a set charge for filing different types of applications. These fees were supposed to pay the costs for hiring and training new immigration examiners who were needed to adjudicate the ever increasing number of applications for benefits.

There is supposedly some magical formula that the Office of Management and Budget uses to determine how much the government should charge for each application. The fees are then paid to Homeland Security at the time the application is submitted.

For those lucky souls who have not ventured onto the Homeland Security website and located the Immigration Forms and Fees page, allow me to give you a quick peek. The following are just a few examples of the fees associated with immigration applications (updated July 30, 2007).

- I-485A Supplement to I-485 Application to Register Permanent Residence, $1,010.
- I-600 Petition to Classify an Orphan as an Immediate Relative, $750.

- I-526 Investor Petition, $1,435.
- N-400 Application for U.S. Citizenship, $675.
- I-90 Application to Replace Permanent Resident Card, $290.
- I-539 Application to Extend/Change Non-immigrant Status, $300.

One can see these charges are by no means small. As an American citizen who is married to an immigrant, I have had to pay several similar fees to Citizenship and Immigration Services. Unfortunately I will probably have to pay several more before my wife becomes a U.S. citizen. In my opinion these fees are nothing short of outright extortion by our Federal government. In return, the service is slightly more than non-existent.

As I stated before, I never formerly served as an Immigration examiner. However, I was called upon several times as a young Special Agent to work extra hours adjudicating applications for benefits. In one instance, around 1979, I was sent to Dulles International Airport to help clear a backlog of applications for extensions of stay (I-539's.) In simple terms these were applications filed by non-immigrants who wanted to extend their stay or change their status while still here in the U.S. (e.g. from visitor to student.) The processing time was about six minutes for each application and the fee was about $20. Today the processing time is about the same, but the fee is an astronomical $300.

I know I will be accused of oversimplifying the adjudication process, but facts are facts. The U.S. government is making about $3,000 an hour processing applications like the one mentioned above. (I told my friends at Homeland Security if they paid me $3,000 an hour to work on "extensions of stay," I would quit writing this book and go back to work.)

Most applications for immigration benefits are sent to Homeland Security processing centers located in Dallas, Texas; St. Albans, Vermont; Lincoln, Nebraska; and Laguna Nigel, California. The facilities are all operated by private contractors and staffed with both government and non-government employees.

When an application is received, it is immediately checked for completeness. If the application is in order, the contractor's staff will enter the data into a Homeland Security database, generate a fee receipt, and forward the application for adjudication to immigration examiners. Whether the application is approved or denied, the fee is deposited into the U.S. Treasury, and the applicant is sent a Notice of Action.

On the next page, I have reprinted a Notice of Action sent to an American woman who married a professional athlete from Australia. She applied for a "green card" for her new husband. There are no numerical limitations for this type of visa. Under normal circumstances it should have taken approximately 30 to 60 days for her application to be approved and sent to the American Embassy in Australia for processing. As mind-boggling as it might seem, the notice indicates that her application will take *"between 990 days and 990 days to process."* That is almost three years—and it is not a misprint.

I have had my own personal experiences with Citizenship and Immigration Services. In February, 2006, my wife decided to put her married name on both her "green card" and her Arizona driver's license. For the change on her license, she went to the Arizona Motor Vehicle Department. There she paid $6.00, received an updated driver's license and walked out in less than thirty minutes.

Citizenship and Immigration Services requires just a bit more time and money for exactly the same process. First, she had to mail a completed Form I-90 (Application to Replace Permanent Resident Card) with a check for $260 (now $290). Within two weeks she received a Form I-797C, Notice of Action, advising her, *"The above application has been received and forwarded on for further processing. USCIS WILL SCHEDULE YOUR BIOMETRICS APPOINTMENT. You will be receiving a biometrics appointment notice with a specific time, date and place where you will have your fingerprints and/or photos taken. You MUST wait for your biometrics appointment notice prior to going to the ASC for biometrics processing."* Four months passed and she did not hear a word from Citizenship and Immigration Services. When she called the

Immigration and Naturalization Service

THE UNITED STATES OF AMERICA

RECEIPT NUMBER		CASE TYPE
WAC-04-018-		I130 IMMIGRANT PETITION FOR RELATIVE, FIANCE(E), OR ORPHAN
RECEIVED DATE	PRIORITY DATE	PETITIONER
October 27, 2003		NICOLE L.
NOTICE DATE	PAGE	BENEFICIARY
October 28, 2003	1 of 1	CRAIG A.

NICOLE L.
N GRAYHAWK DR
SCOTTSDALE AZ 85255

Notice Type: Receipt Notice

Amount received: $ 130.00

Section: Husband or wife of U.S. Citizen, 201(b) INA

The above application or petition has been received. It usually takes 990 to 990 days from the date of this receipt for us to process this type of case. Please notify us immediately if any of the above information is incorrect.

We will send you a written notice as soon as we make a decision on this case. You can also use the phone number (800) 375-5283 to obtain case status information direct from our automated system 24 hours a day with a touch-tone phone and the receipt number for this case (at the top of this notice).

If you have other questions about possible immigration benefits and services, filing information, or Immigration and Naturalization Service forms, please call the INS National Customer Service Center (NCSC) at 1-800-375-5283. If you are hearing impaired, please call our TDD at 1-800-767-1833.

You can also visit the INS on the internet at www.bcis.gov. On our web site you can get up-to-date case status information on your case and find valuable information about immigration services and benefits.

s 990 to 990 days f
of the above info

Please see the additional information on the back. You will be notified separately about any other cases you filed.
IMMIGRATION & NATURALIZATION SERVICE
CALIFORNIA SERVICE CENTER
P. O. BOX 30111
LAGUNA NIGUEL CA 92607-0111
Customer Service Telephone: (800) 375-5283

"990 days to 990 days" to process an application. This is NOT a misprint.

National Customer Service Center (1-800-375-5283), they said they had no information about her application in their computer, and suggested she wait another few months. In June, 2007, she was finally notified to appear for her biometric appointment. She did so, and on August 2, 2007, her "green card" arrived—six months after she applied and at a cost of almost $300! (If this is what it takes to get a name changed on a "green card," imagine the machinations an alien must go through to get a work visa for the U.S.)

These are perfect examples of the utter confusion facing most people who attempt to comply with our nation's immigration laws. Every day, people across America are forced to deal with the dysfunctional world of U.S. immigration and the monumental backlog of applications for benefits.

In typical form, Congress took *a bold step* in an attempt to eliminate the backlog. Section 452 of the Homeland Security Act of 2002, established the position of "Citizenship and Immigration Services Ombudsman." Unfortunately, this job is "Mickey Mouse," both literally and figuratively. In July, 2003, the Secretary of Homeland Security appointed Prakash I. Khatri as the first "Ombudsman." Is he a former Immigration officer who might have knowledge about how to improve the system? No. Has he been successful at eliminating the backlog? No. However, Mr. Khatri's resume does indicate he served five years as the Manager of Immigration and Visa Processing for none other than Walt Disney World in Florida. I told you, it is "Mickey Mouse."

Inspections fee account

As one can see from the Delta ticket receipt, every international passenger is charged "an immigration service inspection fee." Although the Homeland Security Inspector General did not give specific amounts collected for immigration inspection fees, his December, 2004, report stated, "Between FY's 1998 and 2002, the former U.S. Customs Service collected $1.1 billion from the airlines."

Delta

*** IMPORTANT FARES INFORMATION ***

1. YOUR FARE INCLUDES A CUSTOMS USER FEE
2. YOUR FARE INCLUDES AN IMMIGRATION SERVICE INSPECTION FEE.

Where does all the "user fee" money go?

In turn, Customs and Border Protection is supposed to receive sufficient funding from the U.S. Treasury to buy computers, train and staff the ports with enough inspectors, and pay for whatever other miscellaneous expenses arise during the work year.

With all that money, have you ever noticed there are never enough inspectors at our international airports? The few Immigration inspectors that are there always seem to be under pressure to keep the long lines moving. In most cases, they have no more than 45 seconds to make the determination whether to allow a person into the country or refer them for secondary inspection.

Should there be so much pressure placed on airport personnel to make such critical decisions in such a short period of time? I think it is dangerous.

Simply put, the money is being paid to the U.S. government and the services are not being provided. Homeland Security officials tell us there is not enough money to pay for a sufficient number of Immigration inspectors.

Where does all the user fee money go?

If the applicants for benefits are each paying hundreds of dollars in "adjudication fees," and international passengers are paying hundreds of millions of dollars in "inspection fees," why are there long lines at U.S. immigration at our international ports of entry, and what could possibly cause a delay of 990 days to process a simple application?

Unfortunately, these user fees have not been properly utilized. Despite the denials of Homeland Security, a serious audit will show that bureaucrats and political appointees have treated these funds as some sort of personal piggy bank. I was always amazed when political appointees and Senior Executives at INS took multiple trips to Europe and Asia and funded the travel with money from the adjudication fee account. At the same time, the backlog of applications was growing into the millions.

The problem is simple. The system used to disseminate funds from these user fee accounts promotes financial irresponsibility and a lack of accountability. No matter how many times I asked, no one could ever tell me how much money was collected, how much money had been spent, and how much money was going to be available.

As an example, I remember being told one year that the inspection fee account did not have enough funds to pay for a small training project at the Immigration Officer Academy. I had requested $75,000 to repair the mock inspections area used during INS practical training exercises. INS Headquarters advised me that, due to an unexpected downturn in the number of European tourists arriving in the U.S., they had not received their projected revenue from the user fees. They advised me they were short of funds for that quarter and could not afford the expenditure.

Three days after I received the thumbs-down on my request, another person in Headquarters from the exact same office called me regarding a completely different project. Without knowing anything about the prior conversation or denial, she claimed there had been an unexpected *increase* in the number of European tourists, and the inspection fees account had a surplus of $11 million. She then asked me if there were any special projects I wanted to fund. (I was going to ask her to fund my trip to the shrink!)

Needless to say, I lost complete faith in the people who handled the user fee accounts at INS Headquarters.

The asylum game

As I discuss in Chapter 6, the Jewish lobby has significantly influenced U.S. immigration policy. In simple terms, American Jews want to make certain that there will never be another Holocaust. More importantly, however, they also want the U.S. to always maintain a wide open-door policy for people fleeing persecution—something that was not available to many Jews who fled Germany in the 1940s.

With regard to refugees, U.S. immigration policy must also fall in line with the agreements and treaties we have signed as a member of the United Nations. Because of these agreements, we accept tens of thousands of refugees and asylum applicants every year.

So as not to confuse my readers, I am going to briefly explain the difference between a refugee and a person granted asylum in the U.S.

- An *asylee* is a person who comes to the U.S. and claims that they have a well-founded fear of persecution if they are forced to return to their home country.
- A *refugee* is a person who makes a claim overseas that he or she cannot remain in their home country, and seeks refuge in the U.S.

In either case, once their application is approved, a refugee or asylee can remain here legally. And, after remaining here for one year as a refugee or asylee, they can then apply for a "green card."

It is known throughout the world that the U.S. is extremely liberal and humanitarian in its treatment of both asylees and refugees. Unfortunately, the system is being badly abused. Despite several attempts to revamp the program, it is still an incredible mess.

Refugee camps in Africa have been plagued with organized criminal activity. Aliens from countries like Somalia, Ethiopia and Sudan are flooding into these refugee camps and paying hefty bribes to officials, who then move the aliens to the front of the processing line. Since the aliens usually have no birth records or any other documentation, those who finally get an interview gather up as many children as possible, claim they are one family and then immigrate a massive "single family" to the U.S. There have been countless stories of women claiming they gave birth to several children two months apart—and countless additional stories of aid workers who believed them! The deception is not just confined to refugee camps.

On many flights to the U.S., aliens still use the old trick of boarding an international flight with a fraudulent passport and visa, and then flushing their documents down the toilet during the flight. As soon as the alien approaches the U.S. Immigration officer, they claim that they have no identification and cannot return home because they fear persecution.

Unfortunately, there are so many people now claiming asylum, there is no jail space to detain all of them. The new Department of Homeland Security does the same thing INS used to do. The aliens are interviewed, given a hearing date at some future time and released onto the streets of America (despite the fact the U.S. government has no idea of their true identity). In many instances, the alien is also given a permit to work in the U.S., and the right to obtain a valid Social Security number.

Many asylum applicants never come back to the immigration court for their hearing because they know the application was a ruse from the beginning. They simply work and remain in the U.S. until Congress passes an amnesty or the alien finds some other method to legally get a "green card."

Our asylum program is problematic for another reason. During its development, asylum advocates at INS felt that normal Immigration officers were too enforcement-minded for the asylum program. The administrators recruited and hired the most liberal individuals they could find, trained them not to deny any application and sent them out to special INS asylum offices across the country. It did not take long before thousands of aliens realized that by claiming political asylum they could subvert the normal U.S. legal immigration process.

Little has changed over the years.

Temporary Protected Status

The "open-border" crowd has expanded another program known as Temporary Protected Status (TPS). This is a legal benefit granted to aliens living in the U.S. (whether legally or illegally) when civil strife or a natural disaster strikes their home country. It basically means that aliens from certain designated countries can remain and work in the U.S. *temporarily* until the situation in their home country is resolved.

I am truly in favor of this program, because it shows America is still one of the most humanitarian places in the world. The only problem with the TPS program is that very few people granted this "temporary" status ever return home. If there is any doubt about this issue, a query of Homeland Security indicates that thousands of people each year are granted Temporary Protected Status. When asked how many have subsequently departed the U.S., Homeland Security will conveniently report that they do not keep statistics on the latter group.

For one reason or another during the last several years countries like Barundi, El Salvador, Honduras, Liberia, Nicaragua, Somalia and Sudan have had their citizens here placed under this "temporary protected status." Whether the aliens were legally here or not, they could come forward, register with immigration and be granted temporary work authorization and legal status. They were also told in no uncertain terms that their right to remain in the U.S. was *temporary,* and as soon as our government took their country off the list, aliens illegally here would have to return home. (As long as they still qualified, legal aliens like foreign students, could have their status returned to what it was before the turmoil began.)

Most of the mainstream media enjoy a feeding frenzy when they see the Federal government attempting to use its legal authority to enforce our immigration laws. Such is case with thousands of Liberian nationals who were granted temporary protected status.

On August 6, 2007, Gerry Smith, staff writer for the *Chicago Tribune,* wrote a lengthy article about the plight of these "refugees" from West Africa. Apparently in October 2007, the U.S. government was going to remove Liberians from the "temporary protected status" list. Most Liberians who had registered for the program were being asked to leave the U.S. and return to Liberia.

Smith's article dealt with a lot more than the facts surrounding Liberia and the immigration status of its citizens. Instead the article discussed Liberians gathering *"in a church basement at Wheaton College"*, and *"... how the flag of Liberia—founded by freed American slaves in 1822—closely resembles the flag of the United States ..."* It also divulged that Liberians are currently sending about $6 million a year to relatives in Liberia.

Obviously the article did not emphasize that this country reached out in a most humanitarian and hospitable way and welcomed the Liberians when they had nowhere else to go in the world. Now that our government has declared Liberia safe, and several attempts in Congress to give the Liberians "green cards" has failed, it is time for them to leave. Guess what? The Liberians do not feel like returning home. So, like most aliens granted "temporary protected status" they will simply thumb their noses at our government's decision and openly violate our immigration laws. Thank you, America.

Chapter 8

U.S. Documents—Our Security Achilles Heel

The U.S. birth certificate—Easy to obtain and easy to abuse

In 1971, Eden Press of Fountain Valley, California, published one of the classic underground documents. *The Paper Trip* was what every criminal, draft dodger, drug dealer, and fugitive needed—a step-by-step description of how to create a completely new identity in the U.S. The book was revised in 1984, but much of what was written in the original book is valid today.

Chapter IV of *The Paper Trip* is entitled "The Birth Certificate Route," and here are just some of the ideas expressed as the author writes about the "The Essential Document."

> *"It is generally true that all I.D. begins with a birth certificate. An individual's original identity (name) is usually recorded at or near his time of birth. The actual document which is prepared by the hospital's staff, signed by the physician, and retained by the county recorder in a 'vital records' department provides the master from which subsequent 'certified' copies are prepared.*
>
> *"With a certified copy of a birth certificate issued by some agency of state or local government, it is relatively easy to apply for and receive virtually any form of ID desired. This type of birth certificate provides a legal basis for the issuance of Social Security cards, driver's licenses, state I.D. cards, even passports.*
>
> *"The foundation for creating an alternative identity is to obtain an 'alternate' birth certificate—one in a name other than your own.*

> *"Go to the files (at the county recorder) open to the public (photocopies of actual documents in bound volumes or on microfilm) and check a book that has death certificates for a year in which you were under five. Every thirtieth to fiftieth death will be that of a young child, usually under one year old. The death certificate will list the birth date, place of birth, race, parents' names and a host of other interesting facts—all you need to know in order to send away for the birth certificate. . . . If all this seems too amazing, you could even look up a copy of the birth certificate you want in the birth files before you order your copy. Just ask a helpful clerk for the appropriate volume . . . "*

If you are not yet convinced about our need to create a National Birth Certificate, I refer you to *How to Create a New Identity,* by Anonymous (1983, Citadel Press).

This book's Chapter 2, entitled "Setting the Cornerstone" begins, *"The cornerstone of all identity is the birth certificate. It is the most widely accepted form of identification in the United States. Birth certificates are almost as varied as the people who possess them. They have no photographs and rarely finger or footprints. Sometimes they have an embossed stamp, can be multiple colors or almost any size, and can be valid even if they are reduced photocopies and simply stamped 'Certified'."*

These books are more than 20 years old, and the U.S. government has done very little to change this massive security loophole. Birth certificates are the best "breeder documents" that anyone can possess, and they are available through the mail to any half-wit who can read an old newspaper and fill out a form.

The Social Security card

After the 9/11 attacks, Jim Huse, Inspector General for the Social Security Administration, testified to Congress that 13 of the 19 hijackers had obtained their Social Security cards legally. Huse said, *"A purloined SSN is as useful a tool for terrorists as it is for identity thieves."*

Why is it so easy to get a valid Social Security card? The "Old School" within the Social Security Administration, the American Association of Retired Persons (AARP), and the Social Security Administration's supporters on Capitol Hill make up one of the most powerful and influential lobbying groups in America. They have also long believed in one simple reality—the easier it is to get a Social Security number, the more money will be collected for the Social Security Trust Fund. For decades they resisted any attempt to allow the Social Security number to be designated as any type of national numerical identifier. Until a few years ago they did everything they could to issue as many numbers as possible and quietly blocked most attempts to tighten their issuance procedures.

In recent years, some progress has been made to prevent illegal aliens from obtaining Social Security cards. Aliens now have to show more supporting documentation, and most immigration documents are finally being forwarded to Homeland Security for verification. (Strangely enough, in 1986, INS officials involved in the Systematic Alien Verification for Entitlements program, advocated that the Social Security Administration verify all immigration documents through the INS, and were told it was politically impossible!) U.S. citizens applying for a number late in life also have to answer a few questions about why they waited so long to get one.

As we have seen with the 9/11 hijackers, we still have a long way to go to eliminate the issuance of valid Social Security cards and numbers to people who should not have them.

Driver's licenses and the REAL ID Act

There is no better example of American knee-jerk reaction than the current debate about illegal aliens, terrorists, and driver's licenses. The 9/11 Commission suggested that we set Federal standards for issuing driver's licenses, and Congress responded with the REAL ID Act. The legislation mandated to the states that they upgrade their driver's licenses or face Federal sanctions in the coming years. Unfortunately, Congress also told the states to pay for the changes themselves. Initially several states started to implement the new measures, but by 2007, several states (like Montana) passed state legislation declaring their intent not to implement the requirements and simply rejected the unfunded mandates of the REAL ID Act.

The states are not to blame. While the intent of the REAL ID Act was honorable, the objective was unrealistic, and had little to do with preventing terrorism. After all, most of the 9/11 hijackers, using the identity documents they had in 2001, would still be allowed to board commercial aircraft today.

The REAL ID Act is simply another legislative initiative to make Americans "think" they are safer. In reality, tightening restrictions on the issuance of driver's licenses is being carried out by state motor vehicle employees who have little or no training about immigration, and in many cases are creating more problems than they are solving.

When I first moved to Arizona in February, 2004, I took a close friend down to the Arizona Motor Vehicle Department to get a driver's license. She happens to be someone who was granted asylum in the U.S. several years ago, and is awaiting her "green card." She carries a document that looks like a U.S. Passport. It is a Homeland Security travel document issued to refugees and aliens who have been granted asylum in the U.S.

When the officer at the Motor Vehicle Division asked her if she was a U.S. citizen, she told him she had been granted asylum in the U.S. and presented her Homeland Security travel document. He told her she could not have a driver's license in Arizona because she did not have a "green card" and she was not a refugee.

At this stage I attempted to intervene. I tried to explain to the officer that the Homeland Security travel document was proof of legal status in the U.S. and she was legally allowed to get a driver's license in every state in America. He said it did not matter. She could not have a license in Arizona.

I then asked to speak with a supervisor. She came out, agreed with the officer and advised me that aliens granted political asylum were not allowed to get an Arizona driver's license. I then asked her to call Homeland Security. She refused. I asked if the Arizona Motor Vehicle Division had access to the Homeland Security databases so they could verify the Alien Registration Number. They said they did not know anything about any Homeland Security database.

As a last resort, I asked to speak with a Motor Vehicle Division security officer. When he arrived a few minutes later, he realized I knew what I was saying about her immigration status. He immediately contacted someone at Homeland Security. Within minutes the security officer and the supervisor received notification from Homeland Security advising them to issue the driver's license. They did so reluctantly.

This personal experience is replicating itself across the U.S. State motor vehicle departments are reportedly not issuing driver's licenses to people they believe are illegal aliens. The problem is that the state officials do not have a clue who is a legal alien and who is not. Most states do not provide any training about immigration documents to motor vehicle department personnel, and very few states are using Homeland Security's E-Verification system.

On the other hand, illegal aliens can buy an entire set of counterfeit immigration documents for about $50 in Mexico. If these counterfeits are subsequently presented to the Arizona Motor Vehicle Division, there is a good chance they will pass as valid. The illegal alien will probably be issued an Arizona driver's license, it will be accepted throughout the U.S., and it will be valid for decades. (My wife's Arizona driver's license expires in 2036.)

Standardization of driver's licenses is a good first step, but it should be just the beginning of a massive overhaul of the entire process. Every state motor vehicle department should be required to check a centralized system before issuing a driver's license. Legally authorized drivers in the U.S. should be allowed to have a valid driver's license in one state at a time. If anyone from a state motor vehicle department claims this is already being done, they are wrong. I have a friend who has three valid unexpired driver's licenses in three different states. He has never been questioned by authorities about any of them.

If the Feds are serious about starting to fix the nightmare we have with America's identity documents, they can do a lot more than pass the REAL ID Act. One place they could start would be to require states to electronically verify the myriad of immigration documents proliferated by Homeland Security.

Illegal aliens and commercial driver's licenses

If The 9/11 Commission really wanted to suggest something to help prevent terrorism, they would have suggested that states stop issuing commercial driver's licenses to illegal aliens and other immigrants who are not authorized to work here.

There is dirty little secret about commercial driver's licenses that state motor vehicle departments refuse to acknowledge. Having a commercial driver's license is basically an authorization to work in the U.S., and these licenses are issued throughout the country with little or no verification of immigration status. The reason again is money. State motor vehicle departments do not want to lose the revenue from tightening their issuance qualifications, so the loophole remains—and it is getting bigger by the day.

Illegal aliens are well aware that, with a commercial driver's license, a whole new world opens up in America. Independent truckers may be "the last of the American cowboys," but they are slowly watching illegal immigrants pour into their rank and file—all because of the ease with which one can obtain a commercial driver's license.

There is also a significant link here to terrorism. Many scenarios constructed by terrorism experts involve the use of large tractor trailers and tanker trucks. Whether it is the smuggling of nuclear devices across our land borders, or a suicide bomber detonating a semi-trailer full of high explosives in a densely populated area, large trucks are the conveyance of choice. With a commercial driver's license, terrorists have easy access to "big rigs" and can move freely throughout the country without fear of any interference from law enforcement officers patrolling our roadways.

I am not suggesting that tightening issuance procedures for commercial licenses, in and of itself, will curtail illegal immigration or prevent a terrorist act. However, terrorists might be discouraged from carrying out a horrific act using a semi-trailer if they cannot obtain the required license to drive one in the first place. Illegal immigrants should also be prevented from obtaining commercial driver's licenses, as this would eliminate one more part of the "employment magnet" that draws them into the U.S.

Once again a simple program could be implemented that would go a long way toward preventing unauthorized persons from obtaining commercial licenses. Simply put, there should be two additional steps for aliens attempting to obtain commercial driver's licenses.

1. The automated Social Security Number Verification System (proposed in Chapter 12) should be used by state motor vehicle departments. Whether the Social Security number is used on the license is not important. All applicants must be required to give a valid Social Security number that is verifiable and valid for employment in the U.S.
2. State motor vehicle departments should also be required to access a Homeland Security database to verify the validity of accompanying immigration documents. When motor vehicle departments use immigration document verification systems, it becomes almost impossible to obtain a state driver's license using counterfeit immigration documents. Such a system is effectively operating in Florida, and it should be done in every state.

The facts and the loopholes about fingerprint checks

After submitting completed applicant fingerprint cards to their state law enforcement agencies and the FBI, thousands of employers and government officials lay claim that their employees have no criminal history and are legally here in the country. The

APPLICANT
LEAVE BLANK
TYPE OR PRINT ALL INFORMATION IN BLACK
LAST NAME NAM FIRST NAME MIDDLE NAME
DOE, JOHN NMN
FBI LEAVE BLANK
SIGNATURE OF PERSON FINGERPRINTED
ALIASES AKA
ORI
RESIDENCE OF PERSON FINGERPRINTED
DATE OF BIRTH DOB Month Day Year
01 23 45
CITIZENSHIP CTZ
COUNTRY
SEX RACE HGT. WGT. EYES HAIR
PLACE OF BIRTH POB
COUNTRY
DATE SIGNATURE OF OFFICIAL TAKING FINGERPRINTS
YOUR NO. OCA
LEAVE BLANK
EMPLOYER AND ADDRESS
FBI NO. FBI
CLASS
ARMED FORCES NO. MNU
REASON FINGERPRINTED
SOCIAL SECURITY NO. SOC
123-45-6789
REF.
MISCELLANEOUS NO. MNU
A12-345-678
1. R. THUMB 2. R. INDEX 3. R. MIDDLE 4. R. RING 5. R. LITTLE
6. L. THUMB 7. L. INDEX 8. L. MIDDLE 9. L. RING 10. L. LITTLE
LEFT FOUR FINGERS TAKEN SIMULTANEOUSLY L. THUMB R. THUMB RIGHT FOUR FINGERS TAKEN SIMULTANEOUSLY

Applicant Fingerprint Card—Many illegal immigrants get "cleared" because they have no fingerprints on file. Full name, Date of Birth, Citizenship, Place of Birth, Social Security Number and Alien Registration Number are rarely verified.

fact is many of these employees are illegal aliens and some have committed serious crimes in their home countries. Since no prints are on file in the U.S. and the biographical information is rarely verified with other agencies, both state law enforcement and the FBI return applicant fingerprint cards with no indication that the person could be an imposter or an illegal alien. Un-

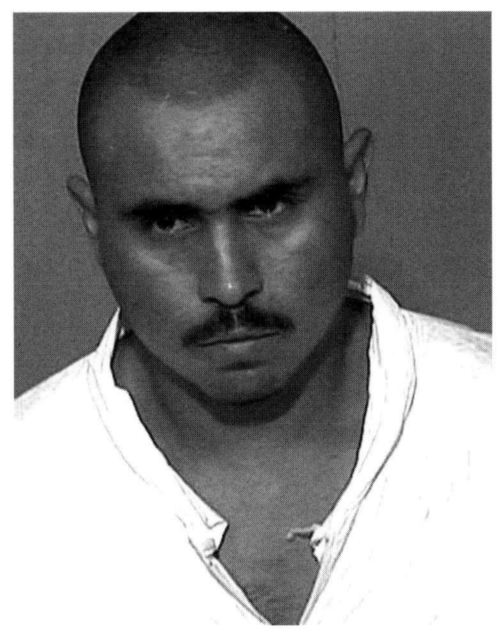

Roberto Lemus-Retana—Illegal alien janitor convicted of raping a 14-year-old girl at a Scottsdale, Arizona high school. Fingerprint check failed to reveal he was an illegal alien.

fortunately our law enforcement officials are doing little to fix this problem.

In late May 2007, Roberto Lemus-Retana (an illegal alien from Mexico) was convicted of raping a fourteen-year-old girl at Saguaro High School in Scottsdale, Arizona. At the time of the assault, Lemus-Retana was employed as a janitor for ABM Janitorial Services and was working at the high school.

Soon after the assault, people in the community began questioning how such a person could have been allowed to work at the school. After all, the contract with the Scottsdale Unified School District mandated that ABM's contract employees undergo a criminal history check and be fingerprinted.

Scottsdale officials and the employer relied heavily on the fingerprint checks, seemingly aware that the process had significant weaknesses. Could it be that those involved were a little more interested in saving a few dollars employing illegal aliens than protecting the children in the community?

Here is why submitting applicant fingerprint cards has only limited value.

- Illegal aliens who are never caught crossing our borders usually have no fingerprints on file anywhere in the U.S.
- Applicant fingerprint cards contain a block for "citizenship," but the information is rarely verified through the Department of Homeland Security.
- Applicant fingerprint cards also have space for a Social Security number, but again the numbers are *not* routinely verified through the Social Security Administration. The same holds true for alien registration numbers listed in the "miscellaneous" section.

Considering the importance fingerprints play in our fight against crime and terrorism, it seems incredible that our law enforcement agencies have not created an automatic verification process to match the biographical information with the prints on *all* fingerprint card submissions.

Employers who rely heavily on applicant fingerprint checks are putting their faith in a less than perfect system and government entities that rely solely on this process could also be putting America's security at risk.

The infamous "green card"

The first day I arrived at the U.S. Border Patrol in Eagle Pass, Texas, in 1976, I knew I had joined an agency that was a little strange. I was filling out some paperwork when I overheard two journeymen Border Patrol Agents discussing a "green card" that had been found near the Rio Grande River. It was my first day on the job, and I noticed that the card they were discussing was not green at all. It was blue. Being the "rookie" I was, I asked them why they were calling a blue document a "green card." One of the journeyman agents gave me a helpful and informative explanation. He said, "Shut up, trainee. Stop asking stupid questions." (Is there any wonder why I consider the day I left the Border Patrol in Eagle Pass, Texas, to be one of the finest days in my life?)

Subsequently I learned the history of the "green card." The term generally refers to the U.S. immigration document issued to an alien who has been granted permanent resident status in the U.S. Resident alien cards were originally green when they were first issued back in the 1950s. Even after the U.S. government changed the color, the term "green card" remained, and has lasted to this day. The term "green card" is also known throughout the world, and many people would sell their soul to get one.

Unfortunately, the "green card" is one of the most *successfully* counterfeited documents in the world. The color, size, style and configuration of the card has changed so many times since it was green, even seasoned Immigration officers have difficulty distinguishing the real ones from the fakes.

Green cards, magnetic stripes, and the budget analyst

During the years I spent developing the Systematic Alien Verification for Entitlements program (the late part of the 1980s), my staff wrote numerous memos asking the people responsible for issuing "green cards" if they would consider putting a magnetic stripe on the back of the card and a portion of the immigrant's Social Security number on the front.

This type of alteration would have required some regulation changes and extra funding. In accordance with INS procedures, the request was forwarded to a budget analyst named Jim. He called and told me that the suggestion was idiotic and said, "According to my sources, magnetic stripes will be a thing of the past by 1990. Furthermore, Social Security numbers have nothing to do with immigration."

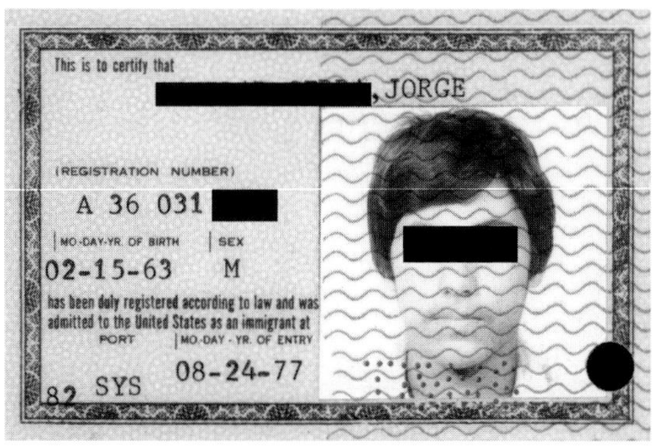

Counterfeits—All of them!

Right then and there, Jim stopped the proposal from going any further. It's now more than 20 years later. I have seven credit cards in my wallet and all of them have magnetic stripes for verification. In addition, there is an absolute linkage between Social Security cards and employment eligibility in the U.S.

This is to certify that
Tatiana
was admitted to the United States on Oct. 13, 1949
at New York
as a NP; Quota immigrant for Perm Res
under Sec. PL-774 of the Immigration Act of 1924 and
has been registered under the Alien Registration Act, 1940.
Visa Application No. I

DATE OF BIRTH	SEX	HAIR	EYES	HEIGHT
Jan. 25, 1947	F	Bld	Grey	3-2

Commissioner of Immigration and Naturalization.
GPO 16—48409-2

A 6 986 (REGISTRATION NUMBER) *This is to certify that*
SISTER M.
was admitted to the United States as an immigrant
on 07 (MONTH) 07 (DAY) 56 (YEAR) (DISTRICT) MIL (PORT)
Y-16 (TYPE) Date of Birth 07 (MONTH) 12 (DAY) 18 (YEAR) F (SEX)
and has been duly registered according to law.
Commissioner of Immigration and Naturalization
UNITED STATES DEPARTMENT OF JUSTICE
If 18 years of age or older, you are required by law to have this card with you at all times.
FORM I-151 (1-10-55)

This is to certify that
, TOM
A-14 057 (REGISTRATION NUMBER)
has been duly registered according to law and was admitted to the United States as an immigrant at

PORT	MO.-DAY-YR. OF ENTRY	CLASS	MO.-DAY-YR. OF BIRTH	SEX
DET	12-18-64	M-3	11-21-60	M

73
Commissioner of Immigration and Naturalization
UNITED STATES DEPARTMENT OF JUSTICE
IF 18 YEARS OF AGE OR OLDER, YOU ARE REQUIRED BY LAW TO HAVE THIS CARD WITH YOU AT ALL TIMES.

Antique "green cards" from the early days of the INS.

As a bean counter, Jim knew little about immigration law enforcement or immigration documents. I was told, however, not to question his wisdom. In turn, he unilaterally short-circuited a program that would have undoubtedly reduced the capability of counterfeiters to create marketable fake "green cards."

Where are the "green card" readers?

The following is one of those stories about INS that is hard to believe. In fact, most of us at INS had trouble believing it, even while it was happening right in front of our eyes.

Back in the mid 1980s and early 1990s, the Mitre Corporation of McLean, Virginia, was the prime contractor for the development of the new, high-tech I-551 Resident Alien Card ("green card"). Mitre was supposedly producing a highly secure and verifiable document that was to be the "be all and end all" of secure documents. Mitre said the new card was going to be impossible to counterfeit because special readers would be located at all U.S. ports of entry, and the readers would immediately identify fraudulent cards.

A couple of years into the contract, everything seemed to be going quite well. The rather unsophisticated-looking "green cards" were being created at a card-producing facility in Texas, and everyone was anxiously waiting for the deployment of the high-tech readers. We waited, and waited, and waited some more. To this day, I do not think a single Mitre reader was ever deployed at a U.S. port of entry.

The result was unbelievable. INS had spent millions of dollars to have a "green card" that could be "read" electronically and the readers turned out to be a figment of someone's imagination.

Barcodes and a mirror for your hair

As if the failure of the I-551 project at Mitre was not bad enough, take a look at the new "green card" issued today. Once again, a contractor convinced the U.S. government to buy a document with almost every security "doo-dad" known to mankind. There is a barcode on the card (so you can compare it with the barcode on toilet paper at your local discount mart). The new "green card" also carries a very expensive copper-colored laser stripe that is mirrored so aliens can use it to comb their hair or put on their make-up. What is missing is an old-fashioned magnetic stripe on the back of the card. These stripes seem to be good

Fancy laser stripe on back of "green cards." Good for checking makeup and hairstyle—that's about all.

enough for five hundred million credit cards, but not high-tech enough for our "green card."

Once again, the U.S. government paid tens of millions of dollars to develop a secure counterfeit-proof "green card," and once again, the government bought a highly sophisticated piece of junk.

The Texas card facility and the rubber stamp

"Green cards" used to be locally issued at INS district offices. Unfortunately, corruption raised its ugly head, and several INS employees were arrested for fraudulently producing and selling valid "green cards" to illegal aliens. To prevent this, INS administrators decided to have all new high-tech cards issued from a single facility in Texas. Unfortunately, the idea was flawed from the very beginning.

When aliens are granted permanent residence in the U.S., they must complete several forms and submit them for processing to a centralized card-producing facility. Depending upon the backlog, some aliens wait months before getting their actual cards. What does INS issue as documentation while the real card is being produced? They place a simple rubber stamp in the alien's passport or on an I-94 Arrival/Departure record.

This little glitch in the issuance process of resident alien cards has become the counterfeiter's "dream come true." The rubber stamp is simple to duplicate, and can be reproduced at most office supply stores. The I-94 Arrival/Departure forms are available on all international flights into the U.S., or in bulk through the U.S. Government Printing Office—no questions asked.

Employers and licensing agencies are all required to accept these stamped I-94 Arrival Records as proof of permanent residence and work authorization in the U.S. And, because there is virtually no way for anyone in the business world to verify the authenticity of the I-94 Arrival Records or the rubber stamps, this glitch in the system has become one of the most widely exploited methods of creating usable forged immigration documents.

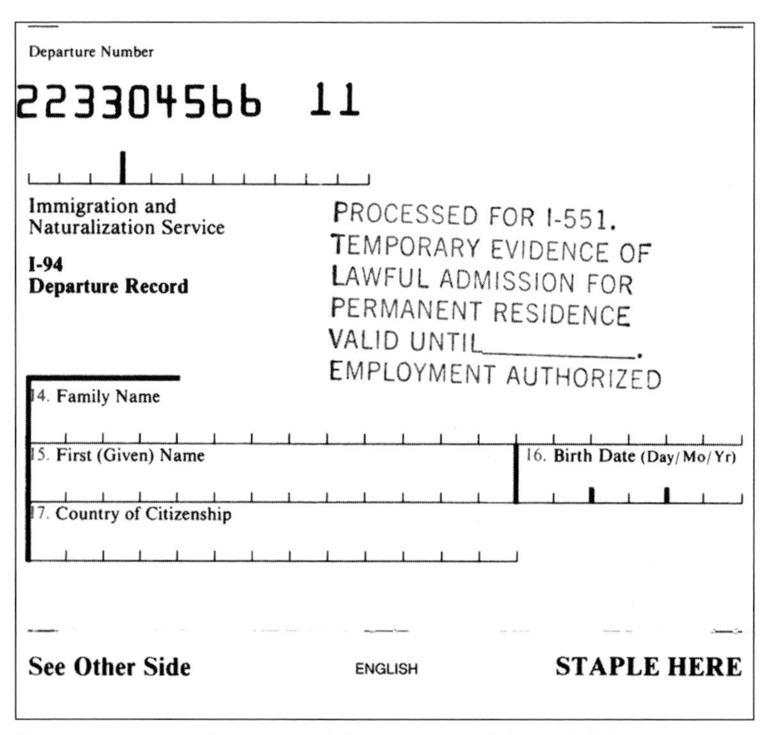
Departure Number

223304566 11

Immigration and Naturalization Service

I-94
Departure Record

PROCESSED FOR I-551.
TEMPORARY EVIDENCE OF
LAWFUL ADMISSION FOR
PERMANENT RESIDENCE
VALID UNTIL________.
EMPLOYMENT AUTHORIZED

14. Family Name

15. First (Given) Name

16. Birth Date (Day/Mo/Yr)

17. Country of Citizenship

See Other Side

ENGLISH

STAPLE HERE

Temporary paper "green cards"—a counterfeiters delight.

I-94 Arrival Records are not only used to obtain employment, but also other state and U.S. government identity documents. Only recently has the Social Security Administration decided to forward these I-94 Arrival Records to Homeland Security before issuing Social Security cards. (My sources tell me that in some Social Security offices, the decision to do a Homeland Security check rests with the intake officer. This significantly increases the chance that a Social Security employee could be compromised.)

No matter how high-tech we make the "green card," this widely used low-tech method of counterfeiting immigration documents is subverting the entire process.

U.S. documents, terrorism and your macaroni and cheese

The next time you see a 75-year-old lady taking off her shoes at an airport screening area, remember this part of my book. The Transportation Security Administration (TSA) is putting us all through these security machinations, while ignoring other massive loopholes. Most of the Transportation Security Administration's pre-flight inspections are more of a "show," than real security. While screening of passengers is important, there is so much more that must be done behind the scenes to protect us from terrorism in the skies. I am not alone in my criticism.

After all we have been promised about airport security, passenger screenings, and employee background checks, how is it that in March 2007, Thomas Anthony Munoz, (a Comair employee) allegedly carried 14 guns and 8 pounds of marijuana aboard a Delta flight bound from Orlando to Puerto Rico?

Whatever excuse the Transportation Security Administration used, there is no excuse. For several years, security professionals have been warning Homeland Security about weaknesses in their screening procedures—especially for employees who work in and around airports. Due to the fact that 9/11 has not been duplicated, most of the warnings have fallen on deaf ears.

Furthermore, many of our major airport facilities are also still vulnerable to terrorist attacks.

According to a December 27, 2006, *News-Press* article by Lee Wolverton, the Government Accountability Office (the investigative arm of Congress) is so concerned about the lack of security at certain airports, they will be sending out teams of undercover officers to try and penetrate airport security. According to the article, the undercover officers will have little difficulty surreptitiously entering most "secure" areas at our nation's 450 commercial airports.

One of the most vulnerable areas relates to off-airport personnel. In the above article TSA spokesperson Sari Koshetz touts the "fingerprint-based background checks and security training for all airport workers." TSA fails to understand that people who work near airports on airport-related business also pose a huge threat to airline security. The following is a good example of how the TSA is overlooking many security weaknesses in this area.

Let's suppose several foreign students enter the U.S. from an innocuous country like Saudi Arabia, Pakistan or Iran. They may be studying English 101 but in reality they are a terrorist cell planning a deadly strike at an American airport.

First thing they will all do is purchase fraudulent immigration documents, Social Security cards and maybe even valid Tax Identification numbers. Within hours they will also obtain valid driver's licenses.

Shortly after obtaining the necessary employment documents they begin researching jobs at local off-airport food service facilities. Before too long they are all hired and begin working a shift that few others want to work. After months of planning, their plot is ready to go.

Fifteen food service carts are loaded with specially constructed bombs set to detonate at 10,000 feet. (Something similar to the device used on TWA Flight 840, April 2, 1986.) The carts are then locked and loaded onto a delivery truck headed for several commercial aircraft.

The unsuspecting driver of the truck clears airport security. After all, he has been cleared by TSA's "fingerprint-based background check" and has his highly secure multi-million dollar Transportation Worker Identification Credential. He delivers all fifteen carts to five waiting aircraft.

During a calm morning, with clear skies, as TSA checks Grandma's shoes, commercial aircraft begin falling out of the sky. Instead of macaroni and cheese for the folks in coach, hundreds and maybe even thousands of people begin losing their lives. And for hours, maybe days, officials will not have a clue what is happening to the planes. As horrible as this scenario may seem, it could take place tomorrow.

The Federal Aviation Administration and the Transportation Security Administration will undoubtedly deny this could ever happen. They will claim they check the documents, the backgrounds and the fingerprints of everyone who has access to our airports. They may be doing a better job than they did prior to 9/11, but their checks are far from sufficient.

As I have shown, readily available and unverifiable counterfeit identity documents can and will continue to be used by terrorists and other criminal aliens. Our weaknesses in this area are well known to professionals and politicians alike. The latter simply do not have the will to do what is necessary to curtail it.

Why do we always have to wait until the planes start falling out of the sky?

Chapter 9

State Department Visas and Immigration Inspections

Obtaining a visa for the United States

For those Americans who are not aware of the process of obtaining a visa to come to the U.S., it's a surprisingly simple system. The State Department's Bureau of Consular Affairs issues nonimmigrant visas at American embassies and consulates abroad. The process requires that the alien produce a completed State Department application, a hefty fee, and proof that the alien does not intend to abandon their foreign residence and then stay in the U.S.

After the alien receives a visa and arrives in the U.S, a Homeland Security inspector at a port of entry is responsible for interviewing the alien and deciding if he or she should enter the U.S. At first glance, this may not seem like a convoluted system, but for most Immigration inspectors, it is a disaster waiting to happen.

Allow me to digress for a moment and give my opinion about U.S consular officers. They are all members of the Foreign Service and most are very intelligent. (It takes a near rocket scientist to pass the Foreign Service Exam.) Every couple of years, they move to another embassy or consulate. These "whiz kids" are also some of the strangest and frustrated government employees I met in my career. After all, what person with a Phi Beta Kappa degree from Harvard wants to make a career of reviewing thousands of visa applications for aliens wanting to visit Disneyland?

Non-immigrant visas

Consular officers supposedly use a set of regulations to determine who gets a visa and who gets denied. This may be the case in some U.S. Embassies, but in many others it is an arbitrary and capricious decision—or it is based on simple corruption.

A few years ago, a former INS official who was stationed at the American Embassy in Mexico City, sent me a very descriptive email complaining about several serious integrity issues at his consular section. The correspondence described how U.S. Embassy personnel were selling everything from visas to spaces in the waiting line. (When I heard about this problem, I looked diligently through the Foreign Service Manual, but I was unable to find the chapter describing the proper method of taking a bribe.) I am certain the vast majority of consular officers are honest, hard-working people. There are, however, a significant number whose integrity is questionable at best. The worst part is the unwillingness of our State Department to do anything about it.

Diplomats are also infamously liberal. They live and work overseas and are usually more interested in diplomacy than they are in denying visas. I will admit that since the 9/11 attacks, things have tightened up a bit. However, diplomats are still in the business of making friends in strange places, and approving visas to the U.S can make consular officers more friends in foreign countries than they ever imagined.

Now let's get back to our aliens. After a non-immigrant visa is placed in an alien's passport, he or she heads off to America. When they arrive at a U.S. international port of entry, they pass through U.S. Customs and Border Protection. It is here that the system breaks down.

Immigration officers have less than a minute to admit the alien or refer them for a secondary inspection. Passengers referred to secondary inspection are usually on some watch list or have triggered some suspicion in the mind of the initial Immigration inspector.

Visa-waiver countries—security versus economics

To make matters worse, there are some 26 countries whose citizens do not even require a visa. They are referred to as "visa-waiver" countries and their citizens can enter the U.S. with nothing more than a valid passport and a completed Customs and Border Protection Form I-94. Visitors from visa-waiver countries are allowed to enter the U.S. for a period strictly limited to 90 days or less.

The history of this non-visa category can be explained quite easily. In the 1980s big business and the U.S. tourism industry (Disney included) teamed up to convince Congress and the Immigration and Naturalization Service that certain countries had very few citizens coming here and violating their immigration status. Lobbyists questioned the need for every single person to obtain a visa, and requested visitors and certain business people be excused from the process. (In fact, they were right. Subsequent studies unquestionably demonstrated that visitors from England, Germany, Japan and others, were not violating their immigration status.) In turn, U.S. citizens could also travel to designated visa-waiver countries without obtaining one of their visas.

During the many heated discussions about this program, the power of IBM and other Fortune 500 companies trumped all of us at the Immigration and Naturalization Service. Many of us expressed serious concerns about America's security, but the visa-waiver program marched onward, like a Disney parade down Main Street.

Almost no one will deny it has proved to be an extremely valuable tool for our tourism industry. Look no further than Orlando, Florida. Every day, thousands of visa-less British nationals walk up and down International Drive buying discount t-shirts and sunbathing their chalk-white bodies at the swimming pool of some cheap Kissimmee motel. Eventually they may even make a visit to see Mickey Mouse and company. The vast majority of these tourists love America, spend their pounds quite freely and return home without incident. (There are some exceptions . . . like the ones who have a bit too much to drink and drive eastbound down the westbound lanes of Interstate 4, all the while proclaiming everyone else is going the wrong way.) While the visa-waiver program may be good for tourism, it is also one of the largest security loopholes in our immigration process. No matter how many security procedures have been instituted at our embassies and consulates around the world since 9/11, terrorists from visa-waiver countries can board a commercial flight for the U.S. and enter virtually unhindered.

After the London train bombings were carried out by British-born nationals of Pakistani descent, U.S. law enforcement officials again realized they had a potential security nightmare on their hands. In a May 2, 2007, *New York Times* article, "U.S. Seeks Closing of Visa Loophole for Britons," London staff writer Jane Perlez divulges that the issue has been raised at the highest levels of the Department of Homeland Security. She states, "American officials, citing the number of terror plots in Britain involving Britons with ties to Pakistan, expressed concern of the visa-waiver loophole. In recent months, the homeland security secretary, Michael Chertoff, has opened talks with the government here on how to curb the access of British citizens of Pakistani origin to the United States." Cancellation of the entire program is now under consideration.

As with most matters relating to U.S. immigration, visa-waivers are a highly charged issue. If the program is cancelled, it will cost the State Department tens of millions of dollars to begin processing the visa applications. This does not take into account the lost revenue from international tourists who might decide to go somewhere other than America because of the hassle and cost of obtaining a visa.

The answer lies somewhere in between. If the U.S. does not cancel the visa-waiver program, Customs and Border Protection must create and implement a very sophisticated profiling system at our international ports of entry. This should include expanded use of biometrics for identification purposes, E-Passports, foreign intelligence and greater cooperation with immigration services worldwide. The alternative is to entirely eliminate the visa-waiver program, creating near catastrophic economic results in several parts of the U.S.

Diplomacy versus security

The State Department uses the Consular Service as a starting place for most of their young diplomats. Many junior foreign-service officers "cut their teeth" interviewing applicants and issuing visas to aliens intending to come to America. (There are also some foreign-service officers who remain in the Consular Corps for their entire State Department career.)

Despite the fact that most young diplomats hate working in the Consular Section, it will be a cold day in hell before the State Department relinquishes its visa issuance authority. It is a money-making machine, an incredible way to establish "friends" in a foreign land, and one of the most powerful tools used by an Embassy to get favors from the host government.

Consider the great nation of Nigeria. Despite the fact that a significant percentage of its students and visitors come to the U.S. and eventually get involved in some form of felonious criminal activity, the U.S. Embassy keeps cranking out non-immigrant visas to Nigerian nationals. Ever wonder why? It's called oil. Simply put, Nigeria has some of the finest crude in the world, and the U.S. Embassy in Nigeria wants to have extremely good relations, to keep both the black gold and the diplomatic-party champagne flowing.

On the other hand, ask any police official in America who has had to deal with the Nigerian crime wave, and he will state that no amount of Nigerian oil is worth the crime that these West Africans have perpetrated on the rest of us.

If Nigeria does not provide a sufficient example of visas for oil, consider the less-than-security-minded deal President George W. Bush quietly made with the Saudi royal family in 2006. Garance Burke of the *Associated Press* divulged this barely publicized agreement in his August 20, 2006, article entitled "Schools Compete for Thousands of Saudi Students." He wrote,

"This school year, college towns from Florida to Oregon will host an estimated 15,000 new Saudi students, nearly all of whom have full scholarships paid for by the Kingdom's royal family. They're part of a new exchange program brokered by President Bush and Saudi King Abdullah last year that will soon quintuple the number of Saudi students studying in the United States."

I am certain college and university officials around the country will hail President Bush as some kind of hero for creating this financial windfall. However, when we consider that most of the 9/11 hijackers were "students" from Saudi Arabia, it appears the President quietly, efficiently and hypocritically opened America's doors to a modern-day Trojan Horse. To me it is unconscionable that the President would authorize these visas in an apparent "sell-out for oil" to the Saudis and, at the same time, demand that the State Department and Homeland Security develop programs to prevent terrorists from obtaining non-immigrant visas.

Before we give in to the interests of our university presidents and the oil cartel with more student visas for Saudis and Nigerians, we would be a lot better off if we developed a reliable and secure visa issuance system to prevent terrorists and criminals from obtaining these non-immigrant visas in the first place. These systems are not currently in place, and the President's actions are simply counterproductive to U.S. efforts to combat foreign terrorism within our own borders.

Secondary immigration inspections

I always enjoyed watching and listening to the interaction between the Immigration inspectors and South Asian passengers referred for secondary inspection at Dulles International Airport Inspections area. In most instances, these aliens were immediately referred for further inspection because they had all the wrong answers to the primary inspectors' questions. As an example, inspectors would frequently ask "What is your reason for coming to the U.S.?" Some South Asians (Indians and Pakistanis mostly) would belligerently respond with comments like, *"I am here to visit friends in D.C. for one week. Besides, who gives you the authority to ask me these questions? I am finished, so please speak to the next passenger."* (Wrong answers—attitude adjustment required.) The inspector would then politely send the new arrival to the secondary inspections area for further questioning.

Inevitably these aliens also had five large suitcases, all with the horrific combined odor of mothballs and curry. Inspectors would do a thorough search of the luggage, looking for the slightest bit of evidence to indicate that the alien might not intend to return home. Here are some examples of what they would find.

- Clue #1: Five heavy winter coats to be used for that leisurely stroll past the White House in the middle of July.
- Clue #2: Thirty-five pots and pans for all that cooking in their motel room.
- Clue #3: A document showing the alien's work schedule in the U.S. for the coming 3 months.
- Clue #4: A letter from someone in the U.S. telling the alien how stupid U.S. Immigration will be when they let him in the country.

The best part would come when the alien was presented with all the evidence indicating he had no intention of leaving the U.S. Without doubt, he would begin waving his hands and arms feverishly, rolling his head from side to side and denying it all. It was always a sight to see.

Welcome to America

For the most part, however, non-immigrant aliens who present themselves to a Customs and Border Protection inspector are usually granted permission to enter the U.S. for a specified and limited period of time.

The feeling among most Immigration inspectors is that, if the State Department reviewed all of the alien's documents and issued a valid visa, the alien should be allowed to enter. Unfortunately, State Department consular officials express the exact same sentiments about Immigration inspectors. Consular officers depend on Immigration officers to stop aliens who do not deserve to get into the U.S. In so many words, the right hand does not know what the left hand is doing.

The result is evident. We allow thousands of "questionable" aliens to enter the U.S. legally. Our government does not have a clue who they are, where they are going, what they plan to do, or when they plan to leave.

The US-VISIT Program

In the summer of 2004, the U.S. government selected the worldwide conglomerate Accenture Corporation to develop the US-VISIT Program—a reliable system to track aliens arriving and departing the U.S.

The Bush Administration and Homeland Security believed this system would help calm Americans' fears, as it would provide U.S. law enforcement and intelligence officials with the information they needed to prevent future terrorist attacks. For those of us who studied the proposed system, the only fears US-VISIT calmed should have been those of Accenture's stockholders. To this day, US-VISIT cannot track all aliens arriving and departing the U.S. After spending billions of dollars, US-VISIT machines at our international airports are quietly being shut down and removed to the scrap heap. The Homeland Security notice on each machine (in 8 different languages) reads,

> *"Effective May 6, 2007, international travelers are no longer required to check out at a US-VISIT exit kiosk. All other exit procedures remain the same. International travelers who received a CBP Form I-94 (Arrival-Departure Record) upon arrival must still return it to an airline or ship representative when departing the United*

US-VISIT kiosk out-of-service at Hartsfield-Jackson International Airport in Atlanta, Georgia.

States. We appreciate the cooperation on international travelers who participated in the US-VISIT biometric exit pilot program."

So what happened to all the hype about US-VISIT? After all, it was supposed to provide an accurate count of the millions of aliens who come to the U.S., and Homeland Security invested billions of dollars to set up the program.

On December 15, 2006, New York Times reporters Rachel Swarns and Eric Lipton authored an article entitled, "U.S. Is Dropping Effort to Track if Visitors Leave."

The article stated,

"In a major blow to the Bush Administration's efforts to secure borders, domestic security officials have for now given up plans to develop a facial or fingerprint recognition system to determine whether a vast majority of foreign visitors leave the country, officials say.

NOTICE

Effective May 6, 2007, international travelers are no longer required to check out at a US-VISIT exit kiosk. All other exit procedures remain the same. International travelers who received a CBP Form I-94 (Arrival Departure Record) upon arrival must still return it to an airline or ship representative when departing the United States. We appreciate the cooperation of international travelers who participated in the US-VISIT biometric exit pilot program.

根據要求，國際旅客無需再於 US-VISIT 出境大廳接受檢查。所有其他出境程序保持不變。入境時取得 CBP 表 I-94（入境出境記錄）的國際旅客從美國出境時須仍將該表交換給航空公司或駐船代表。我們感謝參與 US-VISIT 生物特徵識別出境試辦計劃的國際旅客的配合。**本通知自 2007 年 5 月 6 日起生效。**

À compter du 6 mai 2007, les voyageurs internationaux ne sont plus obligés d'effectuer leur départ en passant par un point de contrôle des sorties pour le programme US-VISIT. Toutes les autres procédures de sortie demeurent inchangées. Les voyageurs internationaux qui ont reçu un Formulaire CBP I-94 (Fiche de suivi des entrées et des sorties) lors de leur arrivée doivent continuer à le rendre à un représentant de la compagnie aérienne ou maritime lors de leur départ des États-Unis. Nous apprécions la coopération des voyageurs internationaux qui ont participé au programme pilote de système biométrique de sortie US-VISIT.

Ab 6. Mai 2007 müssen internationale Reisende nicht mehr an einem US-VISIT-Kiosk auschecken. Alle anderen Ausreisevorgänge bleiben unverändert. Internationale Reisende, die bei der Ankunft ein Formular I-94 (Ankunft-Abreise-Dokument) der US-Zoll- und Grenzschutzbehörde erhalten haben, müssen es weiterhin bei der Ausreise aus den Vereinigten Staaten einem Repräsentanten der Fluggesellschaft oder des Schiffes übergeben. Wir schätzen die Kooperation der internationalen Reisenden, die am US-VISIT-Pilotprogramm zur biometrischen Ausreise teilgenommen haben.

2007년 5월 6일부터 시행, 국제 여행자는 미국-방문 출국 키오스크에서 체크-아웃을 하여야 할 필요가 더 이상 없습니다. 기타 제반 출국 절차는 동일합니다. 그럼에도, 도착시 CBP 서식 I-94(도착 출발 기록서)을 받았던 국제 여행자는 미국을 떠날 때 항공사 또는 해운사 담당자에게 그 서식을 제출하여야 합니다. 시험중인 미국-방문 생체 인식 출국 프로그램에 참여해주신 국제 여행자들의 협조에 감사합니다.

A partir de 6 de maio de 2007, não é necessário que os passageiros internacionais façam o check out no quiosque de saída do US-VISIT. Todos os outros procedimentos de saída permanecem os mesmos. Os passageiros internacionais que receberam o Form I-94 CBP (Registro de Chegada e Partida) na chegada, ainda precisam devolvê-lo ao representante da companhia aérea ou marítima ao sair dos Estados Unidos. Apreciamos a colaboração dos passageiros internacionais que participaram do programa piloto de saída biométrico do US-VISIT.

A partir del 6 de mayo de 2007, no se requiere que los viajeros internacionales registren su salida en un kiosco de salida US-VISIT. Todos los demás procedimientos de salida se mantienen iguales. Los viajeros internacionales que recibieron un formulario CBP Form I-94 (Registro de Arribo y Partida I-94) tras su arribo, siguen teniendo que devolverlo a un representante de una aerolínea o barco cuando salen de los Estados Unidos. Apreciamos la colaboración de los viajeros internacionales que participaron en el programa piloto de salida biométrica US-VISIT.

Simula ng ika-6 ng Mayo 2007, ang international travelers (mga nagbibiyahe mula sa ibang bansa) ay hindi na kinakailangang mag-check-out sa isang US-VISIT exit kiosk. Ang lahat ng ibang mga gagawin upang mag-exit ay pareho pa rin. Paglabas ng international travelers mula sa United States, dapat pa rin nilang isauli sa isang airline o ship representative ang natanggap nilang CBP Form I-94 (Arrival Departure Record) nang sila'y dumating. Nasisiyahan kami sa kooperasyon ng international travelers na lumahok sa US-VISIT biometric exit pilot program.

For more information about US-VISIT, please visit **www.dhs.gov/us-visit.**

International travelers with privacy concerns or questions about the safekeeping of their personal information should visit **www.dhs.gov/trip** or may contact the US-VISIT privacy officer at **usvisitprivacy@dhs.gov.**

$1.7 billion for what?

> *"Domestic security officials had described the system, known as US-VISIT, as critical to security and important in efforts to curb illegal immigration. Similarly, one-third of the overall total of illegal immigrants are believed to have overstayed their visas, a Congressional report says."*

Later in the article came the really interesting news. *"Domestic security officials, who have allocated $1.7 billion since the 2003 fiscal year to track arrivals and departures, argue that creating the program with the existing technology would be prohibitively expensive."*

The boondoggle does not end there. The Government Accountability Office released a report in July 2007, entitled "Homeland Security needs to immediately address significant weaknesses in systems supporting the US-VISIT Program." *Washington Post* reporter Spencer Hsu summed up the findings of the report in his August 3, 2007, article when he stated, *"The*

U.S. government's main border control system is plagued by computer security weaknesses, increasing the risk of computer attacks, data thefts and manipulation of millions of identity records including passport, visa and Social Security numbers and the world's largest fingerprint database."

Laser visas on the Mexican Border Crossing cards

As if the US-VISIT program fiasco is not bad enough. Since 1996, Congress has been pouring tens of millions of dollars into another similar boondoggle. Since 2000, 9.1 million high-tech laser visas have been issued to replace the old Mexican Border Crossing cards at a cost to taxpayers of a mere $28.6 million. (These cards basically allow certain Mexican nationals to enter the U.S. for short visits.) Laser visas look like driver's licenses and contain the recipient's biometric as well as biographic information (two fingerprints, photograph, name, date of birth, etc.).

On May 15, 2007, Associated Press writer Elliot Spagat reported in the *Associated Press IMPACT* section, *"The face-and-fingerprint-matching technology that has been touted over the past decade as a sophisticated new way to stop terrorists and illegal immigrants from entering the country through Mexico has one major drawback: U.S. border inspectors almost never use it."* The article further states, *"Jeffrey Davidow, (U.S. Ambassador to Mexico from 1998 to 2001), recalls members of Congress visiting the border to see the machines, which were never used when the lawmakers were gone."*

The simple fact is, our Federal government wastes billions of taxpayer dollars on projects like US-VISIT and laser visas, and then fails to fully support proven initiatives like the E-Passport. (See Chapter 15.)

The U.S. Department of State introduced a new **BORDER CROSSER CARD**, Form DSP-150 in May 1998. The front of the card has a three line machine readable zone and a hologram. Bearers of this card are **not** entitled to work in the U.S..

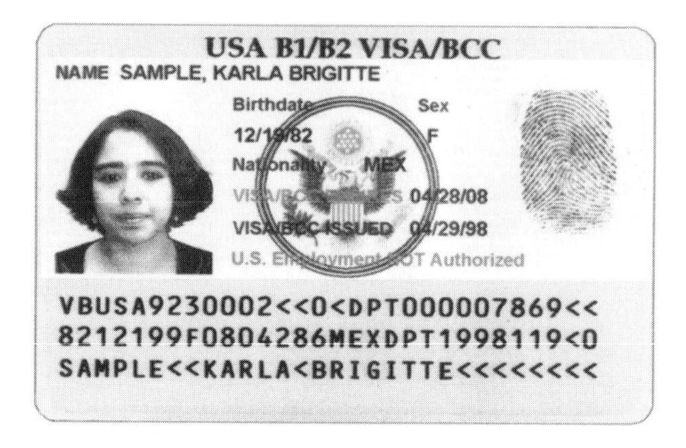

FRONT

REVERSE

The Optical Memory Stripe contains encoded cardholder information as well as a personalized etching which depicts the bearer's photo, name, date of birth, and card expiration date.

Another multimillion dollar high-tech boondoggle.

Chapter 10
Immigration Records Chaos

If there was ever an issue at the Immigration and Naturalization Service that used to turn my stomach, it was the way the agency managed alien files. Diligent record keeping is critical to the success of any government agency, and accurate immigration records are critical to the lives of millions of aliens and citizens residing in the U.S. Unfortunately, INS treated its alien files as if they were meaningless.

The INS Records Services Division was responsible for collecting, storing and disseminating alien files. For the most part, this division was a cadre of untrained and underpaid clerks who were incompetent by no fault of their own. Further exacerbating the problem, Immigration officers had little or nothing to do with this division. Records clerks were rarely properly trained and usually did not have a clue what was supposed to be in an alien's file. Making matters worse, they also did not know why the file was so important or where it was supposed to be stored.

Before now, not much has ever been said publicly about this problem, but it is a bureaucratic quagmire of incredible proportion. Lost and missing alien files are just as dangerous to our security as a wide-open border. The problem has deteriorated to an unconscionable level.

Spenser Hsu, a *Washington Post* reporter, wrote an article on November 30, 2006, entitled, "Immigration agency lost track of 111,000 files." He states that the problem is rampant in 14 of the largest U.S. Citizenship and Immigration Services offices in the country. In one case, Citizenship and Immigration Services granted U.S. citizenship to a man whose file was lost. He apparently had connections with the terrorist group Hezbollah. *Washington Post* reporter Hsu probably doesn't realize it, but his example is again the "tip of the iceberg."

This is not the first time the issue has been brought to the attention of our politicians. Every INS Commissioner in the last 30 years was made aware of the problem, and every Commissioner attempted to solve it in the same way—direct billions of dollars in agency funds to Beltway bandits who claimed to know exactly what to do. The thieves would conduct meeting after meeting with INS officials and then implement a program that did absolutely nothing to solve the records problems. Within weeks after implementation, they would claim the problems were solved, collect their money and head out the door knowing the problems would grow steadily worse.

Immigration officers were forced to deal with the records problem as if it were a bad virus that would not go away. I know from experience that many of my fellow Special Agents, inspectors, examiners and even Border Patrol Agents were totally amazed about the poor quality of INS data. Considering the impact that immigration records now have on our national security, it is about time America fixed this chaotic situation.

For the record

The Homeland Security website states, *"Beginning in 1944, Alien Registration records became the foundation document in a new series of INS records, the Alien Files, or A-Files. After April 1, 1944, INS maintained an individual case file on each immigrant to the United States, containing all papers, records, and documents relating to that immigrant. A-Files remain in DHS custody and subject to the Freedom of Information/Privacy Acts."* (A-files were also known as Administrative Files.)

What Homeland Security does not say on its website (or anywhere else for that matter) is that approximately 20% of the records have serious errors.

Alien files and *Days of Our Lives*

One of my most vivid memories about INS records occurred when I was a Special Agent ("criminal investigator" in those days) at the Washington District Office. Our offices were located at 1025 Vermont Avenue NW, Washington, D.C. (The Boardroom Topless Bar and Restaurant was on the ground floor.)

Agents were required to have an A-file created for every alien arrested, as these files were critical to almost every process at INS. Any alien who came to the INS for any type of action, whether it was to obtain a legal benefit or as an illegal alien, an A-file was created in their name. (The paper A-files were actually ugly manila folders with an Alien Registration number permanently stamped on the label portion of the folder.)

Before I continue with the story, here is a short lesson about what *should* have happened with alien files.

- The A-file number *should* have been used for one alien and only one alien. The A-file sequencing consisted of the letter "A" followed by three digits, a hyphen, three more digits, another hyphen, and then the last three digits, for a total of nine numbers proceeded by the letter "A".(i.e. A022-123-456). This number was subsequently placed on all correspondence and documentation relating to that alien, including their "green card," in the event the alien obtained legal residency in the U.S. (Despite the fact that it has nine digits, the alien registration number has no relationship whatsoever to a Social Security number.)
- A-files *should* contain important and sometimes voluminous information about the alien. Among other things, there could be arrest records, marriage certificates, income tax returns, applications for benefits, photographs, and fingerprints.
- The exact location of every A-file *should* be noted several places in the Department of Homeland Security data systems.

- Every time an A-file is moved, the file location *should* be updated in the Homeland Security computer systems.
- The alien's correct immigration status *should* be in the Homeland Security databases and in the A-file.
- Every document issued to the alien by Homeland Security *should* contain the A-file number somewhere on the document.
- When an Immigration officer or other Homeland Security personnel checks the database by name, date of birth, country of birth, or A-file number, the information *should* be correct and immediately available.

A lot of things that *should* have happened at INS and Homeland Security never happened. Some aliens have five, six or even ten A-files floating around different parts of the world. And, many of them are in one stage or another of being lost. Your training lesson about A-files is over. Suffice it to say there are hundreds of thousands, if not millions, of A-files missing, misplaced or destroyed.

Let's go back to the experience I had when I worked at the INS Washington District Office.

One afternoon I needed to have an A-file created in a hurry. I had arrested an alien earlier in the day, and needed to process him immediately for deportation. Since I needed it in a hurry, and did not have the time to request the file in the normal tedious fashion, I went straight to the file room.

No one was at the front counter to greet me, so I wandered back to the area where most of the files were stored. It was a sight to behold. The place was cluttered with paper plates, alien applications, shoes, various INS documents, coffee cups, and chicken bones. There were boxes of A-files stacked against the windows, under desks and against doors. Loose papers were all over the floor and unopened mail was everywhere.

On the other side of the room were about 15 floor-to-ceiling filing racks. They contained thousands of A-files. Many were barely on the racks, while others were stuffed so far back that no one could even reach them. Hundreds more were just lying on the floor. There was no order to any of it. The place was a disaster.

As I approached one of the clerks sitting at her desk, I observed something I had never seen anywhere in my working life. Sitting at the desk was a young lady with four enormous stacks of files in front of her. Behind the four stacks, she had hidden a small television set with a neat aluminum foil ball scrunched at the far end of the antenna (perhaps a predecessor of DirectTV). The screen was a little blurry, but the sound of *Days of Our Lives* was as clear as a bell. While watching T.V., the clerk was stuffing fried chicken into her mouth with one hand and typing information into her computer with the other. She was a marvel of human capability.

I peered over her shoulder to see exactly what was happening. My worst fears were confirmed. The A-file number on the computer screen was not the same number as the one on the A-file. Not even close! The name of the alien was misspelled and the date of birth was three years off. (Other than that, it was perfect.) I could not believe my eyes!

When an advertisement finally interrupted the soap opera, I brought the errors to her attention. She thanked me and simply stated, "I don't understand all this A-file shit. I do my 50 files a day. I got an Outstanding Award last year, and I'm getting one this year, and that's all that matters."

Unfortunately I learned that my experience in the Washington District INS Records Section was as commonplace in New York, Los Angeles and Miami as it was in D.C.

I never forgot that day, and I never again trusted an INS database.

Mind your own business. EDS will figure it out.

I was obviously not the only one at INS to realize there were records problems. District Directors across the country were bombarded by Congressional aides who wanted to know "Why is Maria's 'green card' taking so long?" or "Why hasn't INS finished with Mohammed's work permit?", and so on. I believe that at least half of all the bureaucratic and administrative problems at the former INS could, in one way or another, be traced to a database error or a missing A-file.

Throughout the reigns of Commissioners Nelson, McNary and Meissner, INS had private contractors come in and attempt to solve the records and information problems. The biggest contractor was EDS. History will show EDS sucked billions of dollars from the INS budgets in the name of solving INS records problems. They solved very little.

EDS was well aware that the data in the INS systems was garbage. They chose to ignore the "garbage-in" factor, and instead invested billions of dollars of INS's funds buying fancy hardware and colorfully bar-coded file jackets. The files looked great, but the expensive exercise did virtually nothing to fix the fundamental problem of erroneous data in INS systems.

Many of us tried to complain, but were forced to watch helplessly from the sidelines. EDS and INS management were content to metaphorically build a skyscraper on a foundation of quicksand—knowing very well that someday the entire structure might collapse.

In the end, the failure was obvious. INS was transformed from an agency with ugly brown A-files and databases filled with erroneous data, to an agency with very colorful A-files and databases still filled with the same erroneous data. The records remain that way today under the care of their new parent, the Department of Homeland Security.

Part 2
Solutions

Chapter 11
Securing America's Borders

Technology, detention, informants and more

In recent years America has developed all sorts of technological gizmos that could be used to better control both our land and sea borders. I was at a briefing a few years ago at one alphabet agency near Washington, D.C. The technician was describing how the U.S. military now has satellites that can read the license plate of a car from miles up in space. As far as I can tell, illegal aliens are a lot bigger than license plates. Why doesn't the Border Patrol have such equipment?

If America decides it truly wants to improve the security of our physical borders, it can be done. Here are some of the most essential programs that should be implemented or significantly expanded.

1. Create camp-like facilities to detain *most* aliens entering the U.S. illegally (60–90 days should be the minimum detention period).
2. Allow the U.S. Border Patrol and the Coast Guard to develop and deploy satellites, to watch the borders of the U.S.
3. Using multiple ground-radar systems and cameras, blanket the U.S.-Mexico border with surveillance equipment for constant observation of the entire area.
4. Utilize drone aircraft to help patrol certain high-risk areas.

5. Double-fence, triple-fence and place sensors in high-traffic areas near major metropolitan areas and known crossing points. (In many areas better fences *will* make better neighbors.)
6. Use current Border Patrol resources to respond to surveillance information, rather than patrolling large areas of the border.
7. Charge our intelligence services (White House "finding") with gathering information on alien smuggling and illegal immigration into the U.S.
8. Use paid informants to infiltrate alien smuggling operations.
9. Digitally fingerprint and photograph every alien apprehended illegally entering the U.S.
10. Negotiate border security and surveillance agreements with Mexico and Canada.

Sheriff Joe Arpaio's tent city detention facility in Maricopa County, Arizona. Similar facilities could be constructed in several localities along the U.S.-Mexico border.

The vast majority of aliens caught illegally entering from Mexico are never detained more than a day. They are returned to Mexico after a few hours and then try again and again until they finally get past the Border Patrol.

If the U.S. would detain most of the aliens caught entering illegally for a minimum period of 60–90 days, several things would be accomplished. Illegal aliens who are detained cannot attempt an immediate return, they do not get into the U.S. and get a job, and, they do not earn money to be sent home to their families—which is the original reason most of them attempted to come here in the first place. (Pregnant women, minors and certain other persons would be repatriated immediately.)

I am certainly not the first one to come up with this idea. Creating camp-like detention facilities to detain illegal immigrants has been suggested for decades, yet the concept has never become a reality. Why? Once again, the pro-illegal immigrant lobbyists in Washington, D.C., understand that long-term detention near the border will work to deter illegal immigration. They will do everything in their power to make sure it never becomes a reality.

For years Border Patrol Agents and other immigration enforcement professionals complained about the "catch and release" policy of illegal aliens apprehended near the Mexican border. The idea of catching the same aliens three times in one night, and releasing them back to Mexico each time seemed ludicrous to those serving on the border—but it was politically and diplomatically "correct"—and that was all that mattered to the U.S. State Department and the rest of the "inside the Beltway" crowd.

In 2005, the Department of Homeland Security (under political and public pressure) finally responded to the twenty-five year old complaints about "catch and release." "Operation Streamline" was initiated and Immigration and Customs Enforcement began to detain aliens apprehended near the border for periods of 15 to 180 days. It did not take long before the effectiveness of this policy change became apparent.

In an October 25, 2007, article by award-winning Arizona Daily Star reporter Brady McCombs, several border-related successes were attributed to "Operation Streamline."

McCombs wrote, *"Operation Streamline was initiated on December 6, 2005, in the Del Rio Sector in Texas. U.S. Customs and Border Protection, which includes the Border Patrol, partnered with the U.S. Attorney, U.S. marshal's, Immigration and Customs Enforcement and the U.S. magistrate. By June 26, 2006, the program was being used along the entire 210 border miles of the sector. Overall apprehensions decreased by 38 percent in fiscal year 2006, compared with the previous year and apprehensions of other-than-Mexicans were down 61 percent in that time frame, the Border Patrol says. The Yuma (Arizona) sector began the program in December, 2006, and has seen apprehensions drop 68 percent."*

Of course not everyone is thrilled about a program that appears to successfully deter illegal immigration. One member of the Tucson, Arizona, Border Action Network refuted the statistics and claimed that it would not be an "effective deterrent."

Despite the fact "Operation Streamline" is still in its infancy, it has already shown that extended detention of illegal immigrants will work, and the program should be expanded along the entire U.S.-Mexico border. Only time will tell if Congress will support a massive expansion of this program.

While border control is not the total solution to our immigration problems, it is obviously a large part of it. America must skillfully and diplomatically convince the Canadian and Mexican governments that America is not the world's patsy, and we have the right to protect our borders and our sovereignty.

Our politicians are playing a dangerous game with American security. We now have millions of airline passengers having their shoes examined, while Congress winks at our porous borders.

Solving some of our visa issuance problems

Considering that approximately 40% of the illegal aliens in the U.S. obtained valid visas or entered the country legally as citizens from visa-waiver countries, it appears the U.S. must immediately change our current visa issuance system. The first step to making it more secure would be to turn the entire process over to Homeland Security. After all, aliens who cross our borders legally with the intention of violating their immigration status are no different than the worker who illegally crosses the Rio Grande or the Arizona desert.

Changing visa issuance procedures may seem like a huge undertaking, but it will be well worth the trouble in the long run. The real problem will be the State Department's reluctance to give up this coveted authority.

Here are the some advantages to making this change.

- Aliens will have only one agency to contact both overseas and domestically.
- Immigration officers are better trained and have more familiarity with visa requirements. They spend years working with immigration-related activities.
- Immigration officers can be moved from domestic ports to overseas and back to the U.S. without disrupting their careers.
- Databases and watch lists that must be checked before visas are issued can all be maintained by Homeland Security.
- Biometric and biographic data collected at U.S. embassies will automatically be available to Homeland Security components.
- Homeland Security can use this biometric and biographic information to obtain travel documents for aliens who have been ordered deported from the U.S. (This will help solve a massive problem encountered during the deportation process. In many instances certain "sending" countries refuse to issue travel documents to their citizens facing deportation. This results in long delays in the deportation process and excessive detention costs for the U.S. government.)

I realize I am advocating a drastic change at our embassies worldwide. If this solution is totally unacceptable, Congress and the President should at least mandate that Homeland Security place more senior Immigration inspectors to serve alongside Foreign Service officers in Consular Sections at high-risk U.S. embassies.

The 9/11 Commission divulged that a lot of questionable procedures facilitated the attacks on the U.S. The lack of communication and coordination between the State Department and INS (with regard to the issuance of visas) was unquestionably one of those procedures. Allowing Homeland Security to take over the entire process of issuing visas is just another commonsense solution that will help us curtail illegal immigration and make America more secure.

Chapter 12

Controlling Illegal Immigration Now—Social Security Number Verification

"A computer registry to verify that a Social Security number is valid and has been issued to someone authorized to work in the U.S. is the most promising option for eliminating fraud and reducing discrimination, while protecting individual privacy."

U.S. Commission on Immigration Reform, Sept.1994

Illegal immigration will never be stopped by hiring more Border Patrol Agents, or for that matter, by completely securing our borders. After all, almost half of the illegal aliens in the U.S. came by air or sea, and never crossed the Mexican or Canadian borders. America must reduce or eliminate the employment magnet that draws illegal immigrants to this country. We have known this for decades. Unfortunately, the vast majority of our representatives in Congress are slaves to powerful lobbies that do not want to curtail illegal immigration for one reason or another.

While most employers comply with the requirement of filling out Form I-9 with their employees, most Americans are under a false impression that the government somehow verifies the information. I have spoken with thousands of Americans about this process and most believe when they first go to any job their Social Security number is immediately validated by the Social Security Administration. Nothing could be further from the truth.

Currently, there is no U.S. government law that requires employers to immediately verify that a Social Security number is valid, and that it has been legally issued to the employee. In fact, the Form I-9 is usually placed in the employee's personnel folder

SOCIAL SECURITY ADMINISTRATION
Application for a Social Security Card

Form Approved
OMB No. 0960-0066

1 NAME TO BE SHOWN ON CARD — First / Full Middle Name / Last
FULL NAME AT BIRTH IF OTHER THAN ABOVE — First / Full Middle Name / Last
OTHER NAMES USED

2 MAILING ADDRESS Do Not Abbreviate — Street Address, Apt. No., PO Box, Rural Route No. / City / State / Zip Code

3 CITIZENSHIP (Check One) — ☐ U.S. Citizen ☐ Legal Alien Allowed To Work ☐ Legal Alien **Not** Allowed To Work (See Instructions On Page 1) ☐ Other (See Instructions On Page 1)

4 SEX — ☐ Male ☐ Female

5 RACE/ETHNIC DESCRIPTION (Check One Only - Voluntary) — ☐ Asian, Asian-American or Pacific Islander ☐ Hispanic ☐ Black (Not Hispanic) ☐ North American Indian or Alaskan Native ☐ White (Not Hispanic)

6 DATE OF BIRTH — Month, Day, Year

7 PLACE OF BIRTH (Do Not Abbreviate) — City / State or Foreign Country / FCI — Office Use Only

8 A. MOTHER'S MAIDEN NAME — First / Full Middle Name / Last Name At Her Birth
B. MOTHER'S SOCIAL SECURITY NUMBER — ☐☐☐-☐☐-☐☐☐☐

9 A. FATHER'S NAME — First / Full Middle Name / Last
B. FATHER'S SOCIAL SECURITY NUMBER — ☐☐☐-☐☐-☐☐☐☐

10 Has the applicant or anyone acting on his/her behalf ever filed for or received a Social Security number card before?
☐ Yes (If "yes", answer questions 11-13.) ☐ No (If "no", go on to question 14.) ☐ Don't Know (If "don't know", go on to question 14.)

11 Enter the Social Security number previously assigned to the person listed in item 1. — ☐☐☐-☐☐-☐☐☐☐

12 Enter the name shown on the most recent Social Security card issued for the person listed in item 1. — First / Middle Name / Last

13 Enter any different date of birth if used on an earlier application for a card. — Month, Day, Year

14 TODAY'S DATE — Month, Day, Year

15 DAYTIME PHONE NUMBER — ( ) Area Code / Number

DELIBERATELY FURNISHING (OR CAUSING TO BE FURNISHED) FALSE INFORMATION ON THIS APPLICATION IS A CRIME PUNISHABLE BY FINE OR IMPRISONMENT, OR BOTH.

16 YOUR SIGNATURE ▶

17 YOUR RELATIONSHIP TO THE PERSON IN ITEM 1 IS: ☐ Self ☐ Natural Or Adoptive Parent ☐ Legal Guardian ☐ Other (Specify)

DO NOT WRITE BELOW THIS LINE (FOR SSA USE ONLY)

NPN	DOC	NTI	CAN	ITV

PBC	EVI	EVA	EVC	PRA	NWR	DNR	UNIT

EVIDENCE SUBMITTED

SIGNATURE AND TITLE OF EMPLOYEE(S) REVIEWING EVIDENCE AND/OR CONDUCTING INTERVIEW

DATE

DCL DATE

Form SS-5 (3-2001) EF (3-2001) Destroy Prior Editions Page 5

Social Security card application showing some of the data elements that could be used in an automated SSN verification system.

and never seen again. By not mandating that the I-9 information be verified by the government, Congress created a loophole so big that 12 million illegal aliens have crawled through it.

For the most part, I have been critical of Homeland Security's efforts to punish employers who hire illegal aliens. However, after the demise of "comprehensive immigration reform" in 2007, Homeland Security did take a monumental step forward. Regulations were promulgated to notify employers that Immigration and Customs Enforcement intended to utilize Social Security "no-match" letters as a source for their sanctions investigations. According to Mr. Mark Hinkle of the Social Security Administration, these letters are issued *"only to employers who have more than 10 workers whose numbers do not match, when those workers represent at least one-half of 1 per percent of the company's workforce."* (From my experience, the vast majority of "no match" letters also indicated the employees were illegally in the country.)

Russ Knocke, a spokesman for Homeland Security stated, *"We are tough and we are going to be even tougher. There are not going to be any more excuses for employers, and there will be serious consequences for those that choose to blatantly disregard the law."* Furthermore Homeland Security officials said there would be more raids on workplaces across the country.

No sooner did Homeland Security announce the regulations than the howling began. On August 8, 2007, Julia Preston wrote an article for the *New York Times* entitled, "U.S. Set for a Crackdown on Illegal Hiring." Ms. Preston wrote, *"Immigrants rights groups and labor unions, including the A.F.L.-C.I.O., predicted the rules would unleash discrimination against Hispanic workers. They said they were preparing legal challenges to try to stop them from taking effect."* What the immigrant rights groups conveniently forgot to tell the *New York Times* is they are also fearful that these "no-match" letters will help identify illegal aliens and law enforcement will have a valuable tool to locate and deport them.

Homeland Security deserves credit for moving forward with these new regulations. However, as we have seen in the past, initiatives like this usually meet their demise from political pressure. Only time will tell if this program will work and lead to a reduction in the employment of illegal immigrants. The fact that these regulations are even being considered is a huge step in the right direction. (By the way, in 2006 the Internal Revenue Service reported that there were 9.6 million tax submissions using "no-match" Social Security numbers.)

A real solution

In an attempt to stop the flow of humanity across the U.S.-Mexico border the Federal government will soon put up more fences, hire thousands of new Border Patrol Agents, and buy every border-security related gizmo known to mankind. Despite all this, millions of illegal aliens will still find a way to get in here—as long as they can find work!

Congress has been shown time and time again that the U.S. needs a law requiring employers to use a secure automated system to verify the validity of their employees' Social Security numbers. Due to political pressure from powerful lobbying groups, Congress has basically been corrupted and failed to mandate such a system. (What else is new?)

Aside from the business associations whose members utilize illegal immigrant labor, the American Civil Liberties Union and similar groups have continuously been able to convince Congress that implementation of such a system will result in a *de facto* national I.D. card. This is nothing more than a blatant scare tactic, as Social Security number verification does not remotely approach the establishment of a national identity card.

The INS and now Homeland Security have been testing such a system since the 1986 Immigration Reform and Control Act. In fact, the first such project, the Systematic Alien Verification for Entitlements Program, was developed and implemented under my direction during the latter part of the 1980s. Over the years Congress has authorized one test program after another, but has never had the will to mandate Social Security number verification nationwide.

Homeland Security has now developed a web-based system that allows employers to verify both Social Security numbers and immigration documents. The E-Verification System was introduced in the latter part of 2007, after years of being named the "Basic Pilot Program."

(For the sake of simplicity, this chapter will discuss our need for a Social Security Number Verification System. Homeland Security's E-Verification System could be the perfect program for this mandate.)

Here is a step-by-step model of how it might work.

1. Immediately after an employer hires an employee, both the employer and employee would be required to access an automated system using a toll-free number or a computer.
2. The system would first require the employer to provide a unique user access code, such as their employer tax I.D. number.
3. If a valid and recognizable user access code is entered, the system would request the employee's Social Security number and name, exactly as it appears on his Social Security card.
4. Once again, if the data entered matches a name and number in the system, the computer would generate random questions with tone-convertible answers using information currently in the Social Security database (example: date of birth, male or female, last four letters of city of birth, etc.). The employee would be required to supply the touch-tone numerical or lettered responses. These questions would change each time the system was queried.
5. The Social Security Number Verification System would then generate either an authorization number or a denial number.
6. The employer would be required to record the computer-generated authorization or denial on the I-9, along with the applicant's name and Social Security number.
7. Authorized numbers would require no further verification.
8. Denied numbers would require the employee to contact a designated agency (Homeland Security or the Social Security Administration).
9. Denied numbers would also require employers to reverify the employee's Social Security number within a designated period of time and obtain a valid authorization number.

10. If an authorization number could not be obtained, the person's employment would have to be terminated and a specific notification sent to the Social Security Administration. This form would notify the Government of the termination of employment based on the denial code and would protect the employer from legal action in the event of a mistake in the database.
11. The Social Security Administration could issue Personal Identification Numbers (PIN) to be used by employees whose Social Security numbers have been compromised.
12. Employers who properly used the Social Security Number Verification System would not be subject to civil or criminal penalties related to employer sanctions.
13. Illegal employment "sting operations" could be effectively used throughout the country. Illegal aliens using counterfeit documents and fraudulent Social Security cards would begin to fear applying for the "wrong" job.

Licensing agencies *must* also be required to verify Social Security numbers. These would include municipal, county, state and Federal licensing agencies. Currently, such agencies do not verify Social Security numbers with the Social Security Administration or an alien's immigration status with Homeland Security. Aliens who are unauthorized to work simply attend a required training course, pass a state exam and obtain a valid occupational license from a state board or commission. (If a licensing agency does require immigration documentation, illegal aliens simply provide counterfeits.) Illegal aliens are well aware that no mandatory verification program exists, and licensing agencies are not required to verify the authenticity of their immigration documents. Aliens who are not authorized to work frequently use this loophole to obtain state and local business licenses and then appear to be working legally in the U.S.

Here are some other fundamental criteria for the establishment and implementation of a Social Security Number Verification System.

1. *All* employers would be required to use the system to verify the Social Security numbers of *all* employees—aliens and citizens alike. This would virtually eliminate most claims of hiring discrimination based on national origin.
2. Automated verification must be completed immediately after the employee begins work or accepts a position with the employer.
3. Pre-screening of applicants (attempting to verify Social Security numbers before employment) would be a serious violation of law, punishable by fines and possible criminal prosecution.
4. Employers who failed to complete the verification and/or failed to record their employees' authorization numbers would be subject to sanctions.
5. Local, state and Federal law enforcement officers would have the authority to issue citations to employers who failed to verify employees' Social Security numbers.
6. Multiple violations could result in criminal prosecution of non-compliant employers.
7. The database would contain only Social Security numbers of people eligible to work in the U.S. It would not include extraneous data like Social Security numbers of children, dead persons and prisoners serving long sentences.
8. Information relating to the misuse of the system would be supplied to Federal, state and local law enforcement.
9. Congress could authorize the Federal government to pay for all costs associated with the verification program, or employers could be charged a small fee each time they completed a verification.

The benefits of a mandatory Social Security Number Verification System are cited below.

1. This system would significantly help in controlling illegal immigration by giving employers the tool needed to prevent accidentally hiring illegal aliens.
2. Employers who knowingly hire illegal aliens would find it difficult to subvert the system.

3. Most enforcement activity would require few arrests, little detention, and possibly no business disruption.
4. Municipal, state and Federal law enforcement officers would have a tremendous resource with which to assist the Federal government in the enforcement of immigration laws in their respective jurisdictions. Training of local, state and Federal officers for this program would be minimal.
5. Billions of dollars could eventually be added to the Social Security Trust Fund, as employers would be taking a much greater risk by "paying employees under the table."
6. Billions of dollars would be sent to proper Social Security accounts.
7. Fines collected from non-compliant employers could be used to fund the Social Security Number Verification System, pay for detention and deportation of illegal aliens, and help local, state and Federal agencies offset the costs usually associated with illegal immigration.
8. The automated system would also be used to more effectively direct law enforcement to employers who were attempting to either misuse or subvert the verification process.

The primary reason many people fear a Social Security Number Verification System is that they have no idea how it will work. There is a misconception that the U.S. government will have to issue new high-tech Social Security cards to hundreds of millions of people, and that the associated costs will be astronomical. Opponents have also warned that job applicants will be denied employment if there is a mistake in the database, and the government will collect all kinds of information to use against us. These fears are mostly generated in the media and, once again, by organizations like the American Civil Liberties Union. (Of course, right-wing "immigration experts," who propose Draconian solutions, give the liberals all the fuel they need.)

As an example, in a *Time* magazine article about illegal immigration ("Who Left the Door Open?" September 20, 2004), T.J.

Bonner, president of the National Border Patrol Council, told *Time* that the U.S. Government should:

> *". . . issue a single document that's counterfeit proof, that has an embedded photograph, that says this person has a right to work in the U.S. And that document is the Social Security card. It's not a national I.D. card. It's a card you have to carry when you apply for a job and only then. The employers run it through a scanner, and they get an answer in short order that says, Yes you may hire, or No you may not. That would cut off 98% of all the traffic across the border. With your work force of 10,000 border-patrol agents, you actually could control the borders."*

The media frequently portrays individuals like Mr. Bonner as "immigration experts" because of their position in the U.S. Border Patrol. The fact is, the Patrol has little presence in the interior of the U.S. where the 12 million illegal aliens live and work. When these "experts" come out in the media with unachievable solutions to our immigration problems, they seem to do more harm than good.

I know Mr. Bonner has done a wonderful job as a union activist for Border Patrol Agents, but he should stick to patrolling the borders. His proposal about immediately upgrading all current Social Security cards with embedded photographs is scary. His suggestion that all employers obtain some sort of magical scanner is ludicrous. The U.S. government should never develop a verification system that gives a simple "yes" or "no" answer about employment eligibility. (There must always be a secondary-verification process available for people who have been initially denied, in case there is a mistake in the government's database.) Lastly, it is simply crazy to believe any system will "cut off 98% of all the [illegal] traffic across the border."

I am also in favor of *eventually* upgrading the security features of our Social Security card. I am, however, also a realist about changing the way the U.S. government does business. By the time the Social Security Administration gets around to putting a digitized photograph or other biometrics on our Social

Security cards, another 50 million illegal aliens will have slipped past Bonner's Border Patrol.

For the immediate future, the U.S. government should be more concerned about who has a legitimate Social Security number, rather than worrying about making the document more secure. I believe if Congress mandates the use of a Social Security Number Verification System for employers, many security issues involving Social Security numbers will be curtailed. Eventually the government can work on making the card more secure. In the meantime, we should first consider more productive and realistic initiatives.

Day laborers

Social Security number verification will not work in all instances. Many cities in America are now dealing with the controversial issue of "day laborers." In some areas, hundreds of men and women (usually illegal aliens) stand near designated street corners or parking lots waiting for contractors to drive by, pick them up and take them to some one-day job that requires unskilled physical labor.

In many areas these sites have become an eyesore, and some communities are using taxpayer dollars to build shelters for the workers. Needless to say the citizenry is sharply divided about this situation.

And for those who think this must be a border issue, think again. One of the most notable cities in America with a "day labor" problem is Herndon, Virginia. (I was a resident there for five years.)

Since it is almost impossible to enforce employer sanctions against people who employ day laborers, I suggest that the Border Patrol take on more responsibility in this area. Homeland Security could use the Border Patrol to establish a uniformed enforcement presence throughout the interior of the U.S. This is a simple, but very effective solution. Illegal aliens do not hang around street corners when the "mean green" Border Patrol is in the neighborhood; and if the employers can't find the laborers, the entire day labor problem will virtually disappear.

011-44-4365

Golf is one of my passions, and during my career at INS, I assisted numerous people associated with the PGA Tour of America. I was fortunate enough to meet golfers like Sandy Lyle; Nick Price; Ian Baker-Finch; Davis Love, III; Jeff Sluman; Bernhard Langer; Brad Faxon; and Vijay Singh. My acquaintances include players, caddies, equipment representatives and security personnel. I have given advice to many of them about obtaining "green cards," visas, passports and U.S. citizenship. In fact, over the years, some of the players and their caddies have spent a night or two at "Hotel Cramer"—especially when a PGA Tour event was nearby.

I can think of no other way to better demonstrate the need for a Social Security Number Verification System than to pass on a great story about a foreign friend of mine who worked as a Tour caddie. I will simply refer to him as "M," and I have changed some of the digits of his Social Security number. The rest of the story is fact.

In 1994, "M" had a week off before the Master's Golf Tournament so he came to stay at my house on St. Simon's Island, Georgia. He was one of the best caddies in the world and had worked for Sandy Lyle, Seve Ballesteros, Tom Watson and Lee Janzen.

One evening, he related to me an interesting story about foreign PGA Tour caddies and their use of Social Security numbers. Foreign caddies usually enter the U.S. as visitors. As such, they are not supposed to work for U.S. citizen or resident alien players. Most foreign caddies could also care less about U.S. immigration law, and they work for anyone who will hire them. The vast majority work without having a valid Social Security number.

So what happens on payday? What about Social Security taxes? After all, some PGA Tour players are earning $5 million or more annually. If the caddy gets his 7–10%, the Social Security

Administration should be getting a sizeable number of greenbacks for the Trust Fund from the caddy, as well as from the player.

It seems that every good foreign caddie knows exactly what to do when he needs a Social Security number. He creates one. They have all learned that the SSN has nine digits, and it should be a number they can remember week after week.

"M" said his made-up number (011-44-4365) consisted of three parts that he never forgot—"011" were the phone numbers to dial the international operator; "44" were the telephone code numbers for dialing England; and "4365" were the last four digits of his home phone in the Midlands. Thus, Social Security number 011-44-4365.

"M" said he used it for seven years on every payday in the U.S. and never once had a problem. To this day, "M" claims he has never received a single notification of any kind from the U.S. government and doesn't know or care if it was a real Social Security number.

The Tax Identification Number

If ever the U.S. government created a program that facilitates illegal immigration, it is the proliferation of the Internal Revenue Service's Tax Identification Number (TIN).

Ever since the Social Security Administration began to tighten its procedures for obtaining a valid Social Security number, the TIN has become the number of choice for those illegally in the U.S. I am not familiar with the history of the TIN, but I can attest to the fact that it is fast becoming the most important number to illegal aliens and other people desirous of creating multiple and fraudulent identities. It takes nothing more than a phone call to the IRS, and they send out a valid nine-digit Tax Identification Number that can be made to look exactly like a Social Security number. The best part for the illegal alien is the TIN is a validly issued identifier. Therefore, there is no danger that another person will eventually complain about its misuse.

Aliens usually apply for their TIN number, have them printed on a counterfeit Social Security card, and almost no one can tell the difference. Once again, there is no automated system available to verify whether these numbers are valid Social Security numbers or Tax Identification Numbers.

In recent years, large and small banks in the U.S. have been looking for ways to sell illegal aliens products (checking accounts, credit cards, home mortgages, etc.). There was always one large hurdle facing the banking industry. Most illegal aliens did not possess valid Social Security numbers, and banks were required to report customer financial information to the Treasury Department, using a nine-digit numerical identifier. Along came the Tax Identification Number, and a whole new world opened up for the banking industry.

With more than 12 million illegal aliens in the country, banks began to look at this huge population as an untapped resource. And, for the sake of the almighty dollar, banks could care less if their customers are in this country legally or not.

On February 14, 2007, *Los Angeles Times* reporters Reckard, Streitfield and Uribarri wrote an article entitled, "Banking on Illegal Immigrants—A move to issue credit cards to people without Social Security numbers draws anger and praise." The article explained that Bank of America, the nation's largest retail bank, was moving forward with a pilot program to allow Spanish-speaking immigrants who did not possess valid Social Security numbers to obtain bank credit cards. While the bank maintained they were not specifically targeting the illegal immigrant population in Los Angeles, it was easy to see that Bank of America was doing exactly that.

Congressman Tom Tancredo (R-Colorado), a strong advocate of tighter immigration enforcement, hinted that the bank was aiding terrorists, and called for a Congressional inquiry. Others hailed the bank's actions as an attempt to help illegal immigrants get a stronger foothold in the country, despite being illegally here. Immigrant advocacy groups praised the bank for looking at the illegal aliens as customers rather than criminals. Wells Fargo Bank was expected to follow the lead of Bank of America.

The entire controversy of making loans and giving credit cards to illegal aliens is just another part of this growing immigration-related quandry in America. The root cause of this turmoil lies with the Treasury Department, since it began issuing Tax Identification Numbers to every "Tom, Dick and Harry" who applied for one. In any event, a great deal of thanks must go to our IRS for creating a program that sends us another five steps backward in the fight against illegal immigration.

A little history about automated Social Security number verification

The Social Security Number Automated Verification System was a white-paper I authored in 1987, as Director of the INS Systematic Alien Verification for Entitlements (SAVE) program. If there is any question about how much I believe in this system, consider the fact that I submitted this proposal to every INS Commissioner since 1985, the U.S. Congress, the Commission on Immigration Reform, and Vice President Al Gore's Reinventing Government.

My research shows that I was not alone. Social Security number fraud was a matter of concern more than 20 years ago. Documents dating back to the early 1980s indicate that bureaucrats and politicians were well aware of the growing problem and chose to do nothing about it.

Social Security Number Fraud—Investigative Guide, *1984*

In March, 1984, Richard P. Kusserow, Inspector General, Department of Health and Human Services, created a guide for his agents to use in combating welfare fraud. Throughout the entire document there are references to the fraud schemes perpetrated using fraudulent and nonexistent Social Security numbers. And even in the early 1980s the costs associated with this fraud were staggering.

The introduction of the guide states the following:

> *"The Social Security number has become a widespread means of identification in the United States. As its use as an identifier has grown, so has the opportunity for its misuse—often to fraudulently* ***obtain employment*** *[emphasis added] or monetary benefits . . . "*

It went on to say, *"In the Federal Identification Fraud Report made by the Permanent Subcommittee on Investigations, issued in May, 1983, the economic impact of false identification fraud on government and commerce was estimated to be $24 billion annually."*

This was 1983; more than 20 years ago!

Immigration Control: A New Role for the Social Security Card, *1988*

In March, 1988, the U.S. General Accounting Office sent a report to Congressional Committees entitled *Immigration Control: A New Role for the Social Security Card.* It stated the following:

> *"One way to resolve verification difficulties is to designate the SSN card as the only document that can be used as evidence of employment eligibility under Immigration Reform and Control Act. We believe the SSN card would meet the needs of both employers and employees and offer advantages over the present system."*

This GAO report became my Bible. It served as one of the most comprehensive documents regarding the failure of INS to properly implement the Employer Sanctions provisions of the Immigration Reform and Control Act.

Virtually no one at INS read it.

A Social Security Number Validation System, *1988*

In November, 1988, the Department of Health and Human Services, Social Security Administration, published a report mandated by the Immigration Reform and Control Act of 1986 entitled

A Social Security Number Validation System: Feasibility, Costs, and Privacy Considerations. While I have always maintained that Social Security administrators and their supporters on Capitol Hill have long resisted any attempt to develop a Social Security Number Verification System, this in-house study was conducted with integrity.

After conducting a pilot program that allowed certain employers to verify social security numbers telephonically, the report concluded, *"The study found that this type of an SSN validation system is technically feasible, but that considerable lead time would be required to implement such a system."* Is 20 years sufficient time?

The Social Security Administration report also estimated that the cost per verification would be $1.10, and computer hardware and software would be approximately $15 million. If you think that is too expensive, consider the $24 billion in fraud mentioned previously. I would gladly spend $15 million to $20 million to save $24 billion.

The Commission on Immigration Reform, *1993*

In the early 1990s Congress and the Clinton Administration realized that the Immigration Reform and Control Act of 1986 had done nothing to control illegal immigration into the U.S. Rather than simply strengthen employer sanctions by mandating that employers use a verification system, the politicians decided to get "the monkey off their backs" by establishing a Commission on Immigration Reform.

Why not spend millions of taxpayer dollars studying an issue that had already been studied numerous times before? The answer was simple. Most politicians hate the immigration issue, and the establishment of a commission absolves them of all responsibility while the study is ongoing. If most politicians had their way, the Commission on Immigration Reform would have lasted until 2030.

I submitted the Social Security number verification whitepaper to the Commission on Immigration Reform during my tenure as Chief of the Immigration Officer Academy.

In March, 1993, I received a confirmation letter from Susan Forbes Martin, the Executive Director of the Commission on Immigration Reform. The letter confirmed that I had submitted a white-paper detailing the necessity and usefulness of a mandatory Social Security number verification system for employers.

In September, 1994, more than one-and-a-half years later, the Commission on Immigration Reform submitted its report to Congress. It was entitled, *U.S. Immigration Policy: Restoring Credibility.* In the report it stated the following:

> *"A computer registry to verify that a Social Security number is valid and has been issued to someone authorized to work in the U.S. is the most promising option for eliminating fraud and reducing discrimination, while protecting individual privacy."*

It further stated:

> *"For decades, all workers have been required to provide employers with their Social Security number. The computer registry would add only one step to this existing requirement: an employer check that the Social Security number is valid and has been issued to someone authorized to work in the United States.*
>
> *"The Commission believes the computerized system is the most promising option because it holds great potential for accomplishing the following:*
>
> - *Reduction in the potential for fraud.*
> - *Reduction in the potential for discrimination.*
> - *Reduction in the time, resources and paperwork spent by employers in complying with the Immigration Reform and Control Act of 1986 (IRCA) and corresponding redirection of enforcement activities from paperwork violations to knowing hire of unauthorized workers."*

In so many words, the Commission on Immigration Reform recommended exactly what was in my white-paper. The Commission's report was bi-partisan and suggested many other realistic improvements to our immigration system. Implementation

COMMISSION ON IMMIGRATION REFORM
1825 Connecticut Avenue, N.W., Suite 511
Washington, D.C. 20009–5708
TEL (202) 673-5348 • FAX (202) 673-5354

March 25, 1993

Mr. Neville W. Cramer
P.O. Box 421
St. Simons Island, GA 31522-0421

Dear Mr. Cramer:

Thank you for your note and the white paper on a Social Security Number Automated Verification System. The Commission will review this proposal as part of its assessment of the implementation and impact of U.S. immigration policy.

Please continue to keep the Commission informed of your recommendations regarding immigration policy.

Sincerely,

Susan Forbes Martin
Executive Director

of the recommendations would have significantly helped curtail illegal immigration. Despite the fact that the Commission's recommendations were sound public policy, many lobbyists on Capitol Hill (who quietly favored illegal immigration) made it known that any representative who supported the Commission's recommendations would receive little if any financial support during the next round of political contributions.

The U.S. Congress and the Clinton White House buried the recommendations as fast as they could. Why? Because they knew if they implemented the Commission's recommendations, the government would have taken a large step forward to successfully curtailing illegal immigration.

Reinventing the Federal government—The National Performance Review

My last significant attempt to implement a Social Security Number Verification System came when Vice President Al Gore announced his National Performance Review. He wanted to reach out to Federal employees and ask for their insight into solving some of the U.S. government's problems. A noble idea, and the reward was a "Golden Hammer" from the Office of Vice President Gore (I'm not kidding about the award).

Since illegal aliens were pouring the concrete for the new sidewalks in front of my house on St. Simon's Island, I thought I would fire off my white-paper for one last chance. No sooner had the announcement of the National Performance Review crossed the lips of the Veep than my white-paper was on its way to the Naval Observatory (home of the Vice President, for those of you who are not familiar with D.C. landmarks).

I was actually quite impressed when a young man by the name of Greg Woods from the Vice President's program contacted me. He advised me that he had received the proposal and had forwarded it to the Social Security Administration for comment.

On July 28, 1993, Andrew J. Young of the Social Security Administration sent the preliminary review (written by Ms. Toni

Lenane) back to Greg Woods at the National Performance Review. Their synopsis read as follows.

> *"Employers in industries known to be at risk for employing illegal aliens would dial into a system that uses Social Security Administration (SSA) data and Immigration and Naturalization Service (INS) data to verify that newly hired employees have supplied accurate Social Security numbers (SSN) and are eligible to work in the United States.*
>
> *"The proposed system would improve on the current employment eligibility process by reducing reliance on documents which can be counterfeited. However, it would lead to increased fraudulent use of valid identities and SSN's by other than the true number holder. This has negative consequences for the true number holder and the government.*
>
> *"SSA's Numident data base can verify the accuracy of SSN's, but has some limitations for verifying employment eligibility; i.e. citizenship or work authorized alien status. In addition, legislation would be needed to authorize SSA to disclose citizenship and alien status information to employers."*

On January 11, 1994, Greg Woods sent me a note attached to the Social Security response:

> *"Neville,*
>
> *Sorry I keep putting this off. Let me know what you think of SSA's response.*
>
> *Greg Woods."*

The next day, I wrote a short response telling Mr. Woods that I was pleased with most of the report. I pointed out that the Social Security Administration had made an incorrect assumption that citizenship and alien status would have to be divulged to employers. I pointed out that my white-paper made no such suggestion.

Having made this clarification, I sent the note back to Mr. Woods and was advised by him that he would send it up the chain to the Vice President's office for further consideration. He told me I would hear something in a couple of weeks.

After a month of waiting, I called the National Performance Review Office. They told me Greg Woods had left the government and all of his National Performance Review projects were thrown away.

So much for my Golden Hammer Award. I gave up.

Social Security numbers—Not for everyone

Preventing the misuse of Social Security numbers and Tax Identification Numbers begins with tightening the issuance procedures. Here are some procedural changes that should be considered to prevent valid numbers from being issued to those who should not have one.

(1) All aliens in the U.S. should obtain their Social Security numbers and Tax Identification Numbers through Homeland Security's Citizenship and Immigration Services. Applications for Social Security numbers by aliens should be verified and forwarded to the Social Security Administration for processing. Aliens in the U.S. will receive their Social Security numbers only after authorization has been given by Homeland Security.
(2) Social Security numbers should not be issued to aliens for an indefinite period of time. This right should be reserved for citizens only.
(3) Individuals whose Social Security numbers have been compromised should be given a Personal Identification Number in addition to their account number.
(4) The Social Security Administration should consider putting magnetic stripes, smart chips, biometrics identifiers and other security features on new Social Security cards.

Current law requires that almost everyone employed in the U.S. must be using a Social Security number. This law also has overwhelming public support. If we implement a mandatory Social

1/11/94

NATIONAL PERFORMANCE REVIEW
AL GORE
Vice President of the United States

NATIONAL PERFORMANCE REVIEW
750 17th St. NW, Box 101
Washington, DC 20006

Nevik

Sorry I keep putting this off. Let me know what you think of SSG's response.

Greg Woods.

Reinventing the Federal Government

I told Greg Woods what I thought, and he disappeared!

Security Number Verification System, employers would be required to take the following steps.

- Keep a record of each employee's Social Security number.
- Keep a record of each authorization or denial code generated by the Social Security Number Verification System.
- Keep other employee biographic data on the I-9 (name, date of birth, etc.).

Opponents of this system will immediately complain that millions will be denied employment because of erroneous data in the Social Security databases. On the contrary, as we saw in the alien status verification program, if protections are put in place (secondary verification), the only ones who will eventually lose their jobs are people who are in the country illegally or otherwise ineligible to accept employment in the U.S.

A Federally mandated Social Security Number Verification System will certainly go a long way in helping America control illegal immigration. However, it is not a panacea by any means, and it must be accompanied by an enforcement mechanism that allows the government to take significant punitive action against employers who fail to verify Social Security numbers.

Chapter 13

Employer Sanctions Using the Social Security Number Verification System

Today's employer sanctions

The employer sanctions program has been virtually dead for nearly twenty years. Since I promised I would stay away from statistics I will keep the promise. Let's just say they are laughable when it comes to immigration enforcement actions against employers in the U.S.

Aside from the fact the sanctions program was sabotaged at INS within weeks after the passage of the Immigration Reform and Control Act in 1986 (see Chapter 3), various influential lobbying groups have quietly and effectively advanced its demise. Legal challenges have also made it quite difficult to prove an employer "knowingly" hired illegal aliens.

The result of virtually no employer sanctions is quite evident. We now have about 12 million or more illegal aliens in the country and employers have a better chance of winning the PowerBall Lottery than being fined for hiring illegal aliens.

Thanks to the efforts of CNN's Lou Dobbs, FOX News' Bill O'Reilly and literally hundreds of America's talk radio show hosts (Limbaugh, Hannity and Humphreys) the problems associated with illegal immigration are in the news everyday. Apparently Homeland Security Secretary Chertoff has been listening to some of them.

Since the establishment of Immigration and Customs Enforcement, Homeland Security has made a sincere effort to bring life back to employer sanctions. Their first big target was Wal-Mart, if for no other reason the headlines. After a massive undercover investigation, several Wal-Mart contractors were arrested and convicted of knowingly employing illegal aliens. Wal-Mart negotiated an $11 million fine and Uncle Sam created headlines about their new intolerance for employers who knowingly employ illegal aliens.

While some Americans may have been "wowed" by the multi-million dollar fine, for Wal-Mart it was simply a "cost of doing business." After all, they probably make $11 million a year just in toothpaste sales!

Since the Wal-Mart operation, Immigration and Customs Enforcement has also raided a major home-building company, a large manufacturer of pallets, a meat packer or two and of course "The Big Mac" McDonald's. While it is true that a few hundred illegal aliens have been arrested and some mid-level company officials are heading to the "Big House" for a year or so, these operations will have no impact whatsoever on America's illegal immigration problem. Political appointee Julie Myers (Assistant Secretary for Immigration and Customs and Enforcement) may be claiming success from this new "crackdown", but who is kidding who? She is well aware that without a mandatory verification system for employers these activities are nothing more than politically driven demonstrations of the absurd.

Speaking of the absurd, Homeland Security has come up with another voluntary program for employers. The project is called IMAGE and it stands for **I**mmigration and Customs Enforcement **M**utual **A**greement between **G**overnment and **E**mployers. (Someone lost a lot of sleep creating that acronym.) These initiatives are supposedly intended to reduce the ability of illegal aliens to obtain employment in the U.S. by allowing employers to voluntarily verify the immigration status of their employees. I think most of these "voluntary" programs are useless gimmicks. Anyone with common sense realizes businesses that use illegal aliens are not going to voluntarily subscribe to any program that will send their workers packing.

Not everything is doom and gloom. In 2007, the Social Security Administration and Homeland Security finally took a bold cooperative step forward in this area. "No-match letters" previously

Social Security Administration
Retirement, Survivors and Disability Insurance
Employer Correction Request CODE V

Office of Central Operations
300 N. Greene Street
Baltimore, MD 21290-0300
Date:
EIN:

EMPLOYER'S NAME
STREET ADDRESS
CITY, STATE ZIP

Establishment Number: MRN: WFID:

Why You Are Getting This Letter

Some employee names and Social Security numbers that you reported on the Wage and Tax Statements (Forms W-2) for tax year 2006 do not agree with our records. We need corrected information from you so that we can credit your employees' earnings to their Social Security records. It is important because these records can determine if someone is entitled to Social Security retirement, disability and survivors benefits, and how much he or she can receive. If the information you report to us is incorrect, your employee may not get benefits he or she is due.

There are several common reasons why the information reported to us does not agree with our records, including:

? Errors were made in spelling an employee's name or listing the Social Security number;

? An employee did not report a name change following a marriage or divorce;

? The name or Social Security number was incomplete or left blank on the Form W-2 report sent to the Social Security Administration; and

? The name or Social Security number reported is false, or the number was assigned to someone else.

IMPORTANT: This letter does not imply that you or your employee intentionally gave the government wrong information about the employee's name or Social Security number. Nor does it, by itself, make any statement about an employee's immigration status.

See Next Page
Visit our website at www.socialsecurity.gov
99-9999999

Sample of No-Match letter (Source: www.ssa.gov)

sent out only to employers will now also be sent to Immigration and Customs Enforcement. ("No-match" letters indicate that an employer has submitted Social Security tax information that does not match the government's records.) If this effort is not struck down by the courts, it could be a giant step forward in combating both illegal immigration and identity theft. It will soon be very difficult for employers to continue to employ illegal aliens with outstanding "no-match letters", and then claim they did not knowingly employ the aliens.

"No-match letters" are a great first step, but their effectiveness will also depend on the willingness of Immigration and Customs Enforcement management to support the effort with the proper resources. Only time will tell.

Whether it is "No-match letters" or the IMAGE Program, nothing will take the place of a mandatory Social Security Number Verification System. Without this system, employer sanctions will remain a "paper tiger", employers will continue to create the "employment magnet" and illegal aliens will continue to pour into America by the millions.

A Homeland Security Immigration Compliance Division

Law enforcement professionals are always faced with choices when it comes to deploying limited resources. Immigration enforcement is no different. During most of the last decade, the INS had a total of 2,000 Special Agents stationed throughout the interior of the U.S. They are now part of the larger Immigration and Customs Enforcement Division in Homeland Security. However, the actual number of Special Agents who understand the intricacies of immigration law enforcement still stands at less than 3,000 for the entire country.

There is an immigration enforcement vacuum in the interior of the U.S. The following facts will come as a surprise to many who believe that illegal aliens throughout America are fearful they will be arrested and deported by our immigration authorities.

- There are extremely few Special Agents who actually seek out, arrest, detain and deport illegal aliens who are working illegally in the U.S.
- Immigration and Customs Enforcement Special Agents are spread thin, working to combat terrorism, alien smuggling, and counterfeiting of immigration documents.
- The few Immigration and Customs Enforcement Special Agents who work in the lower 48 states must conduct criminal investigations to maintain their pay grades within the Federal law enforcement system. Catching an illegal alien at work is *not* considered a criminal investigation.
- Considering the number of illegal aliens in the country versus the number of companies fined, it is fair to say the employer sanctions program is currently not working.
- Border Patrol Agents work in South Florida and on the Canadian and Mexican borders. They have little presence or jurisdiction in the interior of the U.S.
- There is almost no one to investigate administrative immigration violations like visa and marriage fraud.
- It is a well known in American immigrant communities that once illegal aliens get into the interior of the U.S. they are virtually "home free."

As a partial solution to the current lack of interior enforcement, I advocate creating a new type of enforcement division within the Department of Homeland Security—an Immigration Compliance Division.

Among other responsibilities, this division would implement and enforce a more stringent employer sanctions program.

The Homeland Security Immigration Compliance Division would be responsible for these actions:

- assisting the Social Security Administration with the development and implementation of a Social Security Number Verification System;
- assisting the employment community with the implementation of the verification system; and
- hiring and training the immigration compliance officers to enforce employer sanctions and other administrative immigration laws in the interior of the U.S. This will include: arresting, detaining and deporting illegal aliens; investigating administrative violations of immigration law; and assisting other law enforcement agencies with problems associated with illegal immigration.

With the establishment and support of this division, Homeland Security will finally fill a large vacuum of immigration law enforcement that has existed in the U.S. for decades.

New Social Security cards

Despite the failure of "comprehensive immigration reform" legislation in 2007, the proposed law gave some insight into the solutions being considered by Congress. One part of the law called for a new high-tech Social Security card to be developed in two years. While I am in favor of upgrading most government identity documents, I believe we need a system in place in a lot less than two years, and a new card is not the answer, by any stretch of the imagination. Professionals in the business of developing secure identity documents will usually stress verification capability, as opposed to building more gizmos into the document itself. Our current Social Security cards are ridiculously simple and easy to counterfeit. However, the automated information behind each Social Security number is guarded with great care by the Social Security Administration. It is also very accurate. Considering these two facts, a Social Security Number Verification

System—that verifies data rather than the card itself—would be very easy to develop and implement.

I do advocate that someday we pursue a more secure Social Security card. Unfortunately it will take years to develop and maybe decades to implement. We do not have that much time, since our main interest is using Social Security number verification to help deal with our current immigration crisis. A solution for the immediate future is a secure automated Social Security Number Verification System—not some new card.

Employer sanctions and "Credit Card Verification 101"

As soon as the U.S. government develops an employment eligibility verification system, a new employer sanctions program must also be developed, and to sanction an employer must be a very simplified process. (The current method is lengthy and convoluted. It takes months of undercover work before most U.S. Attorneys will consider bringing criminal charges against an employer for "knowingly" hiring illegal aliens.)

How will a new verification system and employer sanctions program operate? Look no further than the credit cards in your wallet.

We can learn a great deal about controlling illegal immigration by looking at our current credit card system. The success of credit cards is based largely on the fact that financial institutions can verify a credit card number almost instantaneously. This capability is based on a system I refer to as "triangulated verification."

1. The financial institution sends a card to consumers, and creates a database using information submitted on the application.
2. When a purchase is made using a credit card number, an electronic process is initiated to *verify* the information by accessing the database of the financial institution that issued the card (i.e. Visa, MasterCard, AmEx, etc.).

3. If the financial institution approves of the transaction, an *authorization number* is generated. If it is not approved, it's simply denied. In some instances, a phone call can be made to see why the authorization was denied.

The authorization number plays a key role in the success of credit-card verification. For every charge made to a card number, an authorization code is generated to prove the financial institution gave approval. When the authorization code is given, the responsibility for payment rests solely with the financial institution. No authorization code, no purchase.

Even with the recent upsurge in identity theft, most experts admit that the trillions of dollars in commerce that result from the use of credit cards far outweigh the costs associated with identity theft. I am the first to admit that our credit card system has flaws. Billions of dollars in losses are reported every year due to fraud and identity theft. I would be a fool not to acknowledge these weaknesses. On the other hand, if these losses are so tremendous, why do I have five credit cards in my wallet?

As the bank advertisement says, "Most credit card fraud is detected before the card holder even knows it happened." Furthermore, great strides are being made to prevent and detect identity theft and credit card fraud.

My proposal for a Social Security Number Verification System is similar in many ways to the credit card triangulated verification process. Employers would be required to use an automated system to verify every employee's Social Security number. In turn, every employer would be issued an authorization or denial code for all verifications completed.

Admittedly some problems have to be overcome, such as existing Social Security numbers issued to illegal aliens in the past. This problem is by no means insurmountable, although in the past it has been used as an excuse to prevent the development of an automated Social Security Number Verification System.

Social Security number verification is nothing more than creating a system to help the government get its act together. Considering the importance of our Social Security system, it is beyond me how we allow billions of dollars in Social Security payments to be sent to accounts that don't exist or belong to someone other than the name associated with the FICA payment.

And, for those who think this system is not technologically feasible, think again. In 1985, I had the rare opportunity to tour the Social Security Administration with then INS Commissioner Alan Nelson. During the tour of Social Security's enormous computer facilities I asked one of their head technicians about the possibility of establishing an automated verification system for employers. He said emphatically, "It could be done in six months if they really wanted to do it." Then he asked me quietly to drop the subject. Apparently it was a very sensitive "non-topic" at the Social Security Administration.

Social Security Number Verification will be the backbone of any effective employer sanctions program.

- Mandatory use of E-Verification will give employers the system they need to properly verify the work eligibility status and Social Security numbers of their employees.
- Systematically issued authorization codes will give employers evidence they need to prove they utilized the system.
- Employers can easily be held responsible for failing to utilize the verification system and knowingly employing illegal aliens.

The end to employment discrimination caused by employer sanctions

In a March 8, 1990, *Wall Street Journal* article titled "Wide Bias in Hiring Blamed on Immigration Sanctions," staff reporter Alfredo Corchado wrote:

> *"With the passage of the landmark Immigration and Reform Act of 1986, the nation's employers were faced with an unappealing choice: play immigration cop or get hit with stiff penalties.*

> *"Their solution, it would appear, hasn't been a happy one for many workers. Many employers simply aren't hiring anybody they think could be an illegal alien—even someone whose work authorization documents appear to be in order—for fear of running afoul of the law. A report to be released later this month by the General Accounting Office, Congress' watchdog, is expected to show that the employer sanctions in the 1986 law have generated widespread instances of bias against job applicants who look or sound as though they may be foreigners."*

The General Accounting Office was wrong. While there was anecdotal evidence that employer sanctions caused concern on the part of some employers, there was no massive discrimination because of the law.

Due to the widespread use of fraudulent documents and the inability of employers to verify documents either by telephone or electronically, employer sanctions became a paper tiger overnight.

Will an effective employer sanctions program using automated Social Security verification result in discrimination? Not if employers are required to verify ALL Social Security numbers, and not if the check is conducted after an offer of employment has been made by the employer.

In fact, just the opposite will occur. Employers who want to hire an alien will have no fear of doing so as long as they receive an authorization code from the computer system or the Social Security Administration. Once the Social Security number authorization is received, employers will not have anything to fear if the checks were conducted in good faith. Proposed legislation in this area has always included a "no fault" provision for employers who properly use the system.

With this is mind, why would groups like the Mexican American Legal Defense and Educational Fund and the American Civil Liberties Union be so adamantly opposed to it? The answer is simple. It will work very effectively to curtail illegal immigration.

Immigration advocates are paid to protect the rights of immigrants. Whether they are Mexican-American groups who support an "open border" or religious groups that want liberal immigration policies, these organizations see any workable immigration enforcement program as the "devil in disguise."

Another foe of effective immigration enforcement is most of America's mainstream media. As soon as illegal immigrants are removed from their employment in large numbers, or several are deported, the government is portrayed as the bad guy.

One of the most effective ways used by advocacy groups and the liberal media to prevent a Social Security number verification system has been to tie it directly to the establishment of a National I.D. system. They complain that the government is collecting all sorts of information, and all of our rights are going down the drain. So far, they have been successful—to say the least.

To set the record straight, automated verification of Social Security numbers is not creating a National I.D. system. It is simply verifying information currently being sent to the Social Security Administration. Advocacy groups can portray it as Big Brother, Draconian, Orwellian, or some other term typically used to raise the fears of the general public. As I have demonstrated, Social Security number verification is good public policy and should be implemented, whether it stops illegal immigration or not.

How enforcement will work using the Social Security Number Verification System

There is no better way to explain this proposed system than to give examples of typical enforcement actions against non-compliant employers.

For the sake of this explanation, let's suppose the fine for a first offense is $1,000 for each employee, and another $1,000 for each day thereafter that "unverified" employees are kept on the payroll. Let's also suppose that local, county, state, and Federal law enforcement officers could issue a citation to employers for failing to verify employees' Social Security numbers.

Scenario #1—A small business has 15 employees and the owner simply refuses to use the Social Security Number Verification System.

In this case, the investigating officer visits the business suspected of hiring illegal aliens and requests that the employer produce the following for each employee: (1) Social Security numbers; (2) an approval code for each Social Security number verified; and (3) an I-9 for each employee.

When the employer states that he *simply* does not use the system, he *simply* gets a citation for each one of his 15 employees. Take my word for it, after a couple of $15,000 fines, he will not only use the system, he will embrace it!

Scenario #2—An employer who has 15 employees decides he is going to make up his own approval codes.

Once again the investigating officer audits all employee Social Security numbers, corresponding approval codes, and the I-9 forms. The officer then accesses the verification system database and notes that the approval codes have been contrived. They may look real, but were never issued by the system. Within minutes, our employer is looking at $15,000 in fines, and possible jail time for fraud. It won't be long before he too will be convinced about the benefits of compliance.

Scenario #3—An honest employer unknowingly hires an imposter.

Once again, the enforcement officer audits the employer's records. The employer provides the Social Security number, the valid approval code, and the I-9.

If an employee has truly used another person's Social Security number and successfully obtained a valid authorization code, the employer will not be held liable. This is assuming the employer did not intentionally assist the employee in the fraud.

Scenario #4—Smuggled aliens.

I have saved the best for last. Every year the media have countless stories about aliens being smuggled into the U.S. Whether the story is about the desperation of aliens dying in our southwest desert, or the ruthlessness of alien smugglers, the stories have been ongoing for at least the last century. There does not seem to be an end in sight.

What would happen if the U.S. government concentrated more of its anti-smuggling resources on locating illegal aliens after they arrive for work, instead of always trying to stop organized smugglers at the border?

As an example, let's look at Chinese-alien smuggling. Most Chinese illegal migrants smuggled into the U.S. know exactly where they will be working before they ever leave China. The migrants pay upwards of $50,000 to get to the U.S. After their arrival, they begin an odyssey that closely resembles indentured servitude. Chinese-alien smuggling is one of the most sophisticated, highly organized criminal activities in the world. It is also impossible to stop because Chinese merchants around the world thrive on the system. So far, law enforcement agencies have not been able to take the financial rewards out of human trafficking from China.

Several years ago, the New York Office of the U.S. Immigration Service was faced with a Chinese-alien smuggling deadly crisis. A ship named the *Golden Venture* pulled into New York harbor carrying a load of smuggled Chinese migrants. When the word got to the ship that Immigration was going to search the vessel, aliens began diving into the water in New York Harbor. Several of the aliens drowned. Many others were arrested and incarcerated for months. Some of the ringleaders were prosecuted and sent to prison.

The *Golden Venture* prosecutions were considered a huge success by the U.S. Department of Justice and the U.S. Attorney's Office.

Consider these facts about the *Golden Venture* case, and you decide whether it was a success or not.

- The prosecution cost the U.S. government hundreds of thousands, if not millions, of dollars.
- A few people were convicted of serious crimes and sent to prison, costing the government even more money.
- Thousands of law enforcement staff hours were spent on the prosecution.
- Most of the smuggled aliens on the *Golden Venture* were kept in the U.S. as material witnesses and eventually given "green cards." (How about that for a deterrent effect?)
- New York politicians, liberals and conservatives alike, were given a great media opportunity to pontificate about how they were working to stop the scourge of Chinese-alien smuggling.
- Chinese-alien smugglers didn't even blink. Their massive, organized, worldwide exploits in human trafficking continue unabated to this day.

While I agree that immigration law enforcement officers must continue their efforts to prevent alien smuggling, I believe that new and alternative methods of enforcement must be considered.

If the Chinese merchants in New York had been required to use the Social Security Number Verification System, and law enforcement officials had an effective program of employer sanctions, there may have been a much more humane and effective way of handling the *Golden Venture* smuggling case.

New York and Federal law enforcement agents could have conducted surveillance on the ship and watched where the aliens were taken after arrival. Further surveillance would have divulged critical information about where the aliens were going, and more importantly, who was going to employ them.

Shortly after the *Golden Venture* migrants went to work, immigration agents, accompanied by other law enforcement officers, could have conducted a raid on the employers. The result would have been much different from what happened that fateful day in New York harbor.

- The employers would have been fined hundreds of thousands of dollars.
- The employers could have been arrested and convicted of conspiracy and sentenced to decades in jail, if it was determined they ordered the migrants from China. (This would have sent shock waves of fear through the Chinese-American merchant community, and Chinese employers who previously ordered illegal laborers from China would think twice about doing it again.)
- The illegal aliens would not have been able to remain in the U.S. They would have been deported to China, sending a strong deterrent signal to others desirous of working here illegally.
- The organized criminal alien smugglers in China (known as "snakeheads") would have lost millions of dollars and their human smuggling operation would have been significantly disrupted.

If Chinese-alien smugglers and Chinese-American employers (who order illegal migrants) continuously faced stiff fines from the U.S. government and local law enforcement, Chinese-alien smuggling to America would eventually become cost-prohibitive for all concerned.

I could construct many other scenarios, but the point has been made. By enforcing Social Security number verification, law enforcement could prevent the vast majority of illegal aliens from gaining employment in the U.S.

Computerized profiling and automated verifications

In my discussion about credit card fraud, I mentioned that financial institutions are getting much better at stopping credit card theft. This is primarily due to profiling by the bank's computer systems. It may be a dirty word for searching certain people at the airport, but profiling by a computer to detect fraud is perfectly acceptable.

In the case of the proposed Social Security Number Verification System, profiling will be the fear of every imposter. While the computer may be fooled into issuing a valid authorization code, it will also be programmed to look for suspicious verification patterns—like the same Social Security number being used in 11 states by 20 people within a week's time.

In this case, each employer would receive a follow-up notice or telephone call requesting further documentation from the employee. The person to whom the Social Security number was legitimately issued will have no difficulty proving it is his number. If the imposters are smart, they will pack up and leave—quickly.

Two other benefits are derived from locating imposters using computer-assisted profiling. A compromised Social Security number can be flagged as a problem number, and the rightful owner can be issued a secret personal identity number for future verifications. Once this happens, persons who attempt to fraudulently use these valid Social Security numbers will find themselves in a constant state of flight. Within minutes, they are located as imposters, fired, and forced to flee law enforcement. In addition, their purloined Social Security numbers and stolen identities become absolutely useless.

"Lack of political will" versus real solutions

I realize this will be a very controversial chapter. People who do not understand illegal immigration will probably call these proposed enforcement programs "overzealous" or a step toward a National I.D. program. Immigrant rights groups will fight to prevent the U.S. government from even trying them. Others will joke about "immigration cops with ticket books." I have heard it all before.

Every American who is concerned about these issues must require politicians to answer specific questions about immigration enforcement. Isn't it time to realistically reduce the jobs magnet that draws so many illegal aliens to America?

If we do not create an interior enforcement mechanism, like the one I have proposed, the result will simply be more illegal aliens, more social welfare and educational costs, and a lot less security. It is time we convince our representatives in Washington, D.C., that it is time to stem the tide. Instead of excuses about our "lack of political will," let's require our elected representatives to enact mandatory Social Security number verification and an effective employer sanctions program. Once these are in place, then Congress can consider their "guest worker" program, "Z-visas," "touchback," or whatever other "comprehensive immigration legislation" they desire. Or does America simply have to live with the fact that Congress does not have the capacity to legislate meaningful solutions to our growing immigration problems?

Chapter 14

Immigration Enforcement—State and Local Role

"Wet in public"

Personally, I had many experiences with illegal aliens, both as a police officer in South Tucson, Arizona, and as an INS Special Agent in Chicago and Washington, D.C. I have a pretty good idea of what local police officers think about the issue.

Most street cops want Immigration agents to do one thing when the police officer arrests a suspected illegal alien—take the alien off their hands and deport him. That way, they receive credit for "assisting another agency," and the Immigration officers are stuck with both the alien and the paperwork.

These arrests got so out of hand in Arlington County, Virginia, in the 1980s, cops termed the alien's crime as being "wet in public" (as in "wetback"). When things got a little slow on the midnight shift, Arlington County police officers would simply walk up to people they thought were illegal aliens (mostly from El Salvador), and ask them for their "green cards." If the aliens could not produce a card, the officers would arrest them, and call INS. The Arlington police officers did not have a clue as to what constituted a valid immigration status, yet they were literally enforcing Federal U.S. immigration law. In so doing, they violated the rights of many people who had legal status in the U.S. The officers finally stopped these arrests when INS became overwhelmed and ran out of money to pay for the detention of aliens who were determined to be illegally here.

Don't misunderstand my attitude toward state and local law enforcement. Police officials are certainly in favor of assisting other law enforcement agencies. However, in the case of immigration, most police agencies are hesitant to take on immigration enforcement responsibility because the Federal government consistently fails to hold up its end of the bargain. Just as it was 30 years ago, many times the new Immigration and Customs Enforcement agents advise local law enforcement they are either not interested or don't have the resources to detain and remove the aliens. Local police get frustrated and often see the Feds as irresponsible and arrogant.

The problems relating to enforcement of our immigration laws impact everything from small police agencies to the famous New York Police Department. One of the most powerful police organizations in America, the International Association of Chiefs of Police, has also had difficulty developing a definitive policy in this area. After the 9/11 attacks, the International Association of Chiefs of Police published a policy paper entitled, "Enforcing Immigration Law: The Role of State, Tribal and Local Law Enforcement. The document states, *"It is the IACP's belief that the question of state, tribal or local law enforcement's participation in immigration enforcement is an inherently local decision that must be made by a police chief, working with their elected officials, community leaders and citizens."*

After publishing the above policy paper, the International Association of Chiefs of Police was inundated with requests from their constituency to provide more specific information about how to deal with illegal immigrants. The IACP responded in July, 2007 with a comprehensive Project Response publication entitled "Police Chiefs Guide to Immigration Issues." While the document does not give specific instructions on how to enforce immigration laws, thankfully it discusses a wide variety of some very sensitive issues.

IACP President Joseph C. Carter states in his introductory letter, *"This Project Response document provides police chiefs with an overview of the issues surrounding immigration, both legal and illegal, provides background information on the current resources available to law enforcement, and examines the concerns and obstacles that currently surround the debate over immigration enforcement by the state, tribal and local law enforcement community."* If one could read "between the lines", it would probably say that the pamphlet was produced because illegal immigration is fast becoming a very significant issue for local law enforcement, no matter what the size of the agency. Police chiefs across America are looking for help and guidance.

One famous county law enforcement official is bucking the trend. Sheriff Joe Arpaio of Maricopa County, Arizona, has not left anyone guessing about his intentions when it comes to illegal aliens. "Sheriff Joe, the toughest sheriff in the West" (as he is affectionately called), has authorized his posse to arrest illegal aliens suspected of being smuggled into the country. He then locks them up in his famous "tent city" jails, while vociferously attacking the Federal government for not doing its job.

Sheriff Joe's initiatives have run into some court challenges, but that has not stopped him. He is pressing ahead with what he believes is right for Maricopa County, Arizona. Like him or not, state and local law enforcement officials across the U.S. are studying Joe's initiatives. Many police chiefs and sheriffs realize that they too may eventually be forced to deal with the complexities of enforcing our immigration laws.

Illegal immigration—A Federal problem with local impact

Controlling illegal immigration is a Federal responsibility mandated in the U.S. Constitution. The Department of Homeland Security website states, *"After certain states passed immigration laws following the Civil War, the Supreme Court in 1875 declared that regulation of immigration is a Federal responsibility."*

Unfortunately, the Federal government does not have the will or the capability to carry out this mandate, and the negative effects are being realized in our local communities. Hospitals are being forced to absorb billions of dollars in unpaid bills incurred by illegal immigrants, local school systems are required to educate their children, and crime and gang violence is on the rise in areas where large concentrations of illegal aliens live.

When it comes to law enforcement authority, there is no question as to who is responsible for managing illegal immigration. With few exceptions, the only law enforcement officers who have the authority to enforce immigration laws in the interior of the U.S. are Homeland Security's Immigration and Customs Enforcement Agents. Unfortunately these officers do not have the time or the desire to arrest, detain and deport illegal aliens who are simply working in the U.S.

A December, 2004, Department of Homeland Security Inspector General's report states:

> *"The Department of Homeland Security continues to face challenges in identifying, locating, detaining and removing aliens who have entered without inspection, violated the terms of their visas or committed criminal acts. The current illegal alien population in the United States is estimated to be 8–12 million. Immigration and Customs Enforcement (ICE), the agency responsible for removing the illegal alien population, continues to wage an uphill battle to address this problem. ICE is hampered in part by shortages of special agents."*

Is there anything local law enforcement can do to stop illegal aliens from flowing into their communities? At the present time, the answer is "no," but this may change in the very near future. Local communities are getting involved in immigration law enforcement, and pressure is building on the Federal government to work with state and local authorities on this issue.

Immigration enforcement training for state and local police

Homeland Security has initiated a fledgling immigration enforcement training program for local and state police. It is known by its legal reference name of "287(g) training." If police officials are sufficiently trained as Immigration officers, this could be a very successful program and serve as a significant "force multiplier" when Immigration and Customs Enforcement agents or the Border Patrol need extra manpower.

Current immigration law is extremely complex and the agencies responsible for immigration enforcement are now more dysfunctional than ever. Considering this current state of affairs, unless officers have had the required 287(g) training, it is prudent policy for state and local law enforcement officers to refrain from arresting and detaining individuals solely for violating our immigration laws.

In any future legislation, Congress should help local jurisdictions and specifically define the role of Federal, state and local law enforcement regarding illegal immigration. Until such a law is passed, most law enforcement officials are sadly aware that the responsibility to control immigration in the U.S. still rests solely with the Federal government—and the Federal government has failed miserably with this responsibility.

Changing immigration status—A law enforcement nightmare

Aside from training, there is another reason local and state law enforcement should not be involved in enforcing U.S. immigration law. An alien can be legally in the country one week, illegally here the next, and then back to having legal status again in a month or so.

If a person presents himself with a proper temporary nonimmigrant visa, he is inspected by an Immigration officer, who in turn allows the alien to enter the U.S. for a designated period of time. If the alien complies with the requirements of his visa, he is considered legally here. However, if the individual decides to violate his status either by taking a job without the U.S. government's permission or remaining beyond his legally authorized time (without getting an extension), the alien is then considered an illegal alien.

If an illegal alien files for political asylum (and they do it every day), there is a strong possibility that Homeland Security will be unable to handle the case in less than six months. Because of this ineptitude, the alien more often than not will be issued a document indicating that he is an applicant for asylum. The document will also grant employment authorization. Within a short time after filing for political asylum, an illegal alien becomes legal once again. These back and forth status changes are quite common in immigration law. While immigration enforcement officers are well aware that an alien's immigration status can change from one day to the next, other law enforcement officials find it difficult to understand.

This creates a huge problem for local, state and other Federal law enforcement officers. Since police are unaware of these possible changes in an alien's status, there is a possibility that some police officers could arrest a legal alien simply because they do not understand the complexities of immigration law.

Law enforcement officials, who are faced with a growing presence of illegal immigrants, should not feel that they must get involved in enforcing immigration laws. There is another possible solution.

Employer sanctions enforcement by local and state authorities

If the U.S. and state governments would utilize the proposed Social Security Number Verification System, local law enforcement would have a tremendous tool with which to combat alien smuggling and illegal immigration in its respective jurisdictions. City councils and police departments could work together and dedicate resources to enforce employee work verification at suspect work sites. This in turn would allow towns and municipalities to have better control over stopping illegal immigrants from settling in their communities without actually enforcing Federal immigration law.

Consider the following about the use of the Social Security Number Verification System as a law enforcement tool for local jurisdictions.

- Municipal, county and state law enforcement officers could use the system to fine employers who create the "jobs magnet" for illegal aliens.
- Law enforcement will need little training in the use of the system. All that is required is an audit of employer records.
- Employers would realize that the fines could be easily levied, and compliance would become the norm—much as it is with other regulatory and tax laws.
- In most cases, arrests would not be required and detention costs would be minimal.
- Revenue from fines would go to local jurisdictions to offset some of the hidden costs of having illegal aliens residing in a community.
- Immigration authorities would have a significant "force multiplier" without having to spend millions of dollars for immigration law enforcement hiring and training.

This is not a new concept. Consider the current drug laws in the U.S. The Federal government has laws against illicit narcotics, and Federal agents enforce these laws. In addition, state laws make possession and distribution of illicit narcotics a state offense. When the Federal government does not have the manpower to stop drug dealers in a particular area, local laws allow municipal and state police to conduct their own investigation, and arrest and incarcerate the criminals. When necessary, Federal, state and local police work together in task forces to break up large drug rings.

Why can't this be done with immigration enforcement in the interior of the U.S? If the proposed Social Security Number Verification System is put in place, states could pass their own legislation mandating the use of the Social Security Number Verification System. After all, most states have their own income tax, and the main identifier used for collecting state income tax is the Social Security number.

State and local law enforcement officers could use citations to fine and prosecute non-compliant employers. Within a very short period of time—say two years—we would have illegal immigration under control.

Could this really be so effective? Consider our income tax laws, and part of the answer will be evident. Just as most people pay their income taxes, willfully but begrudgingly, most employers will comply and verify their employees' Social Security numbers.

When an employer is evidently non-compliant, not only Federal agents, but also state and local law enforcement would have a very powerful tool. In many cases, officers from all levels of law enforcement could simply review a "suspect" employer's documentation, and issue a summons for failure to comply with the verification requirements. Jurisdictions that did not want illegal immigrants in their cities and towns could work with their business communities and eliminate the employment magnet. The vast majority of illegal aliens looking for work would look somewhere else.

In most jurisdictions eliminating the employment magnet will eliminate most of the illegal alien population. However, if local law enforcement officials decide they have problems with criminal aliens, they can also participate in the 287(g) training program and work with Immigration and Customs Enforcement on more serious crime related problems.

Chapter 15
The E-Passport

The Malaysian E-Passport

Just before I retired from the INS, I was lucky enough to work on a project involving the Malaysian passport. That's right, Malaysia!

In March, 1999, the Malaysian government introduced the first "E-Passport" (electronically readable passport) in the world. To say the least, it was unbelievable. Imbedded in the back cover of each new passport was a radio frequency identification (RFID) microchip with encrypted data relating to the holder of the document. Simply stated, this means it is virtually impossible to fraudulently change the data on the "face page," and then attempt to use it anywhere that the passport readers are deployed.

The Malaysian government had contracted with IRIS Technologies to build the E-Passport, as well as an airport Autogate system (described below). At the new Kuala Lumpur International Airport, foreign passengers are treated to a sight that few have ever seen before. Malaysian citizens with their E-Passports approach an entry gate that resembles that of a New York subway. Passengers place their passport on a reader and place a designated finger on an automated fingerprint reader. Within seconds, the system compares the biometric and biographic information of the passenger with the information on the passport's chip. If there is no further reason to question the passenger, the gate opens and the traveler proceeds to the baggage claim area. Malaysian citizens returning home are virtually

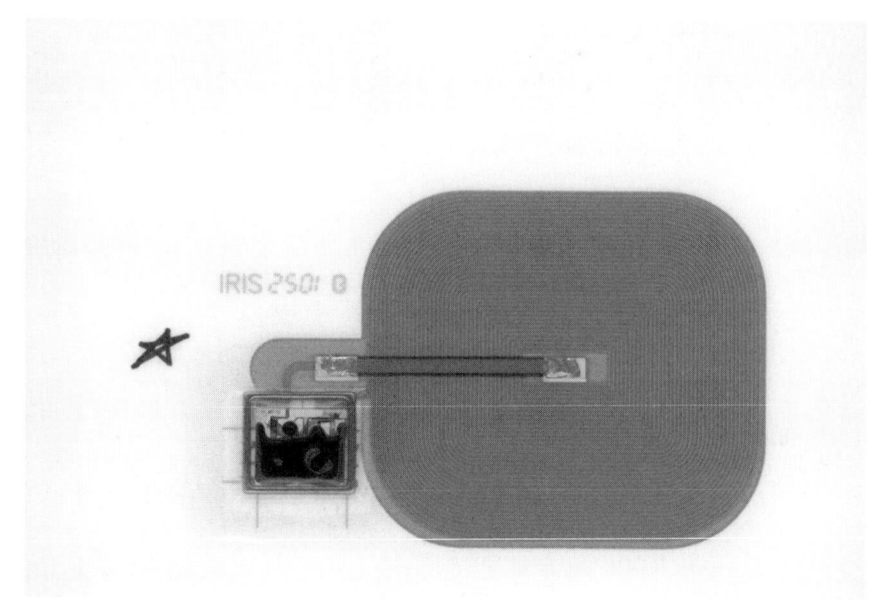

RFID microchip and antenna hidden inside back cover of original Malaysian E-Passport.

"inspected" using automation. Compared to the U.S INSpass Program, the Malaysians are light years ahead of us.

I first learned about the Malaysian passport from the INS Forensic Document Laboratory in McLean, Virginia. Several INS airport inspectors had submitted intelligence reports indicating that there was a strange "bump" in the back cover of new Malaysian passports. As the supervisory Special Agent in charge of Overseas Enforcement, I was asked to contact both the Malaysian government and IRIS Technologies to find out exactly what was in the passport.

When I arrived in Malaysia, I was given the "keys to the castle." The Malaysians were very proud of what they had developed and willing to share their successes with the U.S. The Malaysian immigration authorities, in cooperation with IRIS Technologies, allowed us to purchase some 20 readers for U.S. ports of entry so that we could test their system.

Within days after placing the readers at selected airports, INS inspectors apprehended imposters using photo-substituted

Never a line at the "Autogates" at Kuala Lumpur International Airport, Malaysia.

Neville Cramer, IRIS directors Chas Yap, Dato Tan Say Jim, and Tony "Gizmo" Lee.

Malaysian passports. In Chicago, Honolulu and Los Angeles, Chinese and Singaporean aliens using forged Malaysian passports attempted to pass through U.S. immigration. As soon as the passports were placed on the readers, they indicated that the holder of the document was not the person to whom it was originally issued. I received calls from several INS inspectors asking me why the U.S. did not immediately consider implementing such a system.

The E-Passport field test at actual immigration ports had been a huge success. Or so I thought.

Typically in INS, whenever an idea or product was presented that would truly help the agency control immigration, it immediately met its demise. Need I say more? In December, 2000, I was advised that the Malaysian E-Passport test program was finished, and the U.S. government had no further interest in E-Passports.

That was until we were attacked on September 11, 2001. Within months, there was renewed interest and Uncle Sam did an about-face. The Enhanced Border Security and Visa Entry Reform Act of 2002, now requires all visa-waiver countries to have passports that contain machine-readable biometric identifiers. In other words, they must contain smart chips identical to the Malaysian passport.

In a press release on August 10, 2004, the State Department issued the following statement;

> *"Although the addition of biometrics to the U.S. Passport is not covered by the Enhanced Border Security and Visa Entry Reform Act, the Department of State has been working diligently towards developing U.S. biometric passports. The United States recognizes the benefits of biometric identity verification and strives to remain at the forefront of international travel document security. By the end of 2005, all domestically produced passports will be biometric passports."*

Our State Department is being a little less than truthful (the first time ever, I promise). The U.S. is not in the "forefront of international travel document security." As I demonstrated in Chapter 8, anyone who can read an old newspaper and fill out a form can still fraudulently obtain a U.S. passport. In 2007, the State Department finally began moving forward with the introduction of America's E-Passport—eight years after the Malaysians first introduced it.

How about this for stupidity? One of the greatest proven security aspects of the E-Passport is the ability of Immigration officials to compare fingerprints on the chip to the fingerprints of the bearer. Guess what? The U.S. government decided in 2006, not to include any fingerprints on the chip in our new E-Passports. The only "biometric" on the chip is a digitized photograph. In other words, the most effective biometric security feature is not even being used.

Aside from being several years behind the Malaysians, another slight problem has arisen. Inventor Mr. Chas Yap (of IRIS Technologies Corporation) holds two U.S patents related to the E-Passport process. IRIS Technologies Corporation has also produced more than five million E-Passports currently in circulation, as well as readers to properly decipher the information embedded on the radio frequency identification (RFID) chips. Nevertheless, our government selected other companies to produce the U.S. version. Some people have suggested that this was done because Malaysia is a foreign country and something as important as our passports should be produced in the U.S. Wrong! The inlays that hold the chip for the U.S. passport are currently produced by Smartrac Technology Ltd., Phra Nakhon Si Ayutthaya 13160, Thailand. No one seems to know why Smartrac was selected. (They also have no known "track record" in producing E-Passports, but this apparently never came into question.) Considering the U.S. government's cavalier attitude toward the E-Passport, it should not surprise anyone if the entire system fails.

The U.S. Justice Department also seems to feel it has the legal right to test and then utilize technology invented by someone else, even in violation of U.S. patents. In a letter from the Justice Department, dated January 14, 2003, INS Assistant

Commissioner Michael D. Cronin wrote to IRIS Technologies, *"We very much appreciate your support and assistance during our evaluation of the Malaysian 'smart passport' technology since 2000. As the INS transitions into the new Department of Homeland Security, we will bring with us the lessons learned with this pilot program. These experiences will help us to advocate for improved biometric technologies as the new organization determines appropriate uses for the many, varied methods available for using biometric identification capabilities in modern travel documents."* The Malaysians invented and patented the E-Passport. The U.S. government now uses exactly the same thing and has never given the inventors proper remuneration or recognition. Could it be because they are Malaysians?

Without question, the E-Passport is one of the finest travel-document inventions to come along in decades. It is an understatement to say that Chas Yap and IRIS Technologies have not been given the credit they deserve. Even the technology world does not have their facts straight. Kevin Woodward, associate editor of *Card Technology* magazine wrote a May, 2006, article entitled, "Behind the scenes in International Civil Aviation Organization (ICAO)—New Technologies Working Group (NTWG) wins award for designing the ePassport." The article states, *"Gary McDonald, chairman of the working group, says the award should be shared with an International Organization for Standardization committee that has worked closely with the ICAO group on the technical elements for ePassports."* The article never mentions who patented E-Passports and does not credit either Malaysia or IRIS Technologies for leading the world in inventing this technology.

It appears that Mr. Yap and IRIS Technology's proprietary rights have been seriously violated. As will often happen when one company seemingly uses another company's secrets, the lawyers get involved. In December, 2006, respected New York patent attorney Stephen N. Weiss of the law firm Moses and Singer, LLP (on behalf of IRIS Technologies and Mr. Yap) filed suit against Uncle Sam in the U.S. Court of Federal Claims. After all, Mr. Yap's patents were issued by the U.S. Patent Office. Whatever the outcome of the lawsuit, it certainly indicates that our government is just as capable of buying pirated material as any other country or company in the world.

Revolutionizing immigration inspections

International airlines with flights to the U.S. currently participate in a program titled Advanced Passenger Information System. Passenger manifests for most U.S.-bound flights are forwarded electronically to U.S. Customs and Border Protection. Checks are conducted on the passengers while the flight is heading for the U.S. Considering what could be done with the E-Passport, the Advanced Passenger Information System is antiquated already.

Eventually the U.S. and the rest of world could all have electronic passports, and the technology will revolutionize world travel and immigration enforcement. While I am not going to bore you with an elaborate description of the technical aspects of the E-Passport, it is important to know that the bearer's photo, fingerprints and biographical information can be embedded on the silicon chip. The chip has a "write-only-once" space that makes it almost impossible to change the data once it is encoded on the chip.

E-Passports are read with special readers. The readers send a sophisticated message to the chip and it responds by sending the data to the computer screen. If someone has changed a photo, or even a date of birth, it is immediately shown on the monitor screen. Furthermore, the data from the chip can be stored for future access. The transaction creates a permanent record of entry into the country, including biographic and biometric data. It is truly a revolutionary advancement, especially to someone who has worked for years with passports and visas.

When I first demonstrated this to the Bush Administration in September, 2002, I had a little difficulty explaining the advantages to a 23-year-old White House staffer who had an answer for everything. After seeing the demonstration of the E-Passport, he told me the entire process was useless. He said, "I could destroy the chip by placing the passport in a microwave oven."

I told him he was absolutely right. However, if destroying the chip and bringing the wrath of God upon himself after a 10-hour flight was his idea of a fun time, he should be living in St. Elizabeth's Mental Hospital instead of working at the White House. I also told him he did not have to waste the electricity of the microwave. All he had to do was cut his passport in four pieces and he would accomplish the same thing.

The fact is, the last thing imposters and terrorists want to do is draw attention to their documents. They want a passport that looks good, feels good and allows them to travel around the world unabated. It won't happen with an E-Passport.

And for all of you *24* and Tom Clancy fans who have already conjured up that the intelligence techies will just create a new chip, forget it. The biometric data will also be stored in a database, and once a person's biometrics have been received and recorded, it will be virtually impossible for a person to change their recorded identity without changing the information on the chip and in the database. Take my word for it, the average alien smuggler, criminal, drug dealer or terrorist should start worrying about E-Passports.

For those of us who are not interested in traveling around the world as someone else, and who just want to get through immigration as fast as possible, there is great news. If the U.S. government uses the E-Passport the way it is intended, most U.S. citizens returning home may never have to talk to an Immigration inspector again.

Consider this scenario. At the time of check-in for a U.S.-bound international flight, a traveler's E-Passport is first read at the check-in counter. The information (including the passenger's photograph, fingerprints and biographic data) is forwarded to U.S. immigration authorities at the flight's intended destination. The data is automatically checked against terrorist watch lists, as these initial checks should be done immediately—even before passengers arrive at the departure gate.

For further security, the E-Passport could be read again before the passenger is allowed to enter the boarding area. During the time of the flight to the U.S., Customs and Border Protection will have hours to check the passengers against all sorts of databases. If the passengers are checked and the U.S. government has no need to speak with them, their names would be so designated in a special "cleared entry" database. Instead of waiting in line to have an inspector stamp the passport and say "welcome home," passengers would be directed to use an Autogate.

Returning U.S. citizens would place their E-Passport on the Autogate reader, look into a camera and place a designated finger or fingers on the reader. When the gate opens (if the passenger has been cleared), they proceed through to baggage claim. The reader would match biometric data, as well as biographic data that was first obtained when the passenger checked-in for the flight. Of course, if the Autogate does not open, the passenger probably has a small issue to clear up—like six felony arrest warrants for child molestation.

Here are the possible benefits of this system.

- U.S. Customs and Border Protection will have hours to check biometric as well as biographic information on arriving passengers.
- There will be an electronic record created for all entries into the U.S., including flight information and other pertinent data.
- No one will be able to board an aircraft, destroy their travel document, and claim they did not have one (a common practice used today).
- U.S. citizens will no longer wait in line when returning to the U.S.
- U.S. Customs and Border Protection can concentrate on more critical initiatives—like stopping terrorists from entering the U.S.

The U.S. government has been aware of the huge security benefits and other advantages of the E-Passport for many years. The State Department has now finally decided to move forward on this project. However, by not requiring fingerprints to be captured and placed on the U.S. passport's chip, they are making a huge, irreversible blunder. Passports are issued for ten years, so all E-Passports issued now will be useless for another decade for fingerprint verification. It is difficult to understand how so many brilliant people work in our State Department, yet their policy decisions about the E-Passport have been so shortsighted.

Chapter 16
Identity Documents—Do We Really Need a National I.D.?

A National Birth Certificate

Americans can argue all they want about the necessity for a National I.D. card. The first thing we need to develop is a National Birth Certificate issued by the U.S. government. The Department of Health and Human Services should be responsible for issuing the document (immediately after birth), and a National Birth Certificate should be the only method by which a citizen born in the U.S. can obtain a Social Security number. In addition, digitized fingerprints must eventually be made part of the automated national birth record database.

Some of the many benefits of a National Birth Certificate are listed below.

- Birth and death records could be easily matched;
- Documentation used to obtain U.S. government employment or benefits would be greatly simplified (military enlistment, security clearances, passports, welfare, student loans, etc.);
- Identity theft would be significantly reduced;
- Establishing "multiple identities" in the U.S. by using other people's birth certificates would be very difficult.

Am I advocating more bureaucracy? You bet. We are now a nation of more than 300 million people. Law enforcement officials will readily admit that identity theft and people using false identities are a huge concern in our fight against terrorism. The 9/11 Commission recommended that Congress also set standards for birth certificates. However, let's hope our representatives in Congress do a lot more than tell state and local governments what color paper to use for their documents.

And speaking about local governments, they are the main reason we do not have a National Birth Certificate. Somewhere along the way local governments were given the right to issue birth certificates, and localities do not want to give up the revenue gained by issuing them.

As with most problems of this kind, Congress will probably not take any affirmative action. It would be 20 years before Americans would realize the benefits of a National Birth Certificate. For most of our politicians, planning ahead that far is completely out of the box.

Who will pay for the National Birth Certificate? Mom and Dad, that's who. I have asked hundreds of U.S. citizens who recently had a child if they would be willing to pay for a U.S. government issued birth certificate which is more secure and very difficult to counterfeit. Not one single person said they were unwilling to pay.

Immigration documents

The two most widely known and accepted immigration documents are the Resident Alien Card ("green card") and the Employment Authorization Document. Aliens in the U.S. apply for these documents for a myriad of reasons. These documents are all produced at one or two locations, and it now takes up to one year for Citizenship and Immigration Services to create them and deliver them successfully to waiting immigrants.

Twenty years ago, this centralized issuance process seemed like a great idea. Corruption was growing within the INS. Some employees realized they could make a lot of money creating legitimate "green cards" for illegal aliens, since the process of making the cards was delegated to each INS local office. There were very few audits done by outside inspectors and the material to make the cards was readily available to most of the INS examiners. Oversight of the card issuance process was virtually nonexistent.

Unfortunately, when INS centralized "green card" production, they failed to consider several enforcement-related issues, and now the process is completely dysfunctional. For example, employers are required to ask for certain immigration documents from aliens in order to properly complete the Form I-9. At the same time, Citizenship and Immigration Service is telling legal aliens (those who are authorized to work) that they must wait months for their legal documents to be issued. (Interim documents issued by Citizenship and Immigration Services are paper-based and very susceptible to counterfeiting.) The entire process of properly documenting legal aliens is a disaster.

The solution is simple. Go back to the old days. Great advances have been made in card security technology. Agencies can locally produce high quality, counterfeit-resistant electronically verifiable documents. These secure cards could be issued at local INS offices and ports of entry. Shortly after an alien completes his or her application for their "green card," they could be issued a secure U.S. government document.

I admit that there must be significant firewalls put in place to prevent corruption at the issuance locations. However, security experts who handle these issues claim they have developed methods to prevent a single employee from issuing documents either erroneously or when conspiring with other employees.

There is currently a massive security loophole that was created by having aliens wait months for their actual immigration documents. Homeland Security is yet to devise a more secure interim document. Considering the advances made in document issuance security, maybe it is time for Homeland Security to begin issuing a secure and verifiable Employment Authorization Card and/or the "green card" from offices and ports of entry around the country.

The myriad of other immigration documents

Aside from the infamous "green card" and the Employment Authorization Document, illegal aliens have a virtual arsenal of documents to counterfeit and use in America. Homeland Security issues all sorts of rubber-stamped I-94 Arrival/Departure Records to indicate that an alien has authorization to work in the U.S. If the counterfeiters are foiled creating one card they simply try another one.

The Department of Homeland Security should simplify alien documentation—especially when it comes to documents that authorize aliens to work. The following two documents should be the only acceptable forms of proof that an alien has been granted employment authorization in the U.S.:

1. The Resident Alien Card ("green card");
2. The Employment Authorization Document.

It doesn't matter if an alien is applying for a driver's license or getting a job. These documents should be the only acceptable forms of identification. Furthermore, these documents should all be verifiable by automation.

Automated document verification instead of a National I.D. card

At the present time, we do not need a National I.D. card, and there is nothing in this book that proposes or advocates that we create such a system. Some of the same people who advocate this as a solution to illegal immigration are also marching around proposing that we completely close our borders and stop all immigration to America.

There are many other programs that can be implemented before we make such a drastic change to our lifestyle. I am far from a supporter of the American Civil Liberties Union, but every now and then they are right. In the case of the National I.D.

card, they raise crucial and important questions. If we require everyone to carry the card at all times, I have no doubt the system will be abused. Databases will have to be established, and no matter how many safeguards are put in place, some officials will find a way to misuse the data and collect intrusive and unnecessary intelligence on law-abiding U.S. citizens.

The U.S. Supreme Court has recently said that police officers have the right to ascertain the identity of any person they come in contact with, even if the suspect's name turns out to be incriminating. Considering this decision, if we had a National I.D. card, the Supreme Court would certainly uphold a requirement that it be presented to a police officer on demand. This is what every American should fear.

On the other hand, automated document verification is a critical component to reducing illegal immigration and enhancing our national security. Improved verification systems using emerging technologies could prevent the usage of many types of counterfeit documents. The advances will not only add a valuable tool in the fight against illegal immigration, they will undoubtedly make America a much safer place to live.

Chapter 17
Domestic and Foreign Immigration Intelligence

Domestic intelligence—Infiltrating alien gangs, terrorists cells, and criminal alien organizations

FBI agents continue to be the leaders in the fight against domestic crime and terrorism. In an attempt to prevent another 9/11, other U.S. law enforcement and intelligence agencies have been rapidly expanding their domestic information-gathering capabilities. The passage of the Patriot Act and the creation of the Homeland Security Department signaled this new era for America. It is my hope that Immigration and Customs Enforcement Special Agents will also be used more aggressively in the fight against alien-sponsored terrorism and criminal alien organizations. Their expertise and unique authority has been overlooked for many years, and could be utilized to thwart future terrorist acts against America. Part of the following chapter outlines some of these unique immigration-related enforcement programs that should be considered for widespread use throughout the U.S. and the world.

Criminal illegal aliens: No data-no proof

Believe it or not, very few studies have conclusively linked illegal immigration to an increase in crime. While it has long been suspected that illegal aliens are involved in a higher percentage of crimes than the rest of the U.S. population, it has never been proven using reliable data.

There are two major reasons. First, anyone who even suggests conducting such a study is immediately viewed as racist, xenophobic, mean spirited, and of course, un-American. The second reason is a lot simpler. Alien status is not a statistic that most law enforcement organizations understand or report.

Crime statistics are gathered throughout the U.S. using a long standing and sophisticated system known as the Uniform Crime Reporting Program. The FBI website says, *"The Uniform Crime Reporting Program was conceived in 1929 by the International Association of Chiefs of Police to meet a need for reliable, uniform crime statistics for the nation."* Approximately 17,000 law enforcement agencies use the Uniform Crime Reporting system, and it is overseen by the FBI.

There is very little in the Uniform Crime Report relating to immigration status, whether it is about victims, suspects or convicts. In all my years of service with the Border Patrol and the INS, I was never asked by another law enforcement officer to determine an alien's status for the sake of correctly reporting it in the Uniform Crime Report.

Immigration-related Uniform Crime Report statistics are usually supplied by the U.S. Border Patrol. Other than information about the apprehensions made along our borders, there is little else. Since most local and state law enforcement officers cannot legally determine if someone is an illegal alien, the nexus between criminality and immigration status is almost never made. Immigrant advocacy groups have long known about this vacuum of data, and they use it to their advantage. Without statistics, no one can say with certainty that illegal aliens cause an increase in crime.

Due to increased interest from Congress and the public, the Federal Bureau of Investigation has recently added some new statistical categories regarding illegal aliens and crime. Immigration advocates are not happy with the results. Some groups have gone so far as to claim the statistics are racist and falsely reported by a U.S. law enforcement community that is anti-

Hispanic. Nevertheless, reports are being circulated based on the FBI's most recent statistics. They show that illegal aliens are apparently involved in much more criminal activity than previously reported.

www.immigrationshumancost.org

I have said before, statistics are not my thing. However, I do love facts. During the last several years (while the law enforcement community slowly began to collect crime statistics related to illegal immigrants), some private organizations were feverishly compiling story after story on their websites. One such group created www.immigrationshumancost.org. This website was brought to my attention while researching the killing of Phoenix Police Officer Nick Erfle.

On September 18, 2007, Erik Martinez, an illegal alien from Mexico, was stopped by Erfle for jaywalking. Erfle started to arrest Martinez because the suspect used a fictitious name. Before the officer could complete the arrest, Martinez pulled a gun and killed the officer. (Erfle had twice survived cancer and left a wife and two young children.)

As horrific as this crime may seem, Erfle is just one in a long line of law enforcement officers murdered by illegal aliens. Some of those killed include Houston (Texas) Police Officer Rodney Johnson, U.S. Park Ranger Kris Eggle, Los Angeles County (California) Sheriff's Deputy David March, Oregon State Trooper Bret Clodfelter, Detroit (Michigan) Police Officer Sheila Herring, Phoenix (Arizona) Police Officer Marc Atkinson, Doraville (Georgia) Police Officer Hugo Arango, Phoenix (Arizona) Police Officer Kenneth Collings, and Oceanside (California) Police Officer Tony Zeppetella. The list goes on and on and on.

In addition to listing the law enforcement officers killed, the website anecdotally tells of dozens of other victims who have been killed or seriously injured at the hands of illegal aliens.

It is unfair to use this information and claim that <u>all</u> illegal aliens are serious criminals. It is a fact however, as this incredible website demonstrates, illegal aliens have been involved in an unusually high number of violent crimes.

The "illegal" mentality

I observed an interesting trend about criminals in my 30 years in municipal and Federal law enforcement. I refer to it as the "illegal mentality," and it is the same among immigrants as it is among U.S. citizens. If a person is caught committing one of their first criminal acts, and *significantly* punished, they frequently develop an immediate respect for our criminal justice system. On the other hand, if a person is allowed to commit crime after crime with impunity, they usually have no respect for law enforcement and find few reasons to stop their criminal activity.

Millions of immigrants initially enter the U.S illegally or violate their immigration status once here. When this is done on a large scale, and with impunity, aliens lose both respect and fear of U.S. Immigration officers. And, if they don't fear deportation, why should they fear any law enforcement?

I believe the "illegal mentality" is evident in many immigrant communities. Here is one of my favorite examples.

Nigerians—Migrants from "the rogue nation"

Nigerians who come to the U.S. have every reason to think our justice system is a joke. An inordinate number of these West Africans are involved in every conceivable kind of financial and drug-related crime known to mankind, and some we have never even heard about. This is not racism on my part. Secretary of State Colin Powell once referred to Nigeria as "the rogue nation."

Many Nigerians come to the U.S. as foreign students. They attend school for a semester or two, and then turn to fraud, financial crime, and drug dealing as a means of support.

As examples, if you have not received an email requesting a four-million-dollar investment in a "very special deal" in Nigeria, you probably do not own a computer. New York City street cor-

Main Identity

From: <roseobaseki1@terra.es>
Sent: Wednesday, July 11, 2007 6:57 AM
Subject: [Norton AntiSpam] Urgent Payment Notification

PRESIDENCY
OFFICE OF THE PAYMASTER GENERAL
FEDERAL REPUBLIC OF NIGERIA

From: Mrs Rose Obaseki
Secretary to the Government
on Foreign payment Matters

Attn: Honourable Beneficiary

Date:11TH JULY 2007

Our ref:FGN/OPG-0607/0221

Dear Sir/Madam

Irrevocable Payment Release Order

Sequel to the meeting held on Friday the 6TH day of July 2007,between the Federal Executive Council of the Federal Republic of Nigeria,Chief Justice of the Federation,Finance Minister,Governor of the Central Bank of Nigeria and the management of the FIRST INLAND BANK NIG.PLC,this office has been mandated to issue out this notice to all our numerous contractors and fund inheritors that did not receive their payment from our past administrators.

However,from the Records of outstanding Contractors/Fund Inheritors due for payment with the Federal Government of Nigeria, your Name and Company was discovered as next on the list of the outstanding Contractors who have not yet received their payments.

I wish to inform you now that the square peg is now in square hole and your payment has been processed and will be released to you as soon as you respond to this letter.

Also note that from the record in my file, your outstanding Payment is US$10,700,000.00 (Ten Million And Seven Hundred Thousand United States Dollars).

Kindly re-confirm to me the followings:

Your Full Name: ______________________

Your Complete Address (Physical Address with Zip Code not P.O.BOX) : ______________________

An e-mail from "the rogue nation of Nigeria."

ners are filled with Nigerians and other West Africans selling counterfeit everything. In 2007, CNN's Special Investigations Unit produced a documentary entitled, *How to Rob a Bank,* and the main thieves responsible for the multi-million dollar rip-off were Nigerians. And if I am supposed to be impressed with one or two NBA basketball players, I am not. For every Hakeem Abdul Olajuwon, I believe there are 10,000 Nigerian fraudsters living and practicing their trade in America.

My favorite Nigerian was "Nathan." Somehow, he and his wife obtained student visas to come to the U.S. and study at a small private university in southwest Virginia.

Nathan's problems started when he ran out of money and found his wife in bed with another man. Within days of his misfortune, Nathan decided that fraud and violence were better than college, so he quit school and attempted to cut off his wife's arms with a dull hatchet.

Since Nathan also needed money, he decided to sell cassette tapes. Instead of buying music from a wholesaler and then reselling it, Nathan found a faster and cheaper way. He ordered several hundred cassette tapes through the mail from unsuspecting companies like Columbia House in Terre Haute, Indiana. He simply used several different names and five of his neighbor's addresses, and sent away for 3,000 tapes at the discount price of "Buy 15 tapes for only $1."

Shortly after Nathan's assault on his wife, he was arrested by the Virginia State Police. When I showed up a few days later and told them Nathan would probably be deported, the prosecutor reduced the charges and released Nathan to my custody. The State of Virginia could not wait to get rid of him.

Before returning to D.C, I took Nathan to his apartment to get his belongings. It was a sight to see. His bedroom was filled floor to ceiling with boxes of brand new cassette tapes. There was hardly room for a bed. He also showed me his spare axe, in case he encountered another act of infidelity.

During the four-hour ride back to the Washington District Office, I stopped at a Wendy's just off Interstate 81 and bought Nathan a cheeseburger, a Biggie French Fry and a Frosty. While eating his lunch, Nathan confided with me about the Nigerian mindset. He explained that growing up as a youngster in the streets of Lagos, he had to lie, steal, and con his way through life just to get enough to eat. He became so good at lying and cheating, he was able to convince the consular officials at the American Embassy to issue him a student visa. The fact that he did not have 10 cents to his name never seemed to matter to anyone at the Embassy. (Remember, it was Nigeria—a supplier of some of the finest crude oil in the world.)

As soon as Nathan received his visa, he was advised by Nigerian friends to attend a two-week school to learn about life in America. The school, however, was not about democracy, and the red, white and blue. He was taught how to create multiple identities, write fraudulent checks, smuggle narcotics, and a whole host of other ways to illegally make money in the U.S. He was also taught that our justice system was a joke. He told me he never worried about being arrested because jails in the U.S. were like hotels, and if he was deported he would just create another identity and return. (My sources tell me that, to this day, such schools still operate openly in Lagos, Nigeria.)

One week after I arrived back in D.C., Nathan was brought in front of Immigration Judge John Gossart. As a last act of desperation, he told Judge Gossart that it was all a conspiracy against him. He claimed he was not really Nathan, and that I had arrested the wrong man.

After two hours of listening to Nathan's nonsense, Gossart had heard enough and ordered him deported from the U.S. Was that the end of Nathan? Not by a long shot.

Approximately six months later, I received a phone call from an Immigration inspector at Boston's Logan International Airport. He asked me if I remembered Nathan. When I told him I did, he related to me his experience.

"Akim" had apparently entered the U.S. a few weeks after he was deported as "Nathan." At Logan Airport, the Immigration inspector did not know anything about the deportation, but thought something was suspicious. He fingerprinted Akim, and completed an intelligence report. Due to the fact that Akim's visa appeared to be properly issued by the State Department, and no other detrimental evidence was immediately available, the inspector had no choice but to allow him to enter the U.S. His fingerprints, however, were forwarded to the FBI.

Some two months after Akim entered the U.S., the FBI Fingerprint Division returned the fingerprint classification results to Logan Airport Immigration. It indicated that Akim's prints were an identical match to those of Nathan taken by the Virginia State Police and the Washington INS Office. The Immigration inspector at Logan immediately forwarded me a copy of his original intelligence report.

How did this guy re-enter so quickly? After Nathan was deported to Nigeria, he did exactly what he said he would do. He obtained a new passport with a completely different name and date of birth. For a mere $25.00, Nathan became Akim. This time around, the U.S. Embassy issued him a non-immigrant H-visa as a medical doctor destined to a job in Georgia.

I called the hospital in Atlanta that had filed the petition for Akim. They advised me that a Nigerian security guard had obtained the visa for Akim (and several others) using stolen hospital stationery. None of them was still employed, and their whereabouts were unknown.

As a last resort, I called the INS Investigations Division in Atlanta. The Special Agents told me they had no information about Akim or Nathan. And, since they had only three agents to cover Georgia, South Carolina and North Carolina, they were not about to start looking for him. I am certain to this day, Dr. Akim is out there somewhere—hopefully not using his hatchet in some operating room.

Nathan is just one of thousands of Nigerians in the U.S., and he is not an anomaly. U.S. law enforcement has tried for decades to combat the Nigerian crime wave, but success has been limited, to say the least. They are masters at creating multiple identities, drug smuggling, writing fraudulent checks, creating lawsuits from staged accidents, and basically taking advantage of every loophole in our system.

The U.S. is not the only place that Nigerians thrive. They are a worldwide menace, and they seem to be everywhere. Everywhere, except Singapore! In June, 2004, I visited the island state and asked Singaporean Immigration officials if they had a problem with Nigerians. Their answer was "no," plain and simple. They smiled and told me that Nigerian criminals don't like Singapore. The fact that they might be caned 10 times for theft and executed by hanging for drug smuggling seems to be a deterrent.

I could write another whole book about Nigerian crimes. America is like one of their candy stores. They come and go as they please, they take what they want, and they fear no one. Suffice it to say Nigerians are the epitome of the "illegal mentality."

A lot more vigilance at home and abroad

While I have given examples that there is a disproportionate number of Nigerians in the U.S. involved in one sort of criminal activity or another, I certainly do not advocate deporting all Nigerians. I do believe, however, it is about time America realizes that not everyone in the world is coming here seeking a better way of life.

When U.S. law enforcement develops credible and actionable information that certain nationalities are more prone to criminal activity or terrorism, we must not be afraid to openly treat persons from these countries in a more restrictive manner—both prior to and after their arrival in the U.S.

Visa applications for the U.S. from high-risk countries must be closely scrutinized, and applicants must submit not only biographic information, but also biometric data including fingerprints, photographs, and even iris scans. Since the 9/11 attacks, some security programs have improved, but they are far from sufficient.

I suggest that Homeland Security devise a system that requires high-risk aliens coming to the U.S. post surety bonds. We must also require them to properly maintain their status, and if necessary, continuously notify the U.S. government of their whereabouts and activities. And, should the necessity arise, under due process of law, these high-risk aliens must be deported swiftly and without hesitation. I realize Homeland Security has already begun some of these initiatives to combat terrorism. However, this vigilance should be expanded to include countries that export their organized criminals, alien smugglers and drug dealers to the U.S.

Believe it or not, one of the biggest opponents to increased vigilance is our own State Department. In the name of diplomacy, they fought against allowing even the most reasonable law enforcement functions inside the walls of their sacred embassies.

I had many sordid experiences with our State Department. As an example, just after I arrived in 1996, as the supervisory Special Agent in charge of the INS Overseas Enforcement Unit, I was tasked by my supervisor John Cummings to respond to a request from the Office of Management and Budget. They wanted to know what new programs could be implemented overseas that would truly help INS law enforcement. They gave me 24 hours to respond.

I quickly put together a memorandum that described two new initiatives: (1) placing seasoned INS inspectors from our international airports at high-risk U.S. Embassies to assist with visa processing, and; (2) placing fingerprint readers in the U.S. Embassy in Nigeria to capture at least two designated fingerprints from all persons applying for a visa.

I discussed these proposals with my subordinate Agents, and they agreed that the suggestions would significantly help INS enforcement initiatives both domestically and overseas.

Much to my surprise, the suggestion created interest at INS Headquarters and at the Office of Management and Budget. Thus, the memo was sent to the State Department for comment. Needless to say, my suggestions were not well received.

The State Department refused to consider having Immigration inspectors assist consular officers anywhere in the world. They firmly believed that the visa issuance process was working quite well, and they definitely did not need anyone from the lowly INS looking over their shoulders. (So what if a few gang leaders, alien smugglers, organized crime figures and terrorists were getting visas.)

But it was the Nigerian suggestion that resulted in the best response. The thought of actually collecting useful information like fingerprints, put the diplomats in the U.S. Embassy in Lagos into a tailspin. Within days of receiving the suggestion, they created a report to the Office of Management and Budget that stated 100 more personnel would be required and $20 million more would be needed to put the fingerprint readers in the Embassy in Nigeria. (Actually, $20 million could have paid for personnel and fingerprint readers for every U.S. Embassy in the world.)

The bean counters at the White House Budget Office took one look at the dollar projection, realized that the State Department was not too thrilled about the suggestion, and allowed the initiatives to suffer a quiet bureaucratic death.

Shortly after the 9/11 attacks, and more than five years after the initial suggestions were made, INS and the State Department began sending seasoned INS inspectors to high-risk U.S. Embassies and biometric identifiers are now being collected on all visa applicants at U.S. Embassies around the world—including Nigeria. It is unfortunate that it took the deaths of nearly 3,000 people on 9/11 before we decided to correct our visa issuance deficiencies.

I advocated earlier in the book that the State Department be relieved of its visa issuance responsibilities. I doubt it will happen any time soon. However, for as long as they have it, consular officials should be reminded daily that America's security is a critical part of their job.

Other alien criminal organizations

Nigerian criminals are just one example of what a failed immigration system can produce. Here are a few other alien-controlled organizations whose members are quite numerous in the U.S.

- Fundamentalist Muslim terrorist cells from Saudi Arabia, Iran, Pakistan, Syria, Jordan and several other Muslim countries.
- Colombian drug cartels.
- Jamaican posses.
- Asian gangs (Chinese, Cambodian and Vietnamese).
- Numerous Mexican gangs in Chicago and Los Angeles.
- Mara Salvatrucha organization (MS-13) from El Salvador and Guatemala.
- People's Republic of China "snakehead" alien smugglers.

- Russian, Israeli and Armenian organized crime syndicates (some former KGB).
- Italian Mafia (The Sopranos are alive and well).
- YACS (Yugoslavian, Croatian and Serbian) commercial safe burglar groups.

These are just the "tip of the iceberg" and they all have one thing in common. If America had effective immigration enforcement, these organizations would find it extremely difficult to operate in the U.S. (It is a well known fact that deportation was feared by the "godfathers" of the Mafia past.)

An innovative solution—Keeping track of who is here and what they are doing

The 9/11 Commission Report mentioned many weaknesses in our immigration system and intelligence-gathering capabilities. Let's hope the attacks served as a wake-up call. It is now evident that America must know more about the aliens who are here, and definitely more about what they are planning to do. Immigration and Customs Enforcement must play a much more significant role in preventing aliens from carrying out acts of terrorism and other related activity.

Intelligence comes in many forms. What America found out the hard way was that human intelligence is as important as (if not more important than) intelligence gathered technologically. Human intelligence is critical to the success of any law enforcement or military organization.

Whether we want to be kind and use the politically correct term of "informant," or simply say it is, a "snitch" or "spy," we need their information. I believe one CIA Director said, *"Spying is the second-oldest profession in the world, and just as honorable as the first."*

Our intelligence and law enforcement agencies fully understand the value of inside information—whether it be from someone in an *al Qaeda* training camp in Afghanistan or a street gang in Los Angeles. Unfortunately, the law enforcement community is also well aware of how difficult it is to infiltrate certain organizations. Most informants are motivated by self-serving political and/or monetary gains. I believe this is where immigration enforcement can be utilized as a very powerful tool in the fight against organized crime and terrorism.

Expanding the use of the S-visa

In the early 1980s, INS special agents used a gimmick called "voluntary departure" to help other law enforcement agencies establish and reward alien informants. The program was simple. Most illegal aliens we encountered needed some sort of legal status to remain and work in the U.S. As Agents we could not offer residency or "green cards." However, using the "voluntary departure" scheme we could keep an alien in the U.S. legally and under our control for years. (Eventually the "voluntary departure" scheme was eliminated and Congress codified the process with the establishment of the S-visa program.)

The benefits were incredible. We used to work quietly and behind the scenes with the FBI, Drug Enforcement Administration, Secret Service and many municipal and state law enforcement agencies on matters relating to counterterrorism, counterintelligence and major crime cases. By allowing illegal alien witnesses and informants to remain in the U.S. without fear of deportation, we gave other law enforcement agencies a tremendous tool to use in their fight against crime.

If anyone questions the importance of undercover informants in the war against terrorism, consider the events during the first half of 2007. Two major terrorist plots were disrupted by U.S. law enforcement. In both cases an undercover informant was critical to their success.

In May, 2007, several members of the Duka family were arrested for allegedly planning to kill hundreds of soldiers at Fort Dix, New Jersey. The brothers were from an immigrant family and their group had been infiltrated by an FBI informant. In June, 2007, several other Muslim terrorists from Trinidad were arrested when law enforcement broke up a plan to bomb the fuel storage tanks at John F. Kennedy International Airport. Once again, an informant played a major role in the case.

In a June 4, 2007, Associated Press article entitled, "Feds: Informant key to foiling alleged JFK plot", Tom Corrigan, a former member of the FBI-New York Police Department Joint Terrorism Task Force, summed up the importance of informants in the Fort Dix and JFK terrorism cases. Corrigan stated,

> *"These have been two significant cases back-to-back where informants were used. These terrorists are in our backyard. They may have to reach out to people they don't necessarily trust, but they need—guns, explosives, whatever. In most cases, you can't get from A to B without an informant."*

If the informants in these cases had been illegally in the country, it would have been a tragedy if the Federal Bureau of Investigation or some other law enforcement agency was not able to offer the informants legal status to remain here.

For most outside observers, the S-visas might not seem that valuable, but to U.S. law enforcement they are like gold. During the entire time I spent in INS, one of the most unforgettable things I observed was the amount of information I could get from an illegal alien simply by allowing him to remain and work in the U.S. My illegal alien informants rarely wanted money.

Unfortunately, S-visas are utilized almost exclusively by the Drug Enforcement Administration and the FBI. They are the only two agencies who have enough personnel to deal with the immigration bureaucracy and complete the ludicrous amount of paperwork required to obtain this type of visa for their informants. Aside from the tedious application process, S-visas are also rare for another reason. Congress only authorized a very limited number.

U.S. law enforcement needs a new and considerably expanded S-visa program. As our immigrant populations get larger and more diverse, all levels of U.S. law enforcement need informants in the immigrant communities. Without them, it will be impossible to penetrate criminal and terrorist organizations. Law enforcement will be fighting a losing battle.

It is critical that local, state and Federal law enforcement have the ability to keep and maintain informants using legal immigration status as a method of payment. If law enforcement makes it known to immigrant communities that they have this powerful tool available to them, criminal alien organizations, alien gangs and foreign terrorist cells operating within our borders will truly have something to fear.

The people who oppose this type of program will say that we are giving legal immigration status to the criminals who we should be deporting. In some cases, I admit this might be true, but we must be willing to give a little to get a lot.

I advocate that every office of the Immigration and Customs Enforcement be given the authority to offer almost unlimited numbers of S-visas to qualified law enforcement informants within their respective immigrant communities.

Considering the following benefits, it is amazing to me that the International Association of Chiefs of Police and other similar organizations have not demanded that Congress enhance the S-visa Program.

- S-visas cost law enforcement agencies almost nothing.
- Our intelligence-gathering capabilities at the street level will improve tenfold.
- Aliens can be granted or denied immigration benefits depending upon the quality of information received.
- Benefits can be given for temporary or permanent periods of time.
- Immigration authorities will have a powerful tool with which to assist other law enforcement agencies. The result will be a much closer and more cooperative working relationship between other law enforcement agencies and Immigration and Customs Enforcement.
- Informants will have a significant benefit for themselves and their families, provided their information is reliable.
- Criminal alien organizations, alien gangs and even foreign terrorists will have significant fear that someone

within their organization may be working for the U.S. government with an S-visa.

Homeland monitoring and reporting

In the months following the 9/11 attacks, certain aliens in the U.S were required to report to INS on a periodic basis. It was one of the most controversial, yet effective programs ever initiated by our immigration authorities.

Homeland Security officials admit that the reporting requirement was implemented without much forethought. (What else is new?) The result was long lines of people outside INS buildings across the country, waiting to comply with the hastily constructed regulations. The media had a field day interviewing all "the tired, the hungry and the poor" immigrants "yearning to breathe free," while their relatives searched for parking spaces in their BMWs.

I agree that the long lines were stupid, but conceptually the program was a success. Some recent reports on the investigative news circuit (*60 Minutes, 20/20,* etc.) have shown families that were split apart because illegal aliens from Pakistan, Iran and Saudi Arabia went home rather than face deportation. Could a terrorist or two have been among them? My sense is, absolutely.

The post-9/11 registration program may have upset some civil libertarians, but I have not met very many Americans who argue against it. Aliens who come to the U.S. from countries designated by our government as "high-risk" should be subjected to the following types of preventative programs.

- Maintenance of status bonds—money guaranteed to the U.S. government if the alien does not maintain his or her status and depart as required.
- Regular reporting to specified Homeland Security officials at designated times and places.
- Immediate notification to Homeland Security of any address change.

- Immediate notification to Homeland Security of any arrest or detention by local, state or other Federal law enforcement officials.
- Statutory creation of an expanded and expedited deportation process for aliens from "high-risk" countries.

Immigration, the National Security Agency, and the Central Intelligence Agency

I have only one issue with the Central Intelligence Agency and the National Security Agency. For years they had every opportunity to gather, analyze and disseminate information about alien smuggling, document counterfeiting and other immigration-related matters. They claim that they were never given the necessary White House "findings" to gather such intelligence.

As the CIA and the rest of the "intelligence community" begin to implement their new intelligence reform legislation, I hope that immigration-related issues will receive the attention they deserve. Furthermore, it is about time that CIA and the National Security Agency be allowed to use their professional and technological resources to assist Homeland Security in carrying out its immigration enforcement responsibilities.

The programs proposed in this chapter are not "close-the-borders" or "deport-them-all" recommendations. The expanded S-visa program, the increased vigilance at home and at our embassies, and the enhanced assistance from the intelligence community are just common sense solutions to some of America's growing immigration, crime, and security problems. The sooner we implement these initiatives, the safer we will be.

Chapter 18
Fixing Immigration Records

A big program with a massive payoff

Homeland Security has tens of thousands of immigration records that are virtually uncorrectable without human intervention. No computer system in the world can determine that a given alien has an A-file with one number, a "green card" bearing another number, and a database with a completely unconnected third number.

So what is the solution? Those of us who remember cars without seat belts should also remember the signs on every post office wall requiring aliens in the U.S., each January, to complete the Alien Address Report Form, or AR-11. Aliens who did not comply were subject to deportation.

This requirement was suspended in the 1980s because the General Accounting Office found INS personnel were putting millions of unrecorded AR-11 forms in shoe boxes and storing them in broom closets at INS Headquarters. (I don't have the imagination to make this stuff up.)

The law, however, was never repealed. In fact, in the immediate aftermath of the September 11 attacks, INS Agents in some localities actually considered using the statute as a subterfuge to detain aliens who were otherwise legally in the country.

If Homeland Security is truly going to fix the data errors in the INS computer systems, a modified reporting system similar to the old AR-11 program should be implemented.

When I suggested this solution to my adversaries in the Records Services Division, they would laugh and whine, "Cramer wants us to go back to the Middle Ages." Well, not quite, but if we have to go back a few steps to move miles ahead, so be it.

Here is a brief description of what would be required and what it would accomplish.

- Each alien would be required to complete a more comprehensive AR-11 indicating his or her former and current names, current address, A-file number, Social Security number, date of birth, and other pertinent information.
- Each alien would be required to submit both a current photograph and a photocopy of both sides of his or her current U.S. immigration document. This is where the real "fix" begins.
- Utilizing a contractor for administrative support, Homeland Security would compare and update INS records using the alien's submissions and information currently available in their own systems. If the information submitted by the alien correctly corresponds to the data in the A-file and the INS systems, the A-file would then be stored in an active and accessible section of the centralized immigration files storage facility. (During the last few years, INS began to centralize many A-files in a huge salt-mine storage area in Missouri. In the event Congress implements the proposed Alien Address Report program, the costs associated with its implementation will be significantly reduced due to the centralized location of the A-files.)
- Homeland Security databases would be electronically noted that the data had been reviewed and programmatically verified.
- Database errors, mistakes in the A-file, or an error on the alien's documents would be set aside for corrective action.

This program needs to operate for two to three years. U.S. resident aliens residing overseas would be required to submit the forms and data to their nearest U.S. consulate or embassy. If immigrants do not change their address during the registration period, the forms would only need to be submitted once.

Some people have told me the program will never work because the immigrant population will not cooperate. I think they are wrong. The program must be required by law, and failure to participate could be grounds for deportation or exclusion from the U.S. More importantly, immigrants know that this records clean-up would eventually help them and members of their families. I believe the immigrant population in America would be the first to cooperate in this problem-solving initiative.

Who will pay?

I understand there will be a concern about the cost of such an undertaking and I propose a possible funding solution as well. The U.S. Postal Service (USPS) could sell a special mail-in package. This would include instructions in various languages, forms, and a pre-addressed, postage-paid return envelope to a designated Homeland Security facility. All of the agencies involved (U.S. Postal Service, Homeland Security, and the Department of State) could submit independent estimates for their anticipated processing costs. Using the U.S. Census estimate of the number of legal aliens residing in the U.S., a per-immigrant application fee could be determined. The USPS could then sell each package and stamp at a designated price, similar to those issued by the USPS for Priority and Express Mail.

Will Congress do it?

Unfortunately, there is not a computer in the world that can fix what *Days of Our Lives*, fried chicken and ineptitude created. (See Chapter 10.) It will not be fixed with new software, data exchanges, or any of the other so-called technical solutions.

Immigration records are also critical to America's security. For various reasons, law enforcement and intelligence agencies must utilize immigration databases. While no study has ever been conducted to determine the exact extent of the errors, after 26 years in INS, I estimate that more than 20% of the records (in A-files, on documents, or in the databases) need corrective action. It is simply dangerous for our government to continue to treat this situation as if it will just disappear. On the contrary, it is getting worse by the day and it is impacting our national security.

The proposed Alien Address Report program will be a huge step in the right direction. It will allow us to gain faith in our immigration records databases and will assist the millions of citizens and immigrants who are now extremely frustrated with the current situation.

To advocate such a program will take strong leadership in both Congress and the White House. So far, we have not seen that leadership.

Expanding the Systematic Alien Verification for Entitlements program and Immigration Verification Information Services

During the development and implementation of the Systematic Alien Verification for Entitlements program, I defended the program against charges that the poor quality of the INS database would lead to welfare-benefit denials to deserving legal aliens.

I succeeded by demonstrating that the program's two-step verification prevented errors resulting from the poor quality of INS computerized data. The automated check, in combination with a "secondary verification" process, made alien document verification extremely reliable. Furthermore, I proved that this dual method of verification helped INS locate and correct errors in the system.

Today, the same verification system goes under the name of Immigration Verification Information Services at Homeland Security. (The E-Verification System for employers is operated by this division.) This verification system has never been used to its full capacity.

Homeland Security seems reluctant to offer alien status and alien documentation verification to entities like state motor vehicle departments, state licensing bureaus and the Transportation Security Administration. Yet, a significant expansion of the use of the Verification Information Services is exactly how Homeland Security could realistically solve many of the concerns about fraudulent identification raised by The 9/11 Commission.

Chapter 19

U.S. Department of Immigration and a National Immigration Policy Board

A U.S. Department of Immigration

Immigration reform is critical to the future of our country. So much so, I believe the U.S. should create a cabinet level U.S. Department of Immigration. For now, politicians will just shake their heads and say that the last thing we need is more bureaucracy. (If six months before the 9/11 attacks, someone had suggested a Department of Homeland Security, they too would have been dismissed as crazy.)

Unfortunately, we live in a day and age when the only thing that seems to move the U.S. government in a different direction is terrorism, mass chaos, disaster, tragedy, war . . . or Fox News and CNN. When it comes to U.S. immigration, I hope we can make significant changes without a mass disturbance or rioting in the streets. We currently estimate that there are 12 million or more illegal aliens in the country. While this seems like an enormous amount, the situation is not uncontrollable. However, the American public must realize that controlling illegal immigration is becoming more and more problematic by the day. The more we let it continue, the more difficult it will be to bring it under control.

Our politicians are often driven by the press and for years our mainstream media hesitated reporting about the negative effects of illegal immigration. Whether it was caused by a liberal bias or a fear of being seen as racist, media organizations generally treated illegal immigration as some sort of forbidden fruit. In almost a complete turnaround, several radio and television talk show hosts have used illegal immigration to successfully boost their ratings. Fox's Bill O'Reilly and CNN's Lou Dobbs discuss the issue on a frequent basis, and much to the delight of their listening audience. And, needless to say, many politicians are beginning to see the light.

Immigrants, both legal and illegal, have an enormous impact on our daily lives in the U.S. Consider the following list of business, national and social issues. Immigration policy has a significant influence on all of them.

- Agriculture
- Construction
- Service industries
- Education
- Public health
- Crime
- Birth rate
- Population growth
- Terrorism
- Commerce and balance of trade
- Diplomacy
- Traffic and road congestion

As one can see, immigration is not just a border issue. Wherever we live in the U.S., we are impacted by the flow of aliens into this country. Immigration is not just an American issue—it is becoming one of the major social issues of the entire world.

The U.S. needs to create an agency whose sole responsibility is to bring together all of the offices, agencies and functions that make up the immigration equation. Whether this happens in the future will probably depend on how many immigration-related tragedies and disasters befall America.

Most of our leaders are clueless about the impact that immigration has on the U.S. Worse yet, they are unwilling to do anything about it. When Congress establishes a cabinet-level U.S. Department of Immigration, it will be the first sign that they finally realize the importance of this issue. I am not going to hold my breath.

A National Immigration Policy Board

For decades, Congress and the White House have struggled with one immigration crisis after another. Whenever a situation arose, the politicians tried to figure out a strategy that satisfied both the left and the right. (We all know that is impossible.) By the time the political appointees at the Immigration and Naturalization Service, the State Department and the White House figured out what to do, we were proverbially up to our asses in alligators. (U.S. Senate attempts to pass "comprehensive immigration reform" in 2007 should be enough to convince anyone that our representatives in Washington are inept when it comes to immigration matters.)

Remember the Mariel Boatlift? It was a fiasco, and we are paying for it to this day. Hundreds of Castro's criminally insane are still in U.S. prisons at a cost of millions of dollars per year. Could it have been handled differently?

An independent policy board would have managed the crisis in a much more sensible fashion than the Carter White House. The anti-Castro Cuban political machine in South Florida would not have been able to influence an independent policy board the way they manipulated Jimmy Carter. America would have willingly accepted thousands of Cuban refugees who were fleeing Communism and who deserved asylum status in the U.S. At the same time, a policy board would have seen through Castro's nonsense and issued orders to forcibly remove the thousands of crazies dumped on our shores. They would have been returned to Cuba. (To this day I have no idea why they were simply not taken to Guantanamo Bay Naval Station, given a McDonald's Happy Meal, and told to take a hike outside the gates.)

Would an Immigration Policy Board work? For so many years, we have had the Federal Reserve Board and it has always been synonymous with U.S. monetary policy. (Alan Greenspan was the Chairman, and every time the man opened his mouth, the financial world went into spasms.) Why doesn't Congress or the White House determine monetary policy? It's simple. Some decisions regarding the nation's money are best made independently and without significant political intervention. The Federal Reserve and its relationship to monetary policy should serve as an excellent example why an independent Immigration Policy Board would be just what America needs. Difficult decisions about immigration policy need to be decided by professionals, and taken out of the hands of politicians.

Aside from mass immigration emergencies, the following is a list of immigration related issues that the U.S. government struggles with every day.

- Immigrant visa number limitations.
- Non-immigrant visa number limitations.
- Special seasonal non-immigrant visas for agriculture.
- Countries whose citizens should be granted Temporary Protected Status.
- Number of refugees and asylees to be admitted each year.
- Welfare benefits—which aliens receive them and which ones should not.
- Immigration emergencies—who pays and how much.
- Immigration authority—Federal versus state.
- Reviewing S-visa policies and procedures. (See Chapter 8.)

These are just a few of the complex matters that create havoc in Congress, the White House and with government employees who are tasked with implementing U.S. immigration policy. To remedy this bureaucratic turmoil, the Congress should take a lesson from our Federal Reserve Board. They should simply create an independent non-partisan policy board (staffed with immigration professionals) to handle these complex policy issues. It makes so much sense it will never happen.

Chapter 20
Comprehensive Immigration Reform

In the first few months of 2007, the U.S. Senate demonstrated to America just how difficult it will be to pass proper immigration reform legislation. After struggling with the immigration debate for months, and receiving significant pressure from the Bush White House to pass "comprehensive immigration reform," the Senate surprisingly killed any chance of a new law until after the next Presidential election in 2008. Was their failure a good thing? You bet it was.

Aside from all of the snazzy terms that came from the proposed legislation—"Z-visas," "touchback provisions," "guest workers"—almost everyone in the business of immigration reform knew it would have been impossible for the Bush Administration to carry out all of the suggested mandates of Congress. The pro-immigration advocates knew very well the enforcement mechanisms would never be implemented effectively, and were salivating over the idea the government was about to legalize 12 million or more illegal immigrants with the stroke of Bush's pen. Instead, U.S. Senators demonstrated common sense, and did not pander to the White House or the far left. In this case, no legislation was far better than bad legislation. (The debates also proved that curtailing illegal immigration is an issue that is foremost in the minds of many Americans.)

Despite the failure of the overall immigration reform bill, it is important to look at several provisions of the proposed legislation, as many of them will no doubt be raised again in future bills.

Enforcement without amnesty or "guest workers"

Congress has never had the will to promote strict immigration enforcement mechanisms, and the bill that failed in the Senate followed this pattern. In fact, as several of the amendments were debated on the Senate floor, it appeared that "amnesty" was the main portion of the legislation and enforcement was secondary. This may be the main reason the bill met its demise.

While it is seldom discussed, there is a "self-deportation" solution for most of our 12 million or more illegal immigrants. If Congress mandates a mandatory Social Security Number Verification System, accompanied by nationwide and effective employer sanctions, the vast majority of illegal aliens will leave the U.S. voluntarily. I am not totally in favor of this because I believe it will cause severe economic consequences in many industries. However, solely implementing these programs will significantly curtail illegal immigration and force many of the illegal aliens already here to return home.

The "Z-visa" and a "guest worker" program

On November 28, 2006, in Tucson, Arizona, President George W. Bush proclaimed that he was adamantly opposed to an "amnesty" for illegal aliens. Instead, as part of a "comprehensive immigration reform" package, he said he was supporting both a new "Z-visa" for the 12 million illegal aliens in the U.S., and a future "guest worker" program.

The new Z-visa equates to a three-year work permit for illegal aliens currently in the U.S. At the end of three years, they could re-register to remain for another three years. However, at the end of six years the alien will have to depart and return home.

Does anyone really believe that millions of illegal aliens are going to register as "guest workers," work like slaves for three or six years and then return "home"? At the end of six years, this will be their home. And, anyone who truly believes that these workers are going to leave the U.S. is naive.

The "guest worker" program was a little more realistic. Congress debated how many future visas should be available to employers who want to bring in skilled and unskilled labor when there is a shortage of American workers. I have always been a proponent for allowing certain employers to bring in immigrant labor, as long as it is not being done to depress American wages. Despite the claims of many union leaders, there is a labor shortage in the U.S. for certain types of jobs (day care, nursing, and agriculture). If Congress completely yields to the labor unions and continues to deny employers the right to bring in more legal immigrant workers (even after they demonstrate a real labor shortage), they are simply creating a recipe for more illegal immigration.

Whatever future amnesty programs Congress passes, dangerous pitfalls already exist and they are mind-boggling, to say the least. For example, who is going to process all the Z-visas for 12 million illegal aliens? The agency currently targeted to handle the job is none other than Homeland Security's Citizenship and Immigration Services Division. In case you skipped a few chapters, this is the same agency that lost 111,000 alien files, has a current backlog of 4 million cases, charges $300 to change the name on a "green card," and sends out notices saying it will take "990 days" to process a simple immigration application. While I have no intention of prematurely proclaiming that the sky is about to fall, Americans should know there are several recent reports indicating Citizenship and Immigration Services is incapable of handling this massive program.

One suggestion is to allow non-governmental agencies (NGOs) to handle part of the processing. If we allow this to happen it will be a security nightmare. Churches and other religious organizations are not the most responsible agencies when it comes to enforcing U.S. law. Recent news articles listed several religious organizations and non-governmental agencies as supporting the growing illegal alien "sanctuary movement." For the U.S. government to ask these same groups to properly register illegal aliens is virtually "putting the fox in the henhouse." In 1986, non-governmental agencies made millions of dollars processing illegal aliens for amnesty under the Immigration Reform and Control Act, and as expected, the fraud was rampant. If our government cannot find the necessary resources to professionally process the millions of illegal aliens, do not pass the law. It is that simple.

Will the situation be any different if the aliens return home and apply for visas in their home country? Considering the fact it now takes almost a month for some aliens to get a simple visitor's visa, the scenes at our embassies will be chaotic to say the least. The U.S. government will have to hire, train and deploy hundreds of new employees overseas, and then spend billions of dollars for new equipment and infrastructure. Even with these upgrades, there is no guarantee the State Department could handle the proper issuance of millions of work visas.

Of course, if our representatives in Washington, D.C. want to pass "comprehensive immigration reform," they certainly can and will do it—even if it means endangering the security of the U.S. And, the President will sign it. After all, who will be accountable to the American public? The Congress? The Senate? The President? The truth is, no one will be accountable—just as no one was accountable for the failure of the 1986 Immigration Reform and Control Act.

From my experience at INS, I can almost predict what will happen if Congress does prematurely pass "comprehensive immigration reform" legislation. Within two or three years after the law passes, human rights activists will file suit against the Department of Homeland Security claiming that Z-visa holders are being deprived of "life, liberty and the pursuit of happiness" because they are separated from their families. A liberal court (like California's Ninth Circuit Court) will agree and mandate that the U.S. implement a family reunification plan for all. Within months after the decision, Homeland Security will be forced to give "green cards" to all workers with Z-visas. Shortly thereafter the families will be allowed to immigrate. Very quietly an "amnesty" (the one the politicians said would never happen) will occur right in front of our eyes.

"Comprehensive immigration reform" should not be a license to endanger the security of America or to invite future illegal aliens to once again break the laws of this country with impunity."

The DREAM Act

Activists involved with immigration reform (on both sides of the issue) understand that one of the most emotional subjects in the debate concerns children of illegal immigrants. Whether they are "anchor babies" who are born here or minor children who innocently accompany their parents to America, the children are victims of a sort. They do not understand the illegality involved in their parents' actions and for the most part the children are innocent of any criminal intent.

More and more of these children are getting caught up in the growing ant-illegal immigrant sentiment spreading across the U.S. The Supreme Court years ago decided that children of illegal immigrants (U.S. citizens or not) are eligible to attend public school. The Supreme Court did not, however, say this guarantee extended to higher education. Thousands of illegal alien teenagers and young adults now find themselves having to pay full tuition to colleges and universities because they cannot prove they are legal residents.

In an attempt to show the nation our understanding and concern for this problem, Congress has tried for several years to pass a law to allow these children to attend school and eventually gain U.S. citizenship. The most recent version of this legislation is known as the **D**evelopment, **R**elief and **E**ducation for **M**inor **A**ct or DREAM Act. (Who has the time to dream up these acronyms?)

Wikipedia, the online encyclopedia, describes it as a "one time solution intended to provide a path to a permanent legal status for persons brought illegally or legally to the United States by their parents or guardians as children. This includes individuals whose parents attempted to immigrate legally but were then denied legality after several years in application, and whose children thus derived their legal status solely from their parents (the child also becoming illegal upon the parents' denial) as well as those initially brought here illegally."

Nothing is simple or transparent when it comes to immigration law. While I am sympathetic to the plight of these children there is a lot more to this legislation than helping students with their education. Have we already forgotten Elvira Arellano? Americans must realize that legislation like the DREAM Act will eventually result in a legal battle for "family reunification!" After all, immigrant advocates will claim that these students cannot live here without their parents. What about students who are U.S. citizens or legal resident aliens? Why should they have to compete for educational funds with children who do not have the right to be here in the first place?

The DREAM Act appeals to the humanitarian side of every American who ever attended high school or college. There has been growing support for it throughout the country as people see the students as victims. What America must also realize is that the DREAM Act is "amnesty" for tens of thousands of illegal aliens—and eventually their entire families.

Amnesty

"If it walks like a duck and quacks like a duck, it's a duck." If we are going to have another amnesty, our politicians in Washington should tell the public the truth and be willing to take the political heat for their actions. (Of course, we know that will never happen.)

For someone who spent almost half of his life trying to enforce U.S. immigration laws, I guess I should be marching outside the White House with signs saying, "Don't Reward Criminals" or "Send Them All Home!" Unfortunately I have resigned myself to the fact that sooner or later Congress will authorize another amnesty. I am certainly not jumping for joy about it, but almost everyone who has studied our growing immigration crisis knows an amnesty of some sort is inevitable. I am fully aware that this sends the horrible message to the rest of the world. We are, after all, rewarding those who broke our laws. However, as a nation, we created this problem. Despite what some people think, we do not have the manpower or the will to *forcibly* deport millions of people from America.

As we look at any legalization program, we must not forget the millions of people waiting in line to come here legally under our current quota system. Before Congress authorizes a single "green card" to anyone through an amnesty, they must do something to eliminate the current backlog of prospective legal immigrants. (This is one of those "900 pound gorilla in the bedroom" situations that politicians are not willing to discuss.)

As much as I hate to agree to it, the question is not whether we should have another amnesty, but rather when should we have it, what form should it take and what should we do to strengthen immigration enforcement to prevent the need for any future amnesties? Part of the answer has already been given earlier in this book. In addition to "programmatically" securing our borders, the U.S. must implement an effective employer sanctions program, and allow municipal, state and Federal law enforcement officers to enforce it by issuing stiff fines to non-compliant employers. We will then significantly curtail illegal immigration to the point where we may never need another amnesty.

Another problem with an amnesty is fraud. In 1986, the amnesty was supposed to provide relief to illegal immigrants who came to America illegally or those who entered illegally and never left. Included in these two groups were Special Agricultural Workers or SAWs. The Special Agriculture Worker program was especially for farm workers and it was a complete sell-out to the agriculture lobby. It was also riddled with abuse.

To get amnesty through the Special Agriculture Worker provisions, an alien had to show evidence that he or she had been employed for a specified amount of time on a farm or ranch doing work related to agriculture. Agriculture experts were able to convince Congress that if these workers received "green cards," there would then be a sufficient legal agricultural labor force in the U.S. They promised they would never again need to utilize illegal alien labor. The agriculture lobby in Washington may as well have sold Congress the Brooklyn Bridge.

Certain unexpected things resulted from the Special Agriculture Worker program. First, any illegal alien who could spell the word "farm" submitted an application for amnesty, and the entire process became a joke.The program resulted in amnesty for many hard-working agricultural workers, and quite a few other scammers like a Canadian golf pro I met in Arizona. In the story below, I will call him "Mike." As you will read, his "green card" had nothing to do with his "fruit-picking" skills.

Apparently in the early 1980s, Mike was on vacation in the U.S when his car broke down near a dude ranch in Colorado. He rented a room there while his car was being fixed.

The first morning there, Mike noticed the owner of the ranch teaching his son how to swing a golf club. He offered to give the boy some professional golf lessons. The father was so impressed that he asked the guy if he would accept a minimal amount of money to remain for a few days and teach his son the fundamentals of the game. The golf pro willingly obliged. He stayed for a week, gave the kid a few golf lessons and then left.

Years later, after the 1986 amnesty passed, the rancher called the golf pro and told him he was probably eligible for a "green card." The rancher was in the process of legalizing all of his illegal alien laborers and noticed the golf pro had also been an "undocumented employee." After a few mailings back and forth to the ranch, Mike submitted the Special Agriculture Worker application with proof supplied by the Colorado rancher. Low and behold his "green card" arrived. The pro told me it was better than getting a hole-in-one.

Not all of the fraud associated with the Special Agriculture Worker program had innocuous results. According to Ira Mehlman, spokesperson for the Federation for American Immigration Reform, two of the bombers of the World Trade Center in 1993, came into the country using the Special Agriculture Worker program.However, when they were arrested, they were employed a taxi drivers in New York City. (I don't ever recall seeing an orange grove on Fifth Avenue.)

An even bigger unexpected problem arose from the "Special Agriculture Worker" program, after the workers were granted amnesty and given legal resident status. Most of them headed for the cities, for higher wages, and that created a vacuum of farm labor in their wake. Who filled the vacuum? You guessed it—a brand new crop of illegal aliens!

As one can readily see, the 1986 amnesty was moving ahead like a freight train, while the employer sanctions program failed miserably. To prevent this from happening again, Congress must demand that Homeland Security implement proven and effective enforcement mechanisms *before* we have another amnesty or a similar program. If we are once again going to reward those who knowingly and willfully violated our immigration laws, we should at least make certain *this time is the last time.*

Employers of illegal aliens

During my years at INS, I had the opportunity to deal not only with illegal aliens, but also with the people who employed them. One disturbing trend that I observed, over and over, related to the wealth of the employer in relationship to the wages of the aliens he or she employed. Inevitably, wealthy employers paid the lowest wages to their immigrant employees.

I remember investigating one of the largest employers of illegal aliens in the Washington, D.C. area. He was a Greek immigrant who owned several restaurants. During the late 1970s we raided several of his establishments and arrested countless illegal aliens from El Salvador, Nigeria, Ghana, India, Pakistan, and Iran. They were working as busboys, waiters, and dishwashers.

During the interview process at the INS office, most of the aliens told us they were paid minimum wage. They also said they were only allowed to consume restaurant food after they paid for it. The owner charged the workers $5 for a bowl of ice cream, and $2.50 for a cup of coffee. This type of activity did not shock me, as it was commonly known that restaurant employers did not treat their illegal alien employees with the greatest respect.

One afternoon I had the opportunity to see the restaurant owner's house in northwest Washington, D.C. It was a huge and opulent residence. At the time (1989), it was valued at $6 million. Despite the beauty of the home, all I could think when I saw it was the $5 he charged his workers for a bowl of ice cream.

I relate this story because I think it exemplifies what is happening in America with regard to employment and illegal immigration. We are a capitalistic nation, and a person's wealth is measured in dollars—not honesty, not sincerity, not goodness of heart—dollars, pure and simple. For the most part, large and small employers are interested in the bottom line. If it takes a shortcut on labor costs to make the millions they all desire, so be it.

I have nothing against people who take risks and then succeed because of hard work and entrepreneurial skill. I do, however, have a problem with employers who pay their employees almost nothing, charge excessive fees for their products and services, and then sit in their multi-million dollar homes, claiming that America needs foreign "guest workers" because no one else will do the work. I think we should take a very close look at not only the wages that will be paid to "guest workers" but also the cost of the products or services their employers provide.

As an example, look no further than the landscaping industry in Scottsdale, Arizona. People who own large landscaping firms will tell you that they cannot survive without illegal labor from Mexico. They strongly advocate a "guest worker" program. But behind the scenes the numbers show a different story. Most landscapers pay laborers $8 an hour. If the employer uses five laborers for one day to complete the landscaping of an average new residence, his labor cost is approximately $320. In addition, $1000 usually covers the cost for all of his equipment, supplies and overhead. Total actual cost: $1320. The bill to the homeowner (as in my case)—$10,000! These landscapers do not need "guest workers"—they need wheelbarrows to carry all of their profits to the bank.

If we allow U.S. employers to have their "guest workers" under the guise that they cannot find Americans to do the work, the U.S. government must establish some sort of price controls on the products and services they provide. Otherwise, the Federal government is doing nothing more than authorizing certain companies to legally use foreign laborers to depress wages in the U.S., while the company's owners laugh all the way to the bank. The truth hurts.

Immigration reform and accountability of the fee accounts

Every proposed "comprehensive immigration reform" law seems to support massive fines and fees to pay for the increased resources required to successfully implement the legislation. Illegal aliens and their employers will probably pay most of these fees, and needless to say, the receipts will be enormous. If our current situation is any example of things to come, Americans should prepare themselves for fraud, waste and abuse by our Federal government that will make the billions lost after Hurricane Katrina look like a minor accounting error.

In Chapter 7, I indicated that Homeland Security collects billions of dollars in "immigration fees." Whether it is the hidden charges on an airline ticket for every international traveler who passes through our airports or the astronomical application fees paid to Citizenship and Immigrations Services, the U.S. Treasury gets enormous deposits for immigration-related charges. There must be more accountability of these funds.

Unless things have changed drastically in the last few years, these receipts are literally used like a "slush fund" by Homeland Security Senior Executives. The fact is, no one really knows how much money is coming in at any one time, and it makes the system ripe for abuse.

There is a solution to this "accountability" problem with the "fee accounts." Senior Executives, however, will be extremely reluctant to implement any workable solution as they will then be accountable. (God forbid!)The U.S. government must eliminate the guesswork about how much money has been received. In so doing, there will be much less opportunity for employees to misuse the money.

Here are the necessary legal steps that Congress should legislate to help fix the "fee accounts" accountability problem and put an end to this financial boondoggle.

1. Congress should create a special one-time appropriation to cover the estimated receipts that Homeland Security would normally receive in a year from the Adjudication Fees Account and the Inspection Fees Account.
2. During that same fiscal year, Homeland Security must deposit all fee account receipts into two special segregated Inspections and Examinations "reserve" accounts.
3. The amount received during each quarter would then be the designated amount to be spent for that quarter in the coming year (e.g., receipts for the first quarter of 2008, would be the amount available for the first quarter of 2009).
4. Homeland Security would then be able to plan ahead with fee account expenditures. Officials would know exactly how much user fee funds would be available six months before the money was to be spent.
5. Managers would be accountable for all user fee expenditures, and would be required to show exactly where the money was spent and for what. (Goodbye to paying for the junket to Rome and London instead of paying for new inspectors at JFK Airport.)

In 1995, I attempted to send this suggestion "through official channels" to the management of INS. Due to bureaucratic protocol, I was required to send it first to my supervisor. His name was "Dick" and he was an INS Director. A few days after submitting it, Dick summoned me to his office and handed the suggestion back to me. He said, *"This suggestion is stupid. The Budget Office knows exactly where all the money is being spent and there is no need for more accountability."* He simply refused to forward the proposal and it never went any further.

I believe now what I believed then. If a program is put in place that assures sufficient oversight and accountability of the revenue generated from these "fee accounts," there will be sufficient funds to employ and equip more inspectors and examiners. It would also help bring integrity back to our legal immigration system and strengthen our national security.

As we contemplate an overhaul of our immigration system with "comprehensive immigration reform," Congress must demand fiscal responsibility and accountability from the government Senior Executives who run our immigration agencies.

Social unacceptability of illegal immigration

One of the most fascinating observations I have made over the last three decades relates to the capability of Americans to change their living habits based on a perception of its social acceptability or unacceptability.

When I was a police officer in Neptune Beach, Florida in 1975, I can distinctly remember stopping a very well-known and powerful local restaurant owner for Driving While Intoxicated. I stopped him for driving in excess of 100 miles per hour the wrong way over the coastal waterway bridge toward Jacksonville.

A few minutes after I called his license plate in to the dispatcher my sergeant showed up at the scene. He advised me (in no uncertain terms) to lock the car and take him home, as he was a very well-respected member of the community (despite the fact he drove home plastered every night after work). That was then. If the same thing happened today, I am certain the incident would be treated differently. In today's America, no matter how powerful one is and no matter how many restaurants they own, drunks driving cars go directly to jail. He would not pass "Go", and his defense lawyer would be the one getting the proverbial $200—and a whole lot more!

Smoking on airplanes is another issue to reflect on. During my career I had the opportunity to fly on commercial aircraft quite frequently. When I first started to travel for the government, there were always seats at the rear of the plane for smokers and the "No Smoking" light was switched off shortly after the wheels went up. Strangely enough, I have not been on a flight in years when smoking was allowed.

What does smoking on airplanes and drunk driving have to do with curtailing illegal immigration? Quite a bit, I hope.

Currently, employing an illegal alien is a quiet little "game" played throughout the country in our homes and businesses. Whether it is on a farm in Kansas, at a restaurant in New York, on a roof in Arizona or in a grove in Florida, employing an illegal alien is socially acceptable—and illegal. During my entire career I heard jokes like, "Tell Neville he is invited to the party, but he better not touch the help." The comments never bothered me, but it did exemplify the dual standard that exists throughout the nation. Employment is the reason most illegal immigrants come to America. Social acceptability of their presence is what allows them to remain.

In the coming years it is almost a certain Congress will legislate "comprehensive immigration reform." As part of that legislation it would be beneficial to this country if they would support a campaign to make hiring illegal workers not only illegal, but also "socially unacceptable."

Dream on, dream on!

Chapter 21
Immigration Lawyers

How could anyone write a book about immigration and not say a little something about those wonderful lawyers who specialize in this field? Like any other group of people, there are the good ones and bad ones. I knew some good ones—Champagne, Virtue, Ladick and Harmeyer, for example. I also tried to get some others indicted.

More than most client groups, aliens are particularly unequipped to determine whether their lawyer is an ethical attorney or an incompetent crook. Many aliens come from countries where the bar is effectively a conduit for bribes and they expect the same from U.S. lawyers. In addition, they are afraid to file complaints against a lawyer as this brings their illegal immigration status to the attention of the U.S. government.

The vulnerability of the alien population attracts many loathsome characters to the immigration bar. On the other hand, many are bleeding hearts who work tirelessly on labor-intensive paper pushing and immigration file-chasing for years at a time. While I am not shedding any tears for immigration lawyers, I know some who probably earned little more than minimum wage for their efforts. Reportedly, immigration lawyers are some of the lowest-paid lawyers, and have one of the worst reputations amongst their legal colleagues.

As a Special Agent at INS, I had a unique perspective when it came to these officers of the court. While some immigration lawyers were dedicated to their profession, and skillfully battled INS employees on a daily basis, there were others who did not know the law, charged outrageous fees, knowingly prepared fraudulent claims for immigration benefits and literally disappeared when their client's case "went South." As in many cases with our legal profession, remedies were available to weed out the "bad apples." Unfortunately, the Immigration and Naturalization Service had the power to punish the con artists—they just never chose to do it.

Enough said . . . lawyer jokes were created for a reason.

Chapter 22
The End

As the title of this book suggests, our government's policies and practices have created chaos within our immigration system. Part II of this book advocates establishing or enhancing many immigration-related programs. I believe these changes will help improve this rapidly and dangerously deteriorating quagmire.

For those who do not think it is an important issue to the American public, read on. CNN's Lou Dobbs conducted an informal survey on October 4, 2004, and asked if illegal immigration should be an issue in the 2004 Presidential campaign. Eighty-eight percent said it should be, and 12% said it should not. This is a startling statistic.

While the vast majority of Americans want something done to curb the problem, most politicians run from the issue like it was a rattlesnake curled to strike. This time, the issue is not going to go away. Reforming our immigration system continues to be one of the most controversial issues we will have to face in the coming years. "Comprehensive immigration reform" will be one of the major issues in the 2008 Presidential and Congressional elections.

America cannot control its borders by simply adding more Border Patrol Agents. And, we must also understand that securing our borders is only a part of the problem. U.S. immigration is controlled by international push factors and domestic pull factors. Without a significant increase in interior enforcement, a new enhanced employer sanctions program, and a complete overhaul of our legal immigration system, America will do little to curtail illegal immigration.

I believe it is time that our politicians stop saying, "we don't have the political will." Congress must start legislating serious and comprehensive changes to our entire immigration system.

As Part II of this book demonstrates, there are commonsense solutions that will work. It is now time to implement these programs and end America's growing immigration crisis. I am not alone in my thinking. About 88% of Americans agree with me!

Attorney General Ed Meese laughing momentarily. Unfortunately, the chaos at INS was no laughing matter.

Immigration Chaos

by
Neville W. Cramer

Executive summary and recommendations

Whether it is discussing the issue with my friends or working as a guest on a talk radio show, I am always asked some form of the question, "What is the solution to our immigration problem?" The question itself demonstrates one of the biggest problems in America. There is no single solution. There is no "magic bullet."

Despite the sudden popularity of discussing "illegal immigration" by many in the media, the public rarely hears from those of us who have spent our professional lives dealing with this quagmire. And despite the claims of the pundits, I do not know of a single Immigration officer who believes that a fence, the military or even an amnesty will solve our growing immigration-related problems.

Immigration reform must be multi-faceted. It will also be a gut-wrenching exercise that will result in name-calling, political in-fighting and maybe even violence. Unfortunately, it must be done—and done right!

The following pages set forth a series of programs and issues that have been discussed throughout this book. While these recommendations are far from all-inclusive, they do represent common-sense solutions to immigration-related problems that have plagued America for decades.

Securing our borders

The U.S. now has almost 14,000 Border Patrol Agents and approximately 12 million or more illegal aliens. If we keep going at this rate, by the year 2030 we could have as many as 50,000 Border Patrol Agents—and 50 million illegal aliens. Obviously our immigration enforcement strategy must go beyond simply hiring more Border Patrol Agents. Here are other programmatic initiatives to be considered in our attempt to truly control our physical borders.

- Almost all aliens apprehended illegally entering the U.S. should be detained for a minimum of 60 to 90 days. The U.S. military could be used to assist in the construction and maintenance of camp-like detention facilities along the U.S.-Mexico border.
- Physical land borders must be secured using a combination of fencing, sensors, ground radar systems, cameras, surveillance equipment, and satellites.
- Intelligence gathering capabilities (human and otherwise) must be increased significantly to combat alien smuggling, human trafficking and document counterfeiting. Law enforcement agencies operating along our borders must be given greater support by the Central Intelligence Agency and the National Security Agency.

Immigration enforcement throughout America

There is currently a vacuum of immigration enforcement in the interior of the U.S. Aliens who get past the Border Patrol or enter temporarily to visit or study must not be allowed to remain and work illegally in this country. Since jobs are the main reason illegal immigrants come here, Congress must establish programs that will discourage employers from hiring workers who are not allowed to accept employment. Here are some necessary programs that should be implemented nationwide.

- Congress must mandate the establishment and use of an automated Form I-9 and Social Security Number Verification System for all employers.
- Employers must verify Social Security numbers of all employees immediately after employment begins.
- Homeland Security must establish an Immigration Compliance Division. Compliance officers should assist the business community with the implementation of the verification system. As soon as the system is in place throughout the nation, these same officers should be utilized to conduct employer sanctions enforcement and other administrative investigations related to immigration violations in the interior of the U.S.
- A simple "ticket book" employer sanctions enforcement mechanism must accompany a Social Security Number Verification System.
- Local, state and Federal law enforcement officers should receive proper immigration-related training and have authority to enforce employer sanctions provisions of Federal immigration law.
- Local and state governments must be allowed to utilize the revenue generated by employer sanctions violations to offset local costs associated with illegal immigration.
- All agencies issuing work related licenses to aliens (medical, nursing, cosmetology, commercial driver's license, etc.) must be required to verify employment eligibility status with Department of Homeland Security prior to issuing any of these licenses.
- Immigration status information, date of birth, and Social Security number on all applicants and criminal fingerprint cards should be verified through Homeland Security and the Social Security Administration.

Terrorists and criminal aliens

Criminal aliens, illegal aliens involved in gangs, suspected foreign terrorists, and aliens previously deported from the U.S. must be subjected to meaningful incarceration and/or swift deportation. The U.S. must significantly increase the use of informants to infiltrate criminal organizations and terrorist cells located within our borders.

- Congress must authorize sufficient resources for the FBI and Homeland Security to investigate, arrest, incarcerate, and deport aliens who are involved in organized crime, gang activities, and terrorism.
- Special deportation and detention laws must be enacted that pertain to aliens determined to be gang members, members of recognized criminal organizations, or terrorists.
- Congress should authorize a large increase in the number of S-visas available to local, state and Federal law enforcement agencies. The process to obtain an S-visa must be simplified and expedited.
- Designate alien smuggling, human trafficking, and document counterfeiting as intelligence issues and require U.S. intelligence agencies to gather, analyze and disseminate information related to these crimes.

Increased security and verification for government-issued documents

Homeland Security must work with local, state and Federal agencies to prevent the counterfeiting and issuance of fraudulent identity documents.In addition to "setting standards" suggested by The 9/11 Commission, Homeland Security must assist with the creation of the following programs to further enhance the security of driver's licenses, U.S. birth certificates, U.S. passports, and immigration documents:

- Create a National Birth Certificate system for all persons born in the U.S. The National Birth Certificate should be issued by the U.S. government and must eventually contain digitized fingerprints and Social Security number of the citizen. (This is not a National I.D. card.)
- Drivers within the 50 states should be allowed to maintain driving privileges in one state at a time. An automated central database of all driver's licenses should be established, maintained, and funded by the Federal government.
- Motor vehicle departments must be required to check the national system before issuing a driver's license. Possession of multiple driver's licenses would be a Federal crime.
- Federal, state and local licensing agencies must begin issuing standardized documents that contain biometric identifiers embedded in radio frequency identification (RFID) microchips or contact "smart chips." Law enforcement, the Transportation Security Administration, and other government agencies should be able to verify the licenses using automated systems.

The E-Passport and U.S. visas

No system is foolproof and terrorists may always find a way to get into America. However, Homeland Security and the State Department could make it much more difficult by doing a major overhaul of the way we issue visas and inspect passengers coming to America.

- The U.S. must immediately upgrade our E-Passports to include fingerprints, as well as other biographic and biometric information. E-Passport data must be electronically forwarded to the U.S. ports under current "advanced passenger information" procedures to pre-clear citizens and facilitate their immigration inspection upon returning home.

- International pre-flight passenger inspections should be enhanced by using E-Passport scanners at both international airline check-in counters and at international boarding areas. Biometric and biographic checks should be conducted on all passengers prior to their departure for the U.S.
- If the U.S. keeps the visa waiver program (because of economic concerns), passenger profiling and similar techniques must be increased to prevent terrorists from exploiting the visa-waiver process.
- Require visa waiver countries to have E-Passports with pictures, fingerprints, and biographic data.
- Establish E-Passport immigration inspection lanes for all aliens carrying E-Passports.
- Eventually assign all visa issuance responsibilities (domestic and foreign) to the Department of Homeland Security.
- User fees collected for the inspection of persons entering the U.S. should be utilized strictly for hiring, deploying and supporting Immigration inspectors and associated activities at U.S. international inspection facilities.

Improving our legal immigration system

Homeland Security must eliminate the backlog of the millions of applications pending adjudication. Simple processes must not take months to complete and for the sake of our own security, immigration records must be thoroughly "cleansed."Activities related to employment authorization should be closely coordinated with immigration enforcement initiatives.

- User fees must accurately reflect the true costs of adjudicating specific types of applications.
- User fees collected for processing immigration benefits should be utilized strictly for hiring, deploying and sup-

porting immigration examiners responsible for adjudicating benefit applications.

- In order to correct immigration data errors in the Homeland Security automated systems, Congress should authorize a two or three year alien registration mail-in program.
- Congress should overhaul immigration laws relating to family reunification. Strong consideration should be given to eliminating the visa category that allows U.S. citizens to sponsor their parents. This will help to eliminate some of the problems associated with "anchor babies" in the U.S.
- Citizenship and Immigration Services must develop a standardized alien employment authorization document. Local offices and ports of entry must have the capacity to issue the documents. Sufficient safeguards must be put in place to prevent erroneous and illegal issuances. These documents must all be verifiable by employers through an automated or telephonic verification system.
- Congress should consider increasing the number of "unskilled" legal aliens allowed to come to the U.S. for employment-related reasons. This is especially true in areas where studies have shown that Americans are not willing to do the work, and employers are willing to pay proper wages and benefits.

"Comprehensive Immigration Reform"

Congress should make immigration reform a national priority in the coming years.

- Eliminate the old Immigration and Nationality Act and write a new comprehensive immigration law for the U.S.
- Establish a Cabinet-level agency to handle all immigration related activities.

- Establish an independent, non-partisan National Immigration Policy Board to develop, implement and review America's immigration-related policies.
- Fund a national campaign to make employment of illegal aliens "socially unacceptable," as well as illegal.
- As soon as an effective nationwide employer sanctions program is operational, and our borders are secure, Congress should consider some sort of limited legalization program for illegal aliens currently working in the U.S.

Bibliography

The 9/11 Commission Report, Thomas H. Kean, Chairman, W.W. Norton, New York, 22 July, 2004.

The U.S. Commission on Immigration Reform, *U.S. Immigration Policy: Restoring Credibility,* Barbara Jordan, Chair, Washington, D.C., 1994.

Anonymous. *How To Create a New Identity,* Citadel Press, 1983.

Barlette, Donald L., and James B. Steele. "America's Border," *Time,* 20 September, 2004.

Harris, Shane. "Homeland Security could face transition problem," *Government Executive National Journal,* 01 June, 2007.

International Association of Chiefs of Police, *Enforcing Immigration Law: The Role of State, Tribal and Local Law Enforcement.*

Simcox, David. *Secure Identification, A National Need—A Must for Immigration Control,* Center for Immigration Studies, Washington, D.C., 1985.

The Paper Trip I, Eden Press, 1971.

U.S. General Accounting Office, *Federal Programs Show Progress in Implementing Alien Verification Systems,* Washington, D.C., Government Printing Office, 1989.

U.S. Department of Justice, Federal Bureau of Investigation, *Uniform Crime Reports,* Washington, D.C., 2003.

U.S. Department of Justice, Immigration and Naturalization Service, *Report to Congress: Study on the use of a telephone verification system for determining employment eligibility of aliens,* Washington, D.C., October, 1987.

U.S. Department of Justice, Immigration and Naturalization Service, *Telephone Verification System (TVS) Pilot: Report on the Demonstration Pilot, Phase I,* Washington, D.C., 1993.

U.S. Department of Health and Human Services, *Social Security Number Fraud: Investigative Guide,* Washington, D.C., 1984.

U.S. General Accounting Office, *Immigration Control: A New Role for the Social Security Card,* Washington, D.C., 1988.

U.S. Department of Health and Human Services, Social Security Administration, *A Social Security Number Validation System: Feasibility, Costs and Privacy Considerations,* Washington, D.C., 1988.

U.S. Department of Justice, Immigration and Naturalization Service, *A Guide to Selected U.S. Travel and Identity Documents,* Washington, D.C., 2001.

U.S. Government Accountability Office, *Homeland Security Needs to Immediately Address Significant Weaknesses in Systems Supporting the US-VISIT Program,* Washington, D.C., 2007.